# WRITE WELL

## VOLUME 2

## ANGELA E. HUNT

HUNT HAVEN PRESS

~

Paperback ISBN: 978-1969011177
Ebook ISBN: 978-1969011184

Subscribe to Angela Hunt's newsletter for writers:
angelahunt.substack.com

# INTRODUCTION

**Welcome to Write Well**

The older I get, the more I want to share what I've learned about writing and the publishing industry. So in 2024, I decided to start a newsletter for people who want to make a career of their writing.

In late February, I sent out the first **Write Well** newsletter, hoping to create a brief, no-fuss lesson about writing and the publishing business. I wanted to share my knowledge, opinions, and mistakes . . . because we all learn from each other.

Now that we've turned the corner into 2026, I thought it would be nice to make the newsletters available to folks who don't usually read posts online. So here they are: words to increase your writing vocabulary, advice from people who have persevered, tips and tricks to make writing more effective, and insights into the publishing industry. These are designed to be brief, fast, practical reads.

And let me be up front about something: I am a professional writer and a Christian, but I don't write exclusively for Christians. If I were a dentist, would I only work on

Christian teeth? I write a lot of books for faith folks, but I also write for the world at large . . . because that's where I live.

So if you encounter a bit of God-talk in this book, please allow me some grace. I'd do the same for you.

Good writing is good writing.

**Welcome to Write Well.**

Angie Hunt

If you want to join us online, you can subscribe to the newsletter at angelahunt.substack.com.

# ON HATERS, MIRACLES, AND MEANING

Write Well: #46

**Word of the Week: misanthrope (MIS-an-thrope).**

An individual who hates people (*miso*, hate, + *anthropos*, mankind). *To all outward appearances, Scrooge was a misanthrope.*

**Root of the Week: miso**

While we're on the subject of haters, let's look at the root word: *miso*. We see it in *misogynist* (hatred of women—*gyn*), *misogamy* (hatred of marriage—*gam*), *misophonia* (hatred of common repetitive sounds—*phone*), *misophobia* (hatred of dirt and germs—(derived from irrational fear: *phobia*), and *misogynoir* (a 21st century word, coined by an American scholar: hatred of black women—*gyn + noir*).

In 2025, we're going to learn the roots of words, because there's no better way to functionally increase your vocabulary. If you know the roots, you can often infer the meaning of an unfamiliar word. This is how I learned vocabulary, and it's what I used when I taught high school. The system works.

## Q&A

**Question:** It is possible for a popular, successful author to have poor writing skills? Doesn't story take precedence over writing ability?

**Answer:** No, it is not common for successful, popular novelists to have poor writing skills. If a writer cannot express himself effectively, how can he tell a good story? Story *is* important, and readers will excuse a lack of literary technique, but a good storyteller needs good storytelling skills if those stories are expressed via the written word. An oral storyteller requires a completely different set of skills.

## Quote of the Week

Viktor Frankl, a renowned psychiatrist, developed a technique known as "paradoxical intention—" in short, to do the opposite of your goal. In other words, if your goal is to fall asleep, Frankl would advise you to try to stay awake as long as possible.

He came to appreciate this principle when his writing career took an unexpected turn. He had written dozens of books he hoped would change the world, but he grew discouraged when they fell short of his lofty goal. So he set those aside and in nine days he wrote a simple book about how he survived a Nazi concentration camp. He initially published the book anonymously under the title *Man's Search for Meaning*.

The little book sold over ten million copies and is considered to be one of the world's most influential books.

"Success," Frankl said later, "cannot be pursued; it must ensue, and it only does so as an unintended side effect . . . You have to let it happen by not caring about it . . . [It] is a side effect or byproduct, and is destroyed and spoiled to the degree to which it is made a goal in itself."

Don't believe him? When I lived in Virginia, I was called for jury duty. I had to report, when needed, every day for a month. Thrilled by the thought of a new experience, for the first few days I sat up straight in the courtroom, paid attention, and tried my best to look competent.

I was never chosen to serve.

On the last day of my term, I was over it. I sat in the courtroom and read a newspaper, pretty much ignored the proceedings, and guess what? I was chosen to serve. A perfect illustration of Frankl's principle.

If you have been agonizing over a project that is not taking shape, set it aside for a while and work on something completely different. You may be surprised by the result.

### Miracles

My writing pal Alton Gansky once said that God is the only character who is not allowed to be Himself in a novel. That's perplexing until you realize why.

We have previously talked about *deus ex machina* (Greek for "god from the machine"), so let's review that definition. Deus ex machina occurs when the writer reaches into his bag of tricks and suddenly solves all the protagonist's problems. Readers frown on these all-too-convenient endings because the writer hasn't done his homework by properly setting up the ending and allowing the protagonist to work out his own problem.

So God, who is in the miracle-working business, should not suddenly show up in a story and set everything to rights. (Remember our fundamental rule about **coincidence**: if a coincidence occurs in your story, to be believable it must work *against* your protagonist, not in his favor.)

Yet there is a way to allow God to exercise His power in your novel—if you set it up, remind the reader that He's around, and place the miracle at the end of the book. If God doesn't do anything until the final act, you're going to get reviews from irritated readers.

Leif Enger effectively allowed God to work in his amazing novel *Peace Like a River*. As I recall, the protagonist is a young boy whose father is a man through whom God works miracles. Not all the time, mind you. Dad works a miracle at the beginning of the book (to establish the possibility), he works another at the mid-point of the story (to remind the reader), and he works a big one at the end. And because we've seen the possibility and been reminded, we have no trouble accepting the final miracle and being awed by what occurred.

The father in the story encounters his share of unbelievers and scoffers. And God is not presented as a fairy godfather who grant every wish and prayer. Because the boy's father encounters trouble and difficulty, we believe it's possible he *won't* get a miracle at the end of the book. That possibility—even the *probability*—of failure creates tension, and tension is what keeps readers turning the pages.

So if your plot involves a miracle at the conclusion of your story—whether it's the result of God's work, the stars' alignment, fairy dust, or an ancient prophecy—you have to 1) set the stage for the possibility early in your story; 2) Remind the reader that such things happen around the mid-point; and 3) write the climactic miracle with great flair and extravagance. The reader has been primed for it, so don't be subtle. Though your character may be surrounded by scoffers (some folks simply refuse to see), your readers will be convinced.

## SPECIAL EDITION: LIFE-FILLERS AND LIFE DRAINERS

Several years ago I experienced an epiphany: lots of people spend all their time grousing about things they *could* write . . . if they didn't spend all their time grousing.

If you are going to become accomplished at any professional activity, you're going to have to spend hours involved in that activity. For the writer, this means hours with your rear in a chair while you read and write over and over again.

But in order to have something to write about, you have to have a life, and in order to have a life, you're going to have to haul yourself out of your chair and engage with the world.

I've discovered in my sixty-plus years that life is filled with activities that can suck you in like the Mafia. Distractions would love to tempt us from doing what is *best* to what is neutral or merely *good*. The trick is learning to discern which activities are **life-fillers** and which are **life-drainers.** The life drainers deplete us. The life-fillers bring joy and give us something to write about!

What may be a "life-filler" for me may be a "life-drainer"

for you, and vice versa. But here are some examples from my experience.

- Life-drainer: accepting a position on my neighborhood's board of directors.
- Life-filler: starting a neighborhood book club.
- Life-drainer: working seven days a week.
- Life-filler: taking a Sabbath.
- Life-drainer: bad books, bad movies, bad TV.
- Life-filler: good books, good movies, great TV.
- Life-drainer: trying to exercise someone else's gift.
- Life-filler: exercising mine.
- Life-drainer: joining a fitness club.
- Life-filler: hitting the treadmill while watching good videos.
- Life-drainer: trying to be all things to all people.
- Life-filler: finding my God-ordained niche and filling it.

Miscellaneous life-drainers: purposeless meetings, trying to maintain fake nails, window shopping, foolish arguments, email chain letters, and debating politics on social media.

Miscellaneous life-fillers: any time spent with children, a good haircut, time spent with my spouse, shopping with a purpose, riveting debates with wise friends, and learning something new.

In order to write about people, you have to put your feet into the pool of life. In order to maintain your spiritual health, you have to feed your spirit. God has placed you in a specific place, time, and situation, so you need to make sure you're using all your moments in the best ways possible.

"For what is your life?" James asked. "It is only a vapor that appears for a little time and then vanishes away."

Sometimes writers have to erect guards around their writing hours—but it can be just as important to guard the time we spend *away* from the desk.

Life is finite—we are all allotted a certain number of minutes, and you can't get a refund of the minutes you've wasted. So spend your minutes wisely.

# ON ARCHETYPES, CHAPTERS, AND BREAKING UP.

**Write Well: #47**

Peter Funk, author of *It Pays to Increase Your Word Power*, says we have three vocabularies: 1) reading or recognition, 2) listening and 3) writing and speaking. Our recognition vocabulary is the largest, because we can often surmise the meaning of a word by its use in context. Our speaking vocabulary is the smallest, because when we talk to friends, we usually grab the simplest words available.

"Your speaking and writing vocabularies, the smallest of the three groupings, depend directly on the effort you make to acquire new words," says Funk. "If you are lazy, your speech will have a paucity of expression. If you are aware of new words and use them, your language will become rich and your writing and conversation more vivid and interesting."

This is why I include vocabulary words each week. If you want to write vividly, you need the words that will make your writing vivid and exact. Good writing doesn't say what you mean—it paints a portrait and conveys every texture and nuance of your message.

This year I am going to stress the roots of words, because if you know the root, you can discern the meaning of dozens of other words.

**Word of the Week: archetype (ARC-keh-type).**

The original pattern or model from which copies are made. A prototype. *The Hero's Journey is a story formula filled with basic archetypes—protagonist, antagonist, wise old woman, guardian, etc.*

From the Greek *arch* (chief) and *typos* (stamp, pattern). Now that you know the roots, test yourself on the meaning of these words: a*rchenemy. archaic. archbishop. archangel. archaeologist. typography. typo. typology. typecast.*

**Q&A**

**Question:** What is the reason for avoiding the use of "I'" when writing memoirs, fiction, and nonfiction?

**Answer:** The use of first-person, of using "I," in books is not forbidden—in fact, it is frequently used in novels when a character relates his or her own story. It is also frequently used in essays, humor pieces, and other avenues when the writers wants to establish a close bond with the reader.

First person is usually avoided in formal or academic writing, however, because those genres favor a more detached approach. But you can certainly use "I" in informal prose and in fiction whenever a close bond with the reader is desired and/or expected.

**Life Observation**

I don't know why this is true, but it is: **whenever I finish and polish a manuscript and hand it in thinking that it's really good, it's not.** Those are always the manuscripts that require the most revision, if not a complete reworking.

Maybe this is unique to me, but I don't think so. If there's a moral to this story, perhaps it's that when we think we've really hit a home run, that's when we most need an objective editor to remind us that we're not writing for ourselves, but for our reader, who will not be as in love with our concept as we are.

**Quote of the Week**

"It comes back to the question, who are you writing for? Who are the readers you want? Who are the people you want to engage with the things that matter most to you? And for me, it's people who don't need it all spelled out because they know it, they understand it. That's why there's so much I can't read because I get so exasperated. Someone starts describing the character boarding the plane and pulling the seat back. And I just want to say, 'Babe, I have been downtown. I have been up in a plane. Give me some credit.'" — Amy Hempel

**Chapters**

We have discussed sentences. We've discussed paragraphs. Now let's look at chapters. If you're wrestling with the thought of where to put chapter breaks, this info is for you.

I have some writer friends who *write* in chapters, but that has never made sense to me. Since I am always moving scenes around, if I predetermined my chapters, I would run the risk of having some super long chapters and some extra-short chapters. Not that there's anything wrong with that, if you're creating short chapters for pacing purposes.

In **nonfiction**, we suggested that you think of a paragraph as an "idea bucket." Think of the chapter as a bigger bucket. Each chapter discusses an idea in your book.

In **fiction**, chapters can be more arbitrary. You should add a chapter break if there's a huge break in time or place —for instance, if the next scene is five years later, or if the action has moved from Florida to Australia. But sometimes it's advantageous to insert a chapter break at a tense moment—creating a cliffhanger of sorts. Like this:

"Why shouldn't I trust you, Bob? I know who you are!"

"Do you?" He reached into his pocket and slowly unclenched his fist. On his palm she saw a glittering constellation of stolen diamonds.

CHAPTER BREAK.

Sally caught her breath, unwilling to believe what her eyes were telling her.

Your chapters should open with a strong sentences that

lets the reader know—almost immediately—*who* the point of view character is and *where* they are. In the example above, it's obviously that we're still with Sally in the same room with Bob, but if you had switched settings, you'd need to let the reader know if there's a different *who, where,* or *when.* You don't have to relate every detail, of course (keep Amy Hempel's quote in mind!), but you need to reveal enough to prevent the reader from becoming confused.

Use **scene breaks**—that empty line between scenes—and **chapter breaks** wisely. When you have finished your manuscript (and if you've been writing in Scrivener, you can see all your scenes in the left column), insert chapter breaks wherever you have sizable breaks in time and/or place. (You should do this as you are writing—it will feel natural to do so). Your manuscript should already have lots of scene breaks where you were changing locations or switching to a different point of view character.

Now it's time to consider your reader's energy level. Most readers are comfortable with chapters of 15-20 pages—depending on the genre and the action in your story. If your story is a fast-paced thriller, you will want shorter chapters. If you're writing a literary novel, you can stretch the chapters a bit. But readers appreciate natural breaking points where they can put the book down to stretch their legs or turn out the light.

Also consider your story—it may have natural breaks built into it. One of my all-time favorite novels is *The Wednesday Wars* by Gary D. Schmidt. The book takes place over a school year, so each chapter is one month of Holling Hoodhood's seventh-grade life. Does your story suggest a natural way to organize your chapters?

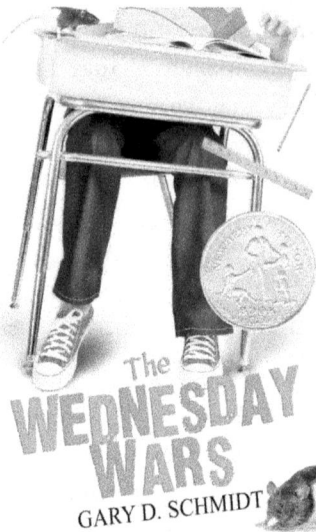

The WEDNESDAY WARS

GARY D. SCHMIDT

If your story is especially long, or if it covers a character's entire lifespan, you may want to include extra divisions. For instance, in my book *Rescued Heart, The Story of Sarah,* I divided the novel in four *books*, with each book covering a season in Sarah's long life. Book One had chapters covering her early years, Book Two covered the first part of her life in Canaan, etc. This organization allowed me to ignore long stretches of years where nothing significant happened and focus on key events in her life—one key event per "book." (Incidentally, I did not start renumbering chapters with each "book" division).

# ON FILTHY LUCRE, SAYING
# IT AGAIN, AND BURNOUT.

**Write Well: #48**

**Word of the Week: lucrative (LOO-cruh-tiv).**

Highly profitable. From the Latin *lucrum*, meaning *gain*. *Writing short stories is rarely lucrative.*

Related words: *lucre*, which has a negative connotation, as money that has been dishonorably gained (and often preceded by the word *filthy*).

Mrs. Williams, my sainted English teacher, always gave us an extra point on our papers when we used one of our vocabulary words. You learn words by using them, so challenge yourself to USE these new words in your writing each week. That's how they actually become part of your vocabulary. (Let's see if I can use *lucrative* in this newsletter.)

## Q&A

**Question:** "Based on our review, we won't be accepting your submission for publication because the book(s) might result in a disappointing customer experience." Why did Amazon's KDP send me this message and block my book?

**Answer:** That message can mean several things—it could be that your book is not properly formatted, or that it contains misspellings, or that it lacks original content. I once received that message because my cover image depicted a spiral binder, and KDP thought readers would expect to receive a spiral notebook instead of a paperback (though the book was clearly labeled "paperback").

Bottom line: your book promises something and KDP feels that it doesn't deliver on that promise. Rather than deal with customer complaints, they are choosing not to publish the book.

You can contact someone in the KDP program (look for the "contact" link on the KDP site) and ask what the specific problem is, then fix the problem.

### Quote of the Week

"Everything that needs to be said has already been said. But since no one was listening, everything must be said again" —Andre Gide.

Mrs. Williams always said that in an essay, "first, you tell 'em what you're going to tell 'em, then you tell 'em, then you tell 'em what you told 'em."

Never worry about repeating what has been said before. Just find a different way to say or illustrate it.

### Can Writers Suffer Burnout?

Published or unpublished, I'm here to testify that yes, writers can suffer burnout. Anyone who does anything every day, without much variation, can fall into a rut and grow weary, especially if their efforts are not regularly rein-forced with some sort of reward. Everyone needs a pat on the back now and then.

Years ago, I was churning out big historical novels, one

every three months, working seven days a week. And I grew weary of it. My joy disappeared.

Someone suggested that I needed to take some time off, but how could I do that with deadlines?

So I decided to put myself into my own version of therapy. I bought a copy of Julia Cameron's *The Artist's Way* and worked through the book, one lesson per week. A lot of that book is new age jargon that didn't resonate with my super-pragmatic nature, but two concepts from that book changed my life:

1. **Daily Artists' pages.** Cameron suggests that artists get a blank journal and fill three pages every morning. It doesn't matter what you write, because no one but you will read it. The value of the practice is that you are getting thoughts out of your head and onto the paper, where they can rest. This act clears the brain in a most amazing way.

2. **Weekly Artist's date:** Cameron also prescribes a weekly "artist's date." Do something just for you —take a couple of hours to do something that fills your artist's well. Whether that's going to a movie, walking along the beach, visiting a museum, painting a picture, or splashing in a creek. Once a week, take two hours to fill your soul.

3. I added a third thing to my new life prescription: **no working on the seventh day.** Ever since that year, I have kept a Sabbath where I do "no ordinary work." I don't write. I may work around the house, watch mindless TV, or train my dogs—but whatever I do, I'm NOT

working on my writing project. (I think God knew what He was doing when He commanded us to rest one out of every seven days, don't you?)

By observing those three principles, I have not experienced burnout since that time. I currently don't write three full pages every day in a journal, but I do jot a few lines in one. (And if something big has happened in my life, I write it out in my journal, taking as many pages as I need to clear my head.) I observe a day of "no ordinary work," usually on Saturday, and I look for things that fill my creative well, taking time to play the piano, paint pictures, or dally in the garden—because we are designed to find joy in doing the thing we were gifted to do.

Writing isn't always fun—it's hard work. (And it's rarely lucrative for the average writer.) But while we may struggle with a difficult scene or shaping a synopsis, the endeavor should be rewarding in itself because we have to wait far too long to hear feedback from readers.

How do you feel when you sit down to write? During my burnout period, I would get a migraine every time I sat in my writing chair. If you're feeling weary, put yourself into creative therapy and start doing artist's daily pages. Take yourself on an artist's date once a week. And take a day to *live*, not to write about living.

This advice is important whether you're published or still in your apprenticeship. Writing is a constant exercise that requires purposeful practice, and we never learn everything we need to know. But joy comes when we do our best, and the reward arrives when our words touch readers' hearts. Sometimes we're even blessed to hear about it.

## ON SWELLINGS, PLAYING IN THE MAJORS, AND SLIPPERY ADVERBS.

**Write Well: #49**

**Word of the Week: tumid (TOO-mid).**

Swollen—literally or figuratively. *During a thunderstorm, the creek behind my house becomes a tumid river. The politician gave a tumid speech. Too many new writers employ a tumid style.*

From the Latin *tumere*, to swell. Associated words: **tumor, tumorigenesis, tumulus, tumefy.** Take a guess at the meaning of these words, then check your answers!

**Q&A**

**Question:** Can a writer with no contacts or an agent self-publish and then get his work picked up by a traditional publisher?

**Answer:** Anything is possible . . . but not likely.

Let's say you're a gifted baseball pitcher. You have an amazing fastball that no one in your neighborhood can hit. So every afternoon you play ball at the baseball diamond in your neighborhood in your small town. Every day you're there, throwing your pitch, striking out players on the opposing team. But who sees you? Only the folks in your neighborhood, and maybe, after word spreads, some folks from your town. And maybe, *just maybe*, other people will come to see you, but only after a long time of pitching and *only* if word of your amazing ability spreads.

Compare that situation to what would happen if you tried out for the New York Yankees and you're signed. There you pitch at Yankee Stadium, and there you strike out lots of other players. Maybe not as many as you would have done in your neighborhood—after all, the competition is keener in the majors—but you've worked hard to achieve excellence in your pitching. And many, many more people will see you play.

That's the difference between self-publishing and traditional publishing. You have a much better chance of reaching lots of readers if you're playing in the majors. And yes, the competition is keener, so you have to keep working on that fast ball. But the odds of a pro scout appearing on your neighborhood baseball field are slim.

### Quote of the Week

In his 1916 book *On the Art of Writing*, Sir Arthur Quiller-Couch wrote: "Whenever you feel an impulse to perpetrate a piece of exceptionally fine writing, obey it — whole-heartedly — and delete it before sending your manuscript to press: *Murder your darlings*."

Now a popular catchphrase among editors, "murder your darlings" admonishes writers to refrain from being pretentious about their prose and to trust in the values of simplicity and efficiency.

I see this a lot in beginning manuscripts—people write to impress, not to tell a story. Their writing is too *writerly*. So don't use a fifty-cent word if a ten-cent word works just as well. I'm *not* saying you should never attempt to stretch your reader's vocabulary, especially if a word is perfect for the situation, but don't do that five times on a page. You will wear out your reader.

**Slippery Adverbs**

An adverb, by definition, is a *word that props up a verb*. Which should tell the astute writer that it would be better to find a strong verb that doesn't need propping up.

I asked ChatGPT to write a paragraph in the style of a beginning writer, and it gave me this:

**The boy eagerly grabbed the baseball and tightly clenched it in his small hand, his fingers nervously twitching as he prepared to throw it. He stepped forward awkwardly, his sneakers scuffing noisily against the dirt, and he swung his arm back wildly. With a quick flick of his wrist, he threw the ball forcefully, the seams spinning furiously as it zipped unevenly through the air. He watched hopefully, his eyes squinting excitedly, as the ball soared briefly before landing roughly in the grass with a dull thud.**

If a high school student wrote this paragraph, they might receive high marks for the imaginative use of language. But this would never work in professional writing —it's too wordy and those adverbs "tell" when it would be better to show. As ChatGPT illustrated, overuse of adverbs is a sign of amateur writing.

This is how I would edit it. First I would do a search and

replace, and ask my computer to fine every *ly* and replace with *LY*. This might not catch every adverb, but it would catch the most superfluous.

The boy eagerLY grabbed the baseball and tightLY clenched it in his small hand, his fingers nervousLY twitching as he prepared to throw it. He stepped forward awkwardLY, his sneakers scuffing noisiLY against the dirt, and he swung his arm back wildLY. With a quick flick of his wrist, he threw the ball forcefulLY, the seams spinning furiousLY as it zipped unevenLY through the air. He watched hopefulLY, his eyes squinting excitedLY, as the ball soared briefLY before landing roughLY in the grass with a dull thud.

Now, for the edit: **The boy** ~~eagerLY~~ **grabbed** (to grab implies eagerness; it's stronger than "took") **the baseball and** ~~tightLY~~ **clenched** (*tight* is implied in a clench) **it in his small hand, his fingers** ~~nervousLY~~ **twitching** (actually, if I wanted to show nervousness, I might have his left eye twitching, or the corner of his mouth) **as he prepared to throw** ~~it~~. **He stepped forward** ~~awkwardLY,~~ (the adverb *tells* —*show* us by saying he stepped forward on unsteady legs), **his sneakers scuffing** ~~noisiLY~~ (scuffing creates a sound) **against the dirt, and he swung his arm back** ~~wildLY~~. (Wildly is *telling*—try a metaphor instead: maybe he pinwheels his arm?) **With a quick flick of his wrist, he threw the ball** ~~forcefulLY,~~ (the force is implied in the next phrase) **the seams spinning** ~~furiousLY~~ (again, a metaphor would be stronger—the seams spinning like— tops would be cliche, so how about "the silver hubcaps on a vintage Mustang) **as it** ~~zipped unevenLY~~ (wobbled?) **through the air. He watched** ~~hopefulLY,~~ **his eyes** ~~squinting excitedly,~~ (this is just wrong—when you're excited, your eyes get bigger, so say his eyes widening) **as the** ball soared ~~briefLY~~ (for a moment woven of eternity) before landing ~~roughLY~~ ~~in the grass~~ with a dull thud (in the grass). (which is more important—the thud or the grass? I think the point is that he threw a bad pitch).

Edited result: **The boy grabbed the baseball and clenched it in his small hand, left eye twitching as he prepared to throw. He stepped forward on unsteady legs, his sneakers scuffing against the dirt, and pinwheeled his arm. With a quick flick of his wrist, he threw the ball, the seams spinning like the silver hubcaps on a vintage Mustang as it wobbled through the air. He watched, his eyes widening, as the ball soared for a moment woven of eternity before landing with a dull thud in the grass.**

How are *your* adverbs? Those slippery little suckers can easily slither into your writing, so do that search/replace for LY and see how you can improve your writing. Think of them as a goad to urge you to do better and think more creatively.

## SPECIAL EDITION:
## SACRED SPACE

I once heard a story about Fred "It's a beautiful day in the neighborhood" Rogers. Seems when Mr. Rogers was in seminary and learning how to preach, he attended a small church and heard another man speak. The minister didn't follow the rules of homiletics and Mr. Rogers didn't find the subject inspiring. He sat in his pew and mentally tore the sermon apart . . . and then he noticed that the woman beside him was totally enthralled. When the speaker had finished, she leaned toward Mr. Rogers and whispered: "That's just what I needed to hear today."

And that's when he realized that the "space" between a minister (or writer or singer) and a listener (or reader) is sacred. From that day forward he promised to not insert himself into someone else's sacred space. He could celebrate the fact that someone, somewhere needed to hear that man's message.

When I was a music major in college, I was nearly ruined for church music. I couldn't listen to another singer or choir without noticing (and quietly cringing) every time I heard a note that was sharp or flat or a vibrato that had wobbled out of control. The little I had learned--and this is when intellect can become a dangerous thing--fostered a critical spirit within me.

Then I realized that all the joy of church music had vanished for me. To restore it *and* an attitude of worship, I had to learn to zip the lip of my inner critic . . . just as Fred Rogers did.

Ah, how the Lord delights in humbling His children. If we don't humble ourselves, He will do whatever it takes to remind us that we are servants . . . and it's in service that true joy lies. It's in the "sacred space" between author and reader, preacher and hearer, singer and listener, that the Spirit works, so who are we to intrude?

So the next time you read an article or a book and find that you don't particularly care for it, be careful what you say about it publicly. Learn what you can from it in private, offer your opinion *if asked*, but if someone else truly enjoyed it, don't drown their delight with the cold water of criticism.

Critics have no place in sacred space.

# ON COSTLY VICTORIES, IMAGE COPYRIGHTS, AND WRITING HISTORY

**Write Well:** #50

**Words of the Week: Pyrrhic (PIR-ic)and verisimilitude**

From the name of a Greek General, *Pyrrhus*, who won many battles but is remembered for defeating the Romans at the cost of most of his army. He is reported to have said afterward, "One more such victory and we are lost." A *pyrrhic* victory is won at such a high cost that victor gains nothing.

**Verisimilitude (ver-ih-SIM-ih-lih-tude):**

the appearance of being actual or real. *Apt details in a novel give the book verisimilitude.* From the Latin *veri* (true) and *similis* (like).

Related words: *veridical, verifiable, verism, veritable, verily, similar,* and *simile.* Now that you recognize the roots, can you surmise the meaning of these words?

## Q&A

**Question:** When I write an article or a blog, can I include pictures I find through Google? Will this cause a copyright issue?

**Answer:** Yes, you can be sued or fined for "borrowing" an image from the Internet. Images have copyrights, and you cannot use an image without permission from the photographer or buying a license. To be safe, only use images from sites that either offer copyright-free images, or where you can purchase a license. If you purchase a license, honor the terms of that license (some licenses are for personal use; others are for commercial use). Many platforms grant permission for a certain amount of time or a certain number of sales, so you need to be sure you have not exceeded the terms of your license.

### Quote of the Week

"The real writer is one who writes, not one who dreams about it." – Anonymous

### Writing History for Modern Readers

So you want to write a historical novel, and you want it to be as accurate as possible. So you do your "big picture" research and write a first draft of your story. What next?

As you work through your second draft, a timeline can help you make sure you haven't contradicted recorded history. (Writers tend to forget about days of the week in the heat of writing, but dates can be significant. The Seleucids were victorious against the Jews in the early years of what would become the wars of the Maccabees because they attacked on the Sabbath, when the Jews would not resist. The Jews wised up, however, and realized that if they didn't make an exception, there wouldn't be any Jews left to observe the Sabbath.)

So make sure that the historic Battle of Waterloo, which took place on Sunday, June 18th, 1815, doesn't occur on a Friday in your story world. If George met Martha for the first time in Vicksburg, you can't have them meeting in Richmond. If you don't correct your mistakes, some expert will read your book and post a review saying you didn't do any research.

What do you do when historical experts don't agree on times, dates, practices, or places? You're more likely to run into this problem when you write about ancient eras—eighteenth dynasty Egypt, for instance, or almost any period of the Old Testament era. In that situation, a novelist is forced to gather as many expert opinions as possible and then make an informed choice. Choose the option that best fits with the other facts you've learned about the period and smile when others disagree. If a date or practice cannot be verified, let it be.

One of the best ways to write about history is to obtain eye-witness accounts or copies of original documents. When I wrote the story of Joseph in ancient Egypt, I found Egyptian poetry from the eighteenth dynasty and quoted it (translated into English, of course). When writing about the lost colony of Roanoke, I used the actual writings of John White, the man who established the colony and sailed back to English for supplies. I had a professor take umbrage with my description of the Native American huts (White had written about *idols* by the natives' doors), and the professor insisted that the native people didn't worship idols. The professor brought the matter to the attention of my publisher, but I was able to point to the eyewitness account, so my research was vindicated. (I actually believe those images were what we would call *totems*, but to a 16th century Englishman, they looked like idols.)

If you're writing for a Christian or Jewish publisher, let the Bible be your chief authority, but consult several translations so you develop a good understanding of the original text. Your modern translation may be a far cry from what the historical biblical writer intended—those writers were fond of euphemisms.

Speaking of historical biblical fiction, some people assume that "Christian fiction" equals "biblical fiction" and vice versa, but nothing could be further from the truth. Furthermore, the best-written biblical fiction is not simply a fleshed-out Bible story, it is a historical novel that includes a biblical character or incident. It's my opinion that novelists who write in this category should include lots of history books in their research and not rely solely on Bible commentaries and books written from a Christian perspective. In writing historical novels featuring Joseph, Moses, Mary Magdalene, and others, I've found fascinating facts in Jewish texts, agnostic accounts, and books written from an Islamic perspective. I don't agree with everything I read, of course, but learning to see historical events from other perspectives helps me sharpen my story world.

I have, incidentally, made it a practice to list my reference books at the end of every historical novel. It's not necessary, but I do it because I think it's only fair that I acknowledge the help these resources have provided.

Furthermore, some readers like to explore time periods further, so a bibliography gives them a great place to start.

As you write about the past, remember that novels are not actual life. They are approximations of life, just as dialogue is an approximation of actual speech.

Since dialog is not real speech, don't be tempted to write phonetically in order to add historical flavor. Writing like this—*luheek thuh suhoond uh doomzdeh*—is too hard to read. (Translation: "like the sound of doomsday" in an Irish dialect.) Instead of foisting strange spellings on your reader, indicate a dialect by word choice: "Sure, and don't I know you're goin' with me?" A single dropped "g" and appropriate word choice can effectively convey an Irish dialect and not distract your reader from the story.

In the same vein, mind your language. The profanity of any era is repulsive to many readers, and you can create the same effect by writing some variation of "He cursed." On the other hand, some words that offend today wouldn't have offended a previous generation . . . but you are writing for contemporary readers.

Historical novelist Stephanie Grace Whitson says, "I don't have my white people calling my black people what white people called black people back then. I do not have my white people thinking about my Lakota people what white people thought about Lakota people back then. And I certainly do not have my people (except the bad ones) *smell* like they smelled back then."

Novels are not real life. And no matter how much research we do, we who have been molded by twenty-first century events may never fully understand the mindsets of previous generations, so I doubt a novelist can ever write a novel that is completely accurate and true to the period. We aim for verisimilitude, we strive to never contradict historical fact, but we must acknowledge that we write for modern readers.

I cringe every time Ricky Ricardo spanks Lucy in the old TV show. That show, which aired its final episode around the time I was born, presents a certain mindset—that it's okay for men to physically discipline their wives—which makes me flinch. Few people flinched in the 1950's; some people probably thought Ricky was being adorable and funny. But perspectives change.

If you want your novel to reach the emotional core of your present-day reader, you must keep his or her attitudes in mind.

Historical fiction pairs story with a rich tapestry of sights, sounds, tastes, aromas, textures, and challenges. When written well, readers come away feeling that they've not only had a moving emotional experience, but they've lived and learned in a fascinating era far beyond the twenty-first century.

Have you tried writing historical fiction or nonfiction? How many sources did you consult? Did your understanding change as you researched?

# ON OBVIATION, CLAY TABLETS, AND PEN NAMES.

**Write Well:** #51

**Word of the Week: obviate (AHB-vee-ate)**

To make unnecessary or prevent by taking proper measures. From the Latin obviates, and obviate, "to meet, to withstand." *She had packed her suitcase with great care, obviating the need for a mad dash to the store for toothbrush and toothpaste.* Related words: *obvious, obviation.*

## Q&A

**Question:** How did authors write novels before the invention of computers?

**Answer:** Before computers, they used typewriters.

Before typewriters? Pen and paper.

Before pen and paper? Papyrus or parchment and quills and ink.

Before papyrus? Clay tablets.

Before clay tablets? They told stories to others who memorized them and passed them along.

The urge to tell stories is as old as mankind.

## Quote of the Week

Hugh Howey only *wanted* to write until someone told him to stop playing video games and start writing. This is part of his story:

"I was at a writing conference in Virginia, and I was there at the time I was reviewing. This is one of the periods of my life where I was reading a book a day. I was getting flooded.

"My stoop every day was just like a pile of books from publishers that weren't out yet, advanced reading copies. I was writing book reviews for a website, and I would every day read a book, write a review, and try to interview the author.

"I was going to book conferences and covering them as well. This is because I had given up on ever writing a book of my own. I had tried for 20 years since I was 12 years old and wrote my first Hitchhiker's Guide to the Galaxy ripoff."

"That was giving me the habit of writing every day, but it was also filling my head with good story and good prose. That's how I finished my first novel, just by someone yelling at me, basically, yelling near me, to just write and by replacing a lot of other things I was doing with my day with that daily habit of writing, it accumulated a lot of words and maybe a little skill. In about a five- or six-year period, I wrote about 15 novels and some of them did well enough that I'm now doing my other dream, which is to sail around the world."

From **The Knowledge Project with Shane Parrish: #63 Hugh Howey: Winning at the Self-publishing Game, Aug 6, 2019**

## Should you Use a Pseudonym?

Whenever I meet someone and mention that I'm a

writer, they invariably ask, "What name do you write under?" Probably because they believe all writers are famous and they've never heard of Angela Hunt. When I say that I write under my own name, they always look a little confused . . .

Should you use a pen name? A *nom de plum*? (pronounced *nahm-deh-ploom*). Probably not . . . unless you should.

In most situations, writers do well to use their own name on their books and articles. After you write several books, your name becomes your brand, and your name begins to stand for something—a voice, a standard of quality, even a genre. You will always have your voice and I hope you will always maintain a high standard of quality, but if you ever make a drastic change in genre, you might want to consider a pen name.

**Nora Roberts** is a prolific romance novelist, but she also writes detective mysteries. Because her mysteries are a far cry from her romances, she uses the pen name **J.D. Robb** for her suspense novels. I'd wager that her chief reason is that she didn't want her romance readers picking up one of her suspense books and being disappointed because they weren't romances. She and her editors may also have hoped that the more masculine "J.D. Robb" might help her pick up male readers who are *not* likely to read a Nora Roberts romance. Most Nora Roberts fans know she uses a pen name—she isn't hiding anything, as her pen name is an open secret.

**Stephen King** once used the pen name **Richard Bachman** for a completely different reason. Back in the day, some publishers liked to restrict their authors to releasing only one book per year. Since many writers can write more than a book a year, King wrote four books under the Bachman name so he could publish more often. That connection was kept secret in the beginning, but once King was outed, he stopped using the name. The Bachman books were in the same style and genre as his other books.

My married friends **Mel and Cheryl Hodde** (he's a physician and she's a writer) write romantic medical suspense together as **Hannah Alexander**. Their primary audience is female, so it made sense to go with a female pen name.

**J.K. Rowling** veered away from magic and fantasy to write crime fiction under the name **Robert Galbrath**. And she initially chose J.K. Rowling instead of her real name, "Joanne Rowling," because she feared boys would not be enthusiastic about reading a book about a boy—Harry Potter—written by a woman. It *is* true that men and boys are often reluctant to read books written by women, but women do not hesitate to read books written by men.

**Agatha Christie**, known for her meticulously plotted murder mysteries, wrote books about love, loss, and psychology under the name **Mary Westmacott**. She kept that secret for nearly twenty years.

In short, there are probably as many different reasons for using a pseudonym as there are authors, but most publishing houses will want you to stick with the name that is your brand. The most valid reason for using a pen name, I believe, is to avoid reader disappointment—if your readers expect X when they open one of your books, they will be disappointed if they find Y instead.

For instance, I have written a few novels for the general market, not Christian publishers. Those stories still have my Christian world view, naturally, and some of them are parables, but I've still had readers leave reviews about how disappointed they were to discover that the general market novels didn't talk about God. Yet I wasn't writing that book for Christians, and the world doesn't understand a lot of God-talk. I did consider writing under a pen name, but my publisher wanted my readers to follow me, so they advised me to stick with my brand.

In the end, you have to do what you feel is best for you. If your output is consistent and your audience does not vary, stick with your own name. That way your readers will be sure to find you.

P.S. The shorter your name . . . the larger it can be on your book cover. (Says the woman who used to use "Angela Elwell Hunt.")

## ON CONGRUITY,
## COUNTING DRAFTS,
## AND FINDING IDEAS.

**Write Well:** #52

**Word of the Week: congruous (CON-gru-us).**

Harmonious, suitable, appropriate. From the Latin *congruus*, meaning *agreeing or suitable* (the Latin *con* means *with*). *The ideas presented in her book were not congruous with prevalent theories.*

Related words: *incongruous, congress, congruence, congruity.* Based on what you've just learned, what do you think these words mean? Check your dictionary to be sure!

**Q&A**

**Question:** Do writers often have difficulty writing after publishing a book?

**Answer:** Not in my experience. Most professional writers—people who write for a living—immediately start another book once they submit their manuscript to a publisher. Since it can take up a year for a book to be published after submission they are likely to have finished that *next* book by the time the first book comes out. So no, most professional writers don't have trouble writing after publishing (no more than usual, that is. Creating something out of nothing isn't easy.) Writing is to them as dentistry is to dentists—it's the day job, what they do all the time.

*On the other hand*, if writers take a long break from writing it can be difficult to get back in the groove—but you could say the same thing of any profession. So the moral of the story, I suppose, is *write regularly.*

## Quote of the Week

Shortly after the release of *Miracle and Wonder: Conversations with Paul Simon*, Malcolm Gladwell talked about the many lessons learned through the deep exploration of Simon's creative process. Simon, Gladwell said, believed that creativity is built on top of craftsmanship. That creative work is a culmination of hours and hours of working, studying, learning, practicing, and revising.

"I responded to that," Gladwell said, "because writing—to my mind—if you sit around waiting for inspiration, you will wait for your entire life. It's not what you do. You have to put in the work."

That reminded him—"one of my favorite things I used to do," Gladwell said, "is whenever I read something I really loved, I would ask the person who wrote it, *how many drafts did you do?* What you would discover is the stuff that you like the most, that you think is of the highest quality, has the most drafts." (Robert Greene's definition of creativity—"creativity is a function of the previous work you put in.")

*From Billy Oppenheimer's Six At Six on Sunday.

## Where Ideas Come From

One of the questions most often asked of writers is "Where do you get your ideas?" Ask ten different authors that question and you're likely to get ten different answers, so let's boil it down to the basics.

When it comes to finding ideas, you must first know if you're writing fiction or nonfiction. Nonfiction writers are seeking to educate, challenge, entertain, persuade, and/or inspire their readers. So they look for material that will be interesting, persuasive, new to the average reader (or a new approach), entertaining, and/or inspirational. One rule of thumb is to consider what your ideal reader already knows, then ask yourself what *more* he wants to know.

I hear from people all the time who assure me that they have an amazing life story. That may be true, but unless they have a TV or radio program, they are not likely to sell their story to a publisher. Why? Because *everyone* has an amazing (to some degree) life story, and unless there's something in that story for the reader, it's not going to be marketable.

When I was just starting out as a writer, my husband and I were trying to adopt. We went through all the heartache and waiting, we did lots of research, and then something fairly miraculous happened—some friends we had gone to college with *just happened* to be missionaries in Korea, and they *just happened* to find a baby on their doorstep, and they *just happened* to call us to ask if we knew anyone who wanted to adopt a baby girl . . . pretty amazing, right?

But even then I knew that our story wouldn't sell on its own merit. *Lots* of adoptive parents have amazing stories. So if I wanted to sell that story—and I did, in part to pay for adoption expenses—I had to add something for the reader. So *The Adoption Option* became a book that included our story, but first and foremost it was a book about how Christian couples could adopt a child.

So if you're looking for a nonfiction idea, take stock of what you know—what life lessons have you learned the hard way? —and then consider how you can make that lesson applicable to *thousands* of readers. Now you're on the right track.

What about fiction? Where do fiction ideas come from? Truthfully, I get ideas all the time, but *good* ideas come once in a blue moon. The best ones usually come when I'm in the shower (can't explain that one, unless taking a shower is so automatic that my conscious mind is free to wander), but good ideas can also be summoned and crafted. Here's how:

I have learned that good ideas involve four elements: **a plot, characters, a setting, and a theme.** All you need is ONE of those elements to get started, but make sure it's an element you're jazzed about.

Years ago, I read an article in the *NYT Sunday magazine* about researchers who work in the top of the rain forest canopy. Up there, they find unique flora and fauna that don't exist anywhere else, and they use these bugs and flowers to make new drugs—a very high percentage of our drugs originate in the rain forest.

After reading that article, I thought, "Wow—what a setting that would make. It's unique, it's thrilling, and it's significant." So I had one element . . . I only had to find the other three.

A few months later I read about a disease called Fatal Familial Insomnia. It's hereditary, it's related to prion diseases like mad cow, and basically you discover that you can't sleep, you eventually go into a coma, and expire. (That's highly over-simplified, of course). And though FFI is not fascinating to those who suffer from it, it was to me. I could give my protagonist—a woman—FFI and send her to the rain forest to search for a cure. But how could I increase the protagonist's stakes so the story was about more than one woman's life? Easy—I'd give her a daughter who will inherit the disease unless she finds a cure.

So I had setting, plot, and protagonist—the woman searching for a cure. I had high stakes. But what about the theme?

I began to research the rain forest and even spent a week there (and yes, I did climb to the top of the canopy, but on stairs, not with climbing gear). But in my research, I discovered a book about an Amazonian tribe who, through nature, had come very close to belief in a single, all-powerful God . . .

I put all those things together and found my theme: through faith in God, people can be healed of physical and spiritual disease.

That book, *The Canopy*, is one of my favorites, but I invented the plot step by step, using pieces that interested me . . . and I knew would interest my ideal readers.

So as you go through life, read magazine articles and books. Watch the news. You will hear about people and stories, so keep a notebook and begin collecting pieces—people, settings, unusual occupations, themes you want to explore, and characters. Don't copy anyone else's combination of those elements, but put together your own set.

And always ask, **"What if?"** What if a divorced woman inherits a funeral home in a small Florida town? (The Fairlawn series.)

What if a newspaper reporter is given a note that has washed up from a plane crash? (*The Note.*)

What if a body language expert meets a man who claims to be two thousand years old—and he's apparently telling the truth? (*The Immortal.*)

Put your story elements on notecards, if you like, and mix them up to create your own combinations. Whatever you do, create ideas that *you* find interesting. Chances are your ideal readers will be fascinated, too.

# ON PEDAGOGUES, SCENES, AND PUBLISHING COSTS.

**Write Well:** #53

### Word of the Week: pedantic (peh-DAN-tic)

preachy; obsessively concerned with learning or teaching. *A major problem with most writers' attempts at children's books is that the books are far too pedantic.* From the Latin *paedagogus,* teacher.

Related words: *Pedagogue, pedagogy.* Take a guess as to their meaning, then consult your dictionary. They have to do with teaching, but *pedagogue* has a negative connotation —an overly strict, humorless teacher.

### Q&A

**Question:** What are the costs associated with publishing on Amazon's KDP program? Why does the author have to pay those costs?

**Answer:** There are, strictly speaking, no out of pocket costs with publishing on Amazon's KDP, but before you are ready to publish on KDP, you should pay for editing, cover design, interior design, etc., unless you have the expertise to do those things yourself. But you pay individuals for those services, not Amazon.

With **e-books**, Amazon makes its money (and pays for book delivery), by taking 30 percent of the retail price, leaving you with 70 percent, which is far more than a traditional publisher. The downside, of course, is that Amazon offers no marketing and no distribution other than its regular online sales channel. You can always pay for advertising on Amazon, but the hard work of marketing your book will be left up to you. With **print** books, the author's royalty is 60 percent of the retail price.

Why do you have to pay for the costs? Because with KDP, you are the publisher, and publishers bear the costs related to publishing. Simple and fair.

**Quotes of the Week**

**Why Bother?**

Because right now there is someone

Out there with

a wound in the exact shape

of your words.

"Why Bother" by Sean Thomas Dougherty from *The Second O of Sorrow* (BOA Editions Ltd. 2018).

**Scenes**

According to Sol Stein, a scene is "an integral incident with a beginning and end that in itself is not isolatable as a story. It is visible to the reader or audience as an onstage event, almost always involving dialogue and other action."

Scenes are the building blocks of a novel. Most of them happen in *one* place, at *one* time, and feature the point of view of *one* character. The first paragraph of a scene establishes these things so the reader is not confused and knows exactly where he is, when this is happening, and which character will be presenting the scene.

Occasionally you will need a scene that opens with a bit of narration to provide information about the passage of time, or things that happen off stage, but after you've done that, you should settle into one place, one time, one POV character.

Example of a typical scene's beginning:

**Tom looked up as Mary approached exactly on time. The sidewalk bistro was less crowded at two o'clock, and she seemed to appreciate the quiet hush of the afternoon as she slid into the chair opposite him. "Hello, Tom," she said, her cheeks brightening. "And how did *you* welcome in the new year?"**

See? Without too much fuss, I've told you where they are, when they're meeting, and who the POV character is. The scene would continue, of course, with the characters each having a goal, then having some sort of conflict, and the scene would end with Tom watching Mary leave. Or not.

Example of a scene with narration at the beginning (assuming that the previous scenes end with Tom and Mary breaking up at high school graduation):

**He thought her all through the years at Harvard and even at law school. How could he not, when every breath of wind reminded him of her earthy voice? Even the English professor, the elderly Dr. Williams, reminded him of Mary and the way her eyes crinkled when she smiled.**

And last night, as Tom had sipped champagne with his college friends, as they joked about the conquests and contacts they would make in the new year, Tom spent the hours thinking about Mary. Was she spending the evening at home? Or had someone asked her out? Was she shivering in Times Square and counting down the last seconds of 2024, or was she sleeping soundly in her bed?

He looked up as the sound of brisk footsteps reached his ear. The sidewalk bistro was less crowded at two o'clock, and she seemed to appreciate the quiet hush of the afternoon as she slid into the chair opposite him. "Hello, Tom," she said, her cheeks brightening. "Have you missed me?"

**Check your scenes.** If they contain more than one major event, if they are spread out over too much time, or if they contain more than one viewpoint character, they need reworking. Think of each scene as a novel within itself—it needs a strong beginning, a solid ending, and some sort of conflict in the middle. Even if your character is alone and reflecting, his thoughts should reflect some sort of turmoil, because no one wants to read about someone placidly sitting and sipping tea.

But as always in writing, there are exceptions. **Single-purpose scenes** exist to serve one purpose only. They are usually brief, so they keep the pages turning.

For instance—let's say a burglar has broken into the house. He's chasing Sally, who has hidden in a closet.

New scene: We see Frank, Sally's true love, at the gas station. He's chewing the fat with the guy behind the cash register, and that fellow mentions that Sally was there a few minutes ago. Frank freezes. "Sally was here? But she's supposed to be in Westchester." The guy shrugs. "She said she had to get something from her house." Frank bolts out of the store because he has arranged for a guy to break into the house and steal a priceless painting. But Sally's not supposed to be there.

The scene with Frank doesn't have to be long or have a beginning, middle, and end. Get in, make the point, and get out. The reader is stuck with Sally in that closet.

This cut-and-jump scene technique is used often in thrillers or at the end of a story. It can work well, but I wouldn't do it more than once or twice in a book. What you can use more than once—in fact, you can use it often—is writing a full scene, breaking at a tense moment, and then beginning a new scene with a different character, thereby stretching out the tense moment over the length of another scene or even chapter. You'll see this in a lot of thrillers.

Scenes are important. Work hard at them so people will *not* want to put your book down.

# ON COPYRIGHT,
# IMAGINATION, AND THREES.

**Write Well:** #54

**Word of the Week: copious (COPE-ee-us).**

Abundantly plentiful. From the Latin *coposus*, from *copia*, meaning abundance. *My English papers, when they returned to me, were decorated with copious notes.*

Related words: *cornucopia*, the "horn of plenty" often seen at Thanksgiving feasts.

**Q&A**

**Question:** Can an idea be copyrighted by one author and then used by another author to write his story? Who would hold the copyright in that situation?

**Answer:** You cannot copyright an idea; only the written expression of that idea. So if Writer A wrote down his idea on a piece of paper ("Two star-crossed lovers end up dying because their families hate each other") and is misguided enough to write ©Copyright 2025 by John H. Smith on that page, he has only copyrighted *the words on that paper*, not the idea itself, because ideas cannot be copyrighted. Writer B is free to write a story using the concept of two star-crossed lovers, because his written expression will look nothing like Writer A's words on the page. And, I hope, his words will look nothing like William Shakespeare's *Romeo and Juliet*, *West Side Story*, or any of the dozens of other stories about star-crossed lovers.

In short, copyright protection does not extend to names, titles, short phrases, ideas, methods, facts, or systems. It does, however, cover *specific creative expression*. For example, copyright does not protect the general idea of a group of friends who journey on a heroic quest to defeat evil. However, it will protect the creative expression of this idea, like the book *A Wrinkle in Time* by Madeleine L'Engle. Click here for more information. https://www.copyright.gov/engage/writers/

**Quote of the Week**

"The true sign of intelligence is not knowledge but imagination." – Albert Einstein

I have always been struck by a comment I heard many times after the terrorist attacks on 9/11. Our national failure, the 9/11 commission reported, was *a failure of imagination.*

Think about that.

I don't know about you, but I grew up in a blue-collar family. I didn't know any doctors or lawyers, so I always assumed those people were smarter than the average bear—and certainly smarter than me.

Then I grew up and began to befriend doctors and lawyers, and I discovered that they weren't smarter than the average person—they had simply taken time to focus on one area.

Writing requires imagination. When writing nonfiction, you must imagine your reader and intuit their needs and desires, then do your best to fulfill those needs and desires.

In writing fiction, you must imagine your reader along with story characters in a story world, who will live out a metaphor that you craft to illustrate a universal truth that is close to your heart and part of your belief system. All fiction writers, no matter what their world view, do this, so never apologize for it.

Just take the time to focus on your work, on your craft, and on your reader. Because in the end, if you want to find a measure of success, you will not write for yourself, but for others. This desire to communicate a message, a story, is the writer's *why*.

**Copyright and AI**

The U.S. Copyright Office has finally released clarification about what you can and cannot copyright if you've used AI to help you write your book or even a scene. Here's the gist: if AI is the sole author—if you simply accept what an AI engine gives you—the material **cannot** be copyrighted. But if you edit it and make it your own, you can copyright the material in your name. For more clarification, watch this outstanding video on the subject. https://www.youtube.com/watch?v=-u6DEow89yo

**The Rule of Three**

I don't know why the number three resonates with us so much, but it does. (Perhaps it's because God is a trinity?) In any case, when in doubt about how many items to put on your coffee table, use three. If you want to create friction in your novel, put any three characters together in a small space. If you want to write an essay, use three main points. If writing a children's picture book, create three complications.

My best-selling book, by the way, is a picture book called *The Tale of Three Trees*. I don't think it would have worked if I had used two trees or four trees.

How many daughters does King Lear have? Three.

How many travel companions does Dorothy pick up in Oz? Three.

How many acts comprise most stage plays and movies? Three.

How many primary colors are there? Three (red, blue, and yellow).

How many men went out on the *Orca* to kill the shark in *Jaws*? Three.

How many little pigs escaped the big, bad wolf? Three. How many bears lived in the house Goldilocks visited? You guessed it—three.

Yes, there are times when you want to use *two* in a dual or chiastic approach (more on that another week), but the majority of the time, your go-to number should be THREE.

Three resonates with the human psyche. Three gives us a sense of completion: father, mother, child. One human: mind, heart, will (to think, feel, and do). God: Father, Son, Spirit. *Echad*, a plural unity.

So when you are plotting your story, keep three in mind. You will have a **protagonist**, a **love interest or best friend**, and an **antagonist**. By the way, *antagonist* does not equal *villain*. An antagonist could be your protagonist's mother. The antagonist is simply someone—and the role can be played by various characters over the course of the story—who stands between your protagonist and his or her goal.

Give your protagonist three major challenges. A full-length novel can have many smaller or even sub-challenges, but make sure there are three important ones.

Look at the *Wizard of Oz*—when Dorothy arrives in Oz, she immediately states her goal: to get back to Kansas. To do that she will have to 1) get to the Wizard of Oz, who will tell her to 2) bring back the broomstick of the wicked witch, and after that she will 3) still have to get in the balloon and fly home.

But between those three big challenges, she faces dozens of smaller ones—she is hungry and has to find food. She is terrified by the cowardly lion, who attacks Toto. The tin man keeps rusting. She is grabbed by flying monkeys, nearly blown up by the wicked witch, and lulled to sleep in a field of opium, er, poppies.

Oz is a children's movie, so the many sub-challenges keep things interesting and keep the characters moving through Oz. But she still has three main tasks before she can make it back to Kansas.

When Maria arrives at the Von Trapp family mansion, with the goal of being a good nanny, three different parties stand in the way of her reaching her goal. First, the children don't want a nanny. Second, after she's won the children over, the captain doesn't approve of her nanny style. And third, after she wins the captain over, the largest obstacle is her own traitorous heart. She can't be a good nanny because this nun-to-be has fallen in love with her employer. So she runs back to the convent.

Finally, look for three in your prose. I picked up a random book on my desk—*Stein on Writing*—and opened to page 153. There I found a quote with a set of three:

"We had been married for three years when, one Sunday, Tom dressed, as usual, in a shirt and tie, **slipped into his handsome jacket, put on his best cordovan shoes, and left the house without his pants.**"

After dressing as usual in his shirt and tie, Tom did three things, and Stein followed up with three questions:

**"What conclusion can the reader come to, that Tom suddenly went crazy? Or is this going to be a wacky comedy about an eccentric? Could Tom be so concerned about something else that he forgot to put on his pants?"**

You don't *always* have to use three, but if it's possible, why not? It resonates. Three gives a sense of completion. And three often works better than two or four or five.

# SPECIAL EDITION: WHAT IS GOOD WRITING?

Someone once asked me, "What is good writing?" There are probably dozens of opinionated answers to that question, so I'll add my notions to the mix.

First, I have to refer to my high school English teacher, who insisted upon giving us *two* grades for every writing assignment: one for technique, one for content. (I did the same thing when I taught English.) In **nonfiction**, content pertains to the information presented: is it unique? Is it useful? Is it applicable to my life? Does it move me to action? In **fiction**, *content* pertains to the story, which is plot plus emotional content.

*Technique*, on the other hand, pertains to how well the writer exercises his craft to create his or her content. Too many errors in technique draw the reader's attention away from the content and diminish the enjoyment of the work. Too many errors and I won't read long enough to notice good content.

What's good technique? The goal is crisp, clear, precise prose. Using the exactly right word, not a word more or less. Oblique dialogue. Clear *interior* dialogue uncluttered by thought attributions and italics. Strong verbs and nouns that obviate the need for redundant adjectives and adverbs. Exposition that flows naturally when needed, not a moment before or after, and definitely not in dialogue between people who would already know the information.

In fiction, I prefer stories that follow the mythical pattern--an interesting, active protagonist strives to reach a goal by overcoming complications, learning a lesson, sacrificing something in the effort, and coming out either a winner or a loser, but wiser for the effort and changed by the struggle.

If I can identify with the protagonist, so much the better. If his world is fascinating, better yet. I also like clear point of view, limited to one person per scene, because, like most of you, I grew up watching moving images and I'm accustomed to stories that unfold like a film.

Yet when all is said and done, the most beautiful writing in the world won't matter if I don't care about the characters by the second chapter . . . some would say the second page. A gripping story will make me forgive--even not notice--all sorts of technique problems. But when I pick up a book and flip through the pages, it's the technique problems that first catch my eye.

So, when it comes to fiction, good writing captivates the reader with story and sympathetic characters.

Good writing is technique that functions like a smooth highway. It paves the way so the story can flow without distracting the reader on the journey.

And for the Christian novelist who wants to make a real difference in the world, art must serve the message, not vice versa.

Don't tell me that novels shouldn't have messages--ALL novels have messages, whether the author intends it or not.

Readers pick up novels because they want to be entertained, enlightened, moved, challenged, or inspired. If a writer can't meet their desires, the writing is not effective. Not every reader is going to love every book, of course, but the writer should write to an ideal reader and satisfy him or her.

Being a novelist isn't about satisfying *the writer's* needs and whims, it's about considering others. A dentist works with craft and skill to care for his patients' teeth. A plumber works to solve his customers' plumbing problems. A teacher strives to impart wisdom to his students. A writer writes to emotionally move readers.

A novelist spins a metaphor to illustrate a particular aspect of life. And in that effort, he or she illustrates universal truths about sin and sacrifice, grace and justice, love and loss.

In nonfiction, a book that achieves its purpose (to educate, persuade, humor, enlighten, or challenge) has been well-written. A novel written with passion, skill, and with the reader in mind is art . . . and good writing.

# ON PROFANITY, SECRETS, AND SNAPSHOTS

**Write Well:** #55

**Word of the Week: rarefy (RARE-eh-fie).**

To make thin, less solid, less dense—NOT to make something more rare. *Constant use had rarefied her wedding band.*

When you see *-fy* at the end of the word, the suffix comes from the Latin *facere*, "to make." Knowing that, you should be able to surmise the meaning of these words: vilify (to make a villain), ratify (to make valid), deify (to make a god), codify (to reduce to a system, or code), certify (to attest to), and fructify (to make fruitful). Now that I've helped you with some, how about these: identify, sanctify, verify, amplify, magnify, modify, mollify, intensify, indemnify, exemplify, stultify, and clarify. Be sure to check the meaning of any words you're not sure of.

How'd you do?

## Q&A

**Question:** What should you do if you have an idea for a

book, but then find out that someone else has already written the same story?

**Answer:** Write your story anyway. Shakespeare wrote *Romeo and Juliet*—did that stop the writers of *West Side Story*? And the zillion other writers who have written about star-crossed lovers? Your idea will be expressed in your voice, with material drawn from your life experiences.

An idea cannot be copyrighted, only the concrete expression of that idea. Some believe there are no more original ideas, and I'm inclined to agree. What makes a story original is the idea plus the author's voice, plus any unique twists added to the concept. So write away!

## Blue Words

I recently heard a podcast about Jerry Seinfeld's start in comedy. A lot of comedians used profanity in their comedy back then, and they rebelled when radio programs and TV networks banned the use of blue words. But Seinfeld said, "Ok. I still wanna play—I'll play by the new rules. I'll get around that." And boy, did he ever.

A lot of writers balk when they hear that some readers—or most readers—don't appreciate profanity in the books they read. They insist that dialogue isn't "real" unless it includes the actual words people speak, but dialogue isn't real conversation. If you wrote a scene using the actual conversation between two people there'd be so many *ums* and *ers* and *you knows* that it'd be almost unreadable.

Dialogue in fiction is an *approximation* of actual conversation, so why not write *he cursed* instead of including words that are going to turn many of your readers off? I'll agree that having a hardened gangster say "fiddlesticks" when he learns he's lost a million dollars is unrealistic. But you could have him "turn the air blue" or throw a coffee mug or slam his fist into the unfortunate soul who delivered the bad news.

When I turn on a movie and every other word is the "f-word," my first thought is that the screenwriter either doesn't get out much or he has a lousy vocabulary.

I learned a trick early on—in my book *The Truth Teller,* I created a very bad man who conned a woman into having her dead husband's baby through IVF, then he inserted a cave man's DNA into the embryo. To work around the lowlifes-frequently-cuss factor, I made my bad guy sophisticated and polished. He was too refined to resort to profanity.

My novelist friend Athol Dickson once pointed out that when a reader encounters a word they find personally offensive—no matter whether it's profane, a racial slur, or scatological—it takes them out of the story. The writer has snapped the reader out of the "fictive dream." We don't want to do that.

For the record, most Christian publishers refuse to accept a novel with profanity in it. I once argued to have a young boy say the word "fart," but after my elderly aunt read the book, she told my mother she wished I hadn't used that word.

I'm not telling you what to write . . . and you may think I'm hopelessly old-fashioned, and that's okay. What I'm saying is this: *choose your words carefully.* You don't want to offend your readers, you want to win their hearts.

**In Fiction: The Secret Snapshot**

Writing novel is more than telling a carefully plotted story. If you want your story to touch hearts and lives, you're going to have to open your heart and show the reader what's inside—even if you don't want to.

Sol Stein talks about the "secret snapshot" technique he uses to get writers to open up and really write. He would ask you to think of a snapshot so private you wouldn't want to carry it in your wallet. Don't think of something embarrassing—you'll get a better result if you think of something deeply personal, some grief or pain from your past.

Now, think about what you're writing. Does your protagonist experience a similar grief? What was her loss? Instead of saying that she felt sad or lonely or hurt, open your secret snapshot and give your protagonist the actions and reactions *you* experienced in your own time of grieving. Your character's situation will be different, but *the emotions will be the same*. That's one reason I love writing historical fiction—times may change, but human nature doesn't. The people of ancient Egypt, Rome, and England experienced the same loves, griefs, and joys we do.

A few months ago, I finished writing Sarah's story, and you may remember that for years—probably more than seventy—she yearned to have a child and could not conceive. I didn't have to struggle with infertility for seventy years, but I struggled for two, so I knew some of the emotions Sarah would have experienced.

I submitted the manuscript to my editor. In one spot, I had written:

*In truth, I had grown accustomed to living with that particular grief. No woman can wrestle with sorrow every day, and over the years I had learned the necessity of protecting myself. I was happy for new mothers and growing families, truly I was, but though I could wish them well from a distance, I could not embrace their joy head-on without ripping the scab off my own wounded heart.*

And my editor commented, "This seems very realistic."

Why? Because it was. When I was grieving, I couldn't go to baby showers, so I sent a gift instead. Sarah probably wasn't invited to baby showers, but she would have seen new babies born to people in Abraham's camp, and she would have kept her distance. I knew how she would have dealt with them because I'd walked a few months in her shoes.

So take a look at your story, and pay special attention to your protagonist's bleakest moment, his loss, or her pain. Have you felt that same pain or loss? How did you react?

Study your secret snapshot and write your truth for your protagonist. That scene, those words, may be the most honest words in your book.

# ON BELIEVING, BOOK COVERS, AND LISTENING TO YOUR WORK.

**Write Well:** #56

**Word of the Week: credulous (CRED-u-lus).**

Gullible, easily deceived, willing to believe. Opposite: incredulous. *My credulous friend believed rabbits laid eggs . . . because of the Easter bunny.* From the Latin *credulus*, from *credere*, "to believe."

From the same root we get *credence, credible, credulity, incredible, credal, street cred, credential, credit,* and *credo.* Can you discern the meaning of these words? Check the dictionary to be sure you've got it right!

## Q&A

**Question:** Why does the same published book often have different covers?

**Answer:** A single title can be issued with different covers for various reasons. Sometimes the original cover becomes dated, so after a few months or years the book is "refreshed." If a book goes out of print at one publisher and is republished by another, the right to the cover did *not* revert to the author, so the cover will be different. Other reasons for a new cover may include an expiration of the license to the art, a mistake in the cover, or an adjustment to better represent the book or genre. Subsidiary editions (large print, audio books, foreign editions) may have different covers because they are produced by specialty publishers. In any case, finding an alternate cover on a book is not unusual.

## Quote of the Week

"The life of every man is a diary in which he means to write one story, and writes another; and his humblest hour is when he compares the volume as it is with what he vowed to make it." —James M. Barrie, author of *Peter Pan*.

"A friend of mine, in the tenth and final year of writing a novel . . . was squirming as he made his way to the finish. . . . One of his anxieties startled and fascinated me. . . . It resulted from the distance between the type of book he had set out to write and the type of book he had, in fact, written." —Susan Bell, *The Artful Edit*

Many of us set out to write a grand vision . . . and find that when reduced to words and phrases, the resulting book is not what we had hoped, but something altogether different. Don't be dismayed. A book often has a mind of its own, and it will be what it wants to be.

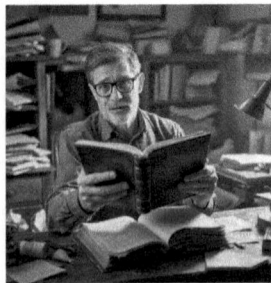

## Move Forward while Writing . . . Listen While Editing

If you've ever sat in one of my classes, you know I'm a

firm believer in moving forward while you're writing that first draft. Too many people get stuck because they keep going back to try to perfect what they've written earlier, and that's a fruitless cause. Your first draft is *supposed* to be terrible, so let it be. Your job in that first draft is to take advantage of forward momentum and keep writing! Editing comes later.

"What would happen," asks Susan Bell, "if you didn't allow yourself to go back to check your output, and only forged forward? You might not need a drastic rupture from your work at the end. You would have created an ongoing distance between you and your work; and your eyes, still fresh, would see pretty well as they read a finished [first] draft." (*The Artful Edit*, p. 13).

"To constantly print out, reread, and perfect your prose," continues Bell, "is usually a trap: after a month of writing, you often have perfectly laid out phrases that say very little, because you paid attention to their sound far more than their purpose."

We all need distance to see our words as they really are, and you can't achieve that emotional distance if you keep peering at past pages. Let them be, and keep writing until you reach the end. Then take a deep breath, take a couple of days to do something else, then begin draft two. For me, draft two is still active writing—filling in details, deepening characterization, adding scenes, and deepening emotion. I don't start editing until draft three, and even then, I'm still doing all of the above.

But by draft four, I'm ready to listen to my work. I thought I was one of the few who had stumbled across this marvelous technique, but apparently it's been around. Some writers like to read their prose aloud to themselves, but I prefer to have the computer read it to me for a couple of reasons. First, if I read it, my eye will continue to skip over the repeated and missed words I've missed in drafts one through three. Second, if I read it, I will supply the emotion, but the emotionless computer will read my words *exactly as they are*. If the emotion isn't in the words (instead of my voice), it won't be on the page.

"There are things that the ear sees that the eye can't hear," writer Bradford Morrow says.

I have also discovered—quite by accident—that viewing my work formatted like an actual book makes me see it in an entirely new light. I discovered this when I was printing out copies of one of my novels for beta readers. I spotted things I wanted to change simply by skimming those formatted pages. Though it makes no logical sense, the words looked different when I viewed them in a formatted book. I'm not the only one who's noticed this. Susan Bell reports that "Jim Lewis discovered that going from Times Roman to Helvetica kicked the complacency out of his eye" (*The Artful Edit*, p. 24). If you don't have a way to format your book, simply changing the font and the page layout (from portrait to landscape) may give you a new perspective.

I write these newsletters without constant editing, then I let them sit, sometimes for weeks. But the week before they are to release, I read them again with an editorial eye. I do this five or six times, making small changes until the day the newsletter releases.

But when my copy shows up in my inbox, I read it *again* with the eyes of a subscriber. Sometimes I find myself making changes yet again, for the sake of those who will read it in the archives.

When you are polishing your draft, read it with distance between the editing and the writing. Read it aloud, or have the computer read it to you. Read it again, changing the font or format so it appears different. Then read it again, imagining that you are the editor or agent or reader on the receiving end.

I'm pretty sure you'll make changes all along the way. We all do.

# ON PROVIDENCE,
# THEME, AND GENRE.

**Write Well:** #57

**Word of the Week: provident (PROV-ih-dent).**

Foresighted, careful in providing for the future. *A provident Girl Scout knew to plan for any contingency when camping.*

You've probably heard people speak of God as *Providence*, but the term isn't referring to his power (that would be His *omnipotence*) . . . it's referring to the fact that He sees what lies ahead and provides for His people. *The American founding fathers saw the hand of Providence frequently at work in the American Revolution and its aftermath.*

From the Latin *providens*, from *providere*, "to see ahead."

Related words: *provide, providence, providential.* Can you deduce their meanings?

**Q&A**

**Question:** I co-authored a book that sold out and would like to do a reprint at my expense. Do I have to share the proceeds with my co-author?

**Answer:** Before proceeding with the reprint, you should talk to your co-author and get his or her permission for the reprint. If he or she is agreeable to forfeit a share of profits in lieu of your bearing the printing costs, great. But create a written agreement to spell out the details of your arrangement and make sure both parties sign before you move forward.

### Quote of the Week

"A theme is not a message. It is an idea written in invisible ink on the backside of your text."—Susan Bell, *The Artful Edit*, p. 85.

### Genre

Why do we write in genres? (By the way, it's pronounced *zhahn-ruh*, not JOHN-ruh.) Why don't we simply write a book and call it "general?"

We write in genres because that's how books are sold in bookstores—they're organized by genre. People know to find the romances in one section, the historical fiction in another, young adult in another. Children's books are usually in the back or along the wall.

Because bookstores like to sell books by genre, publishers like to publish books by genre. In their seasonal lists, they'll have x number of slots for romances, x number for suspense books, x number for children's picture books, etc.

No one knows quite what to do with "general" books because they don't fit anywhere. That's an oversimplification (because there *is* a general category), but if you write a genre book, the publisher and the bookseller will know immediately where your book should go. If you write a book that's not immediately definable, your publisher and agent may not know what to do with it. They can put it in the general category, but who goes into a bookstore thinking, *I want a novel that's not romance, not historical, not time travel, not suspense, not* . . . See the conundrum?

So when you are starting out, choose a genre you enjoy reading— odds are that you'll enjoy writing in that genre, too. Read several books in that genre and study what they have in common. Do they feature a certain tense? A particular point of view? For instance, back in the day, "chick lit" novels featured pink and green covers, had first person protagonists, and were written in present tense. They were about twenty-something girls who left their small towns, entered the big city, and found true love.

If you want to sell a book in a certain genre and you violate one of its standards, your book will have a major strike against it. So study your genre. Some publishing companies offer guidelines for writing in a specific genre or a line within that genre, because *they* don't want to waste time reading manuscripts that don't follow the rules. Check publisher websites to see if guidelines are available.

So don't write a category romance in which the hero and heroine don't get together. Don't write Christian fiction with profanity. Don't write a mystery in which the murder doesn't get solved.

Once you choose a genre and actually publish in it, are you stuck writing in that genre for life? Not necessarily, though most publishers will want you to write several books in that genre. If you're published and selling well in mystery, your publisher might balk if you want to switch to cowboy romance. It takes time to build a fan base of devoted readers, and you risk losing that base if you suddenly begin to write something else. Super-agent Donald Maass says it takes at least *five books* in one genre to become well-established (Writing the Breakout Novel.)

I started out writing nonfiction and picture books—because I was writing books that sprang from ministry and because I had young children at home. I wrote what I was living. But because my husband was a middle school youth pastor, I was with kids of that age all the time, so I wrote some nonfiction for them—on topics like living with a parent's divorce, for instance. Then I realized that kids of that age liked fiction (and I'd grown up reading Nancy Drew), so I started writing mysteries for middle graders. I wrote nine of those, then wrote some slice-of-life books for middle graders. So after writing 25 or so books in those genres, my publisher said, "Why don't you try adult fiction?" and I thought, "Why not?" So I wrote my first adult series, historicals set in medieval times.

I was writing in different genres and had published dozens of books, but the picture book readers didn't know I was writing adult novels, and the adult novel readers didn't know about my picture books. This is the *disadvantage* of writing wherever your interests take you. On the other hand, I was writing things I enjoyed, I was constantly learning new things, and I think I was known as versatile, which led to some interesting collaborative projects.

You're going to have to chart your own path. I'm a big believer that skilled writers can write *anything* as long as they study and follow the blueprints for their selected genres. But be aware that publishers will want you to settle into a genre so you can grow your readership and see repeat sales with each book.

Here's another thought, especially if you happen to be male—romance is the largest-selling genre, and romance publishers are hungry for new books. If my memory can be trusted, I believe Don Maass wrote four romances under a pen name when he first started. I often tell the men in my writing seminars that they should take some version of their wife's middle and maiden names as a pen name and write a romance—they'll learn how to write, get a sale, and get their foot through the door of a publishing house. Why not go where the demand is greatest?

After that, you can write what you love . . . but you'll be much better prepared to write something in your preferred genre.

I've mentioned this before, but some writers use a pen name to write in an alternate genre—for instance, Nora Roberts writes romance under her name, but suspense novels under "J.D. Robb."

So do a survey of all the common genres before you begin to write a novel or nonfiction (Yes, nonfiction has genres: inspirational books, how-to guides, humor, educational, history, etc.) Then study some of those books to see what they have in common. What style does each writer use? What tone, and what point of view?

Then choose your genre carefully. You should probably nest in it until you have developed a base of loyal readers.

What is *your* favorite genre to read? Into which genre would you put the book you want to write? The answer is important.

# ON LIARS, HITTING TARGETS, AND REPUBLISHING OLD WORK.

**Write Well: #58**

**Word of the Week: mendacious (men-DAY-shus).**

Untruthful, lying, addicted to falsehood. A chronic liar. Noun: *mendacity*. *The pretend countess was a mendacious braggart; her mendacity amazed even her interviewers.* From the Latin *mendax*, lying.

## Q&A

**Question:** How do I get opportunities as a writer? I've tried writing books on apps, but I have no views or reads. I've tried writing screenplays. I'd like to try ghostwriting.

**Answer:** Dear reader, you have been shooting in the dark in the *hope* that you might hit a target. Stop wasting your time and start studying books on how to write *on a professional level*. I've written an entire series of craft books (**Writing Lessons from the Front;** they're on Amazon). There are a zillion excellent books on the craft of writing, so get busy learning how to tailor your writing to a specific market.

Once you are *confident in the craft*, get a copy of WRITER'S MARKET and start identifying targets you can hit. Look at what magazines and online sites are buying. *Learn how to write* what they are buying. Come up with ideas and send out query letters. When you focus on a clear target and hit it, you will earn an income and establish your credibility as a writer. No one is going to hire you as a ghostwriter until you have proven that you know how to write professionally. You prove yourself by selling and publishing consistently.

**Quote of the Week**

"If you catch an adjective, kill it!" —Mark Twain

**Should You Republish Old Work?**

From a Write Well reader: **If you've written a novel in the past and it was published, have you ever considered revising that novel and republishing (assuming rights are returned to you)? Do you ever add new chapters or make content revisions, or do you just do new covers?**

I thought I'd spend some time on this topic since the times, they are a'changin'.

Let's look at magazine articles first: If you sell and publish a magazine article, you can certainly resell that article provided you did not sell **all rights** to that piece. In my early days, I often sold rights to articles two or three times (to different magazines)—but there were more magazine markets in those days.

As to books—let's look at nonfiction. Early in my career, I wrote a book on adoption that included our story and lots of information about adoption. It went out of print and I let it languish, but then I thought it might still be useful, although the process of adoption had drastically changed.

So I deleted the out-of-date information, added a new chapter about "snowflake babies" (the adoption of frozen embryos), and added some links for people to find additional information. Then I self-published *The Adoption Option* with a new cover.

I did the same with several other nonfiction titles—updated, re-covered, republished. But I did not attempt to make them into brand new books—I had moved on and was writing other things.

Many of my novels for children and adults had gone out of print, too, so I re-covered and republished them. I wrote them when I was just starting out, so I did some quick editing to cut weasel words. For instance, by simply searching for phrases like "stood to her feet" and replacing it with "stood," along with "clapped her hands" and replacing it with "clapped," I cut over 7,000 words from one book. That's a lot of pages eliminated, so I could sell the book for less money.

Since the advent of e-books, however, publishers are less likely to revert rights to authors. Some do, simply out of the goodness of their hearts, and I'm always grateful when they release the novels that are no longer selling more than, say,

100 copies in a year. But some publishers refuse to revert rights because they keep them in print through a print-on-demand service (which, unfortunately, causes the book to be overpriced) and in e-book format. They have every right to do this according to the contract, so the writer can't *require* them to revert the rights. This is unfortunate, because a refresh and new marketing push could revive the books that are currently on the forgotten backlist. Frankly, it hurts to see a book languish in oblivion when you know you could give it new life by republishing it yourself.

**If you get the rights back, can you sell it to another traditional publisher?** Possibly—I've done it a couple of times—but it was to publishers that didn't directly compete with the previous publishers. That situation doesn't happen often, because publishers, understandably, want new material. If a book didn't do well with Publisher X, they reason, why would we think it would perform better for us?

One more point: should you update novels to reflect changes in technology? I once considered updating a book I had written in 1999—I had people logging onto the Internet via dial-up modem, people did not carry cell phones, etc. I began making changes, then decided to leave the book as originally written. If I completely updated the book—with a different president, different hairstyles and social trends, different technology—I was likely to run into plot problems. (Have you ever realized how many plots would be ruined if someone had simply had a cell phone? *Cujo*, anyone?)

So now I republish old novels as they were. They reflect life at the time they were written (unless they are historicals —which is a lovely thing about writing historicals), and they reflect my skill at the time I wrote it. Sure, you could look at my novels and see me breaking all the principles I'm now teaching you not to break. But I've learned a lot along the way, and so can you.

Bottom line: if you are offered a book contract from a traditional publisher, see if there's a **rights reversion** clause. Ideally, there will be one that specifies exactly when and under what conditions the rights can be reverted to you. Some publishers today have eliminated that clause. You can *ask* for a rights reversion clause, but the publisher may not agree to insert it. At that point, you have to decide if you're willing to say goodbye to your book forever.

I do enjoy having my old novels under my control. I can give them a new cover whenever I please, I can advertise them; I can keep them and their audience alive—but I *do* realize that *they would not have as large an audience if they hadn't first been published by a traditional publisher with great distribution*. The first publisher got the word out. When I republish, I keep them alive.

I hope this is helpful. If you don't need to know about rights reversion now, you soon might!

## SPECIAL EDITION: EARN YOUR QUARTERS.

No, this isn't a post about the financial rewards involved (or not) in publishing. It's a post about self-editing. And it's a tribute to the best English teacher I ever had, Janet Williams. Mrs. Williams is in heaven now, but I hope she knows that the things she taught umpteen years ago have stuck with me.

One of Mrs. Williams' pearls of wisdom was this: After you write your piece, go back and pay yourself a quarter for every word you can cut. As high school students directed to fill $x$ number of pages with words, cutting wasn't our favorite activity. But I quickly saw the wisdom in Mrs. Williams' words, and cutting is something I now do on every draft.

I don't cut the important words and I don't cut hunky verbs. But adverbs almost always bite the dust, as do filler words like *rather, just*, and *very*. *That* is a word I'd rather leave on the cutting room floor whenever possible, along with lots of *wases* and *weres*, which often signal passive voice.

I try to remember that we are children of the video age, so if I write, "The dog was on the floor," the movie in my mind is nebulous. What's the dog *doing* on the floor? Who knows? Instead I could write "The dog was yawning on the floor." Okay, but earn some quarters by saying, "The terrier at his feet yawned." There! Active voice, and a succinct, visible action. Even a specific type of dog.

I cut all backstory out of the first act (the section before the inciting incident) because at the beginning of a novel, the reader wants to move forward, not backward.

I carve out the exclamation points and the explanations because I know my purpose is to hook the reader, not stuff him with answers. I take a scalpel to paragraphs of nothing but description, because I can describe as my characters move through the story.

I try to cut unnecessary and obvious words. "She stood to her feet." (What else would she stand on?) He scratched his forehead with his hand. (What else? But if he used, say, a felt-tip pen, that might be worth mentioning. Particularly if the cap was off and he didn't realize it.) "He clapped his hands" can become "He applauded."

I cut ~~out~~ unnecessary words. He sat ~~down~~. He looked ~~up~~ at the sky.

One of my publishers reissued THE TRUTH TELLER, a book I had written several years before. Before it went to press the second time, I asked if I could edit it again . . . and without changing a word of the plot, I cut 6,000 ~~completely~~ unnecessary words. In the intervening years, I'd learned how to write tighter. It's a skill you pick up and practice makes—well, maybe not perfect, but better.

Suppose I took my car to the shop for a new battery and after an hour the mechanic said, "Oh, Mrs. Hunt, you'll be happy to know that we not only replaced your battery, but we also put in $1500 worth of unnecessary parts."

Eeek! Not only would I not want to spend the extra

money (that's a *lot* of quarters), but unnecessary parts would clank and clunk around in my engine, causing my car to run like a slug--if it ran at all.

The same thing will be true of your story. Get rid of the unnecessary words, and your story engine will run ~~much~~ more smoothly. Plus, think of all you can do with all those quarters . . . perhaps there's enough to craft an entirely new story!

# ON SHADOWS, INTENTIONS, AND BIKE RIDING

**Write Well:** #59

**Word of the Week: vestige**

A shadow or a remnant of something now vanished or lost. From the Latin *vestigium*, footprint. *Since retiring from tennis, she does not have even a vestige of interest in sports.*

For years I have pronounced this word *VEST-teezhuh*, so it's a good thing I don't say it often. It's pronounced *VEST-tij*, rhyming with *best-ridge*.

Related words: vestigial, a small remnant of something that was once larger—*a vestigial pulse of anger at the memory of how he'd been insulted. I once saw a movie in which a character claimed to have the vestigial stump of a tail . . .*

## Q&A

**Question:** Has anyone published their story or experiences before? What was their process, and did they do it independently or with the help of a publisher?

**Answer:** *Thousands* of people have published their personal stories. Some did it independently, some did it through a traditional publisher. But those who were successful through a traditional publisher were celebrities or had stories that were moving and had *something to offer the reader.*

Nearly everyone thinks his or her story is interesting—after all, *we're* vitally interested in our own stories, so we assume others will be, too. But since *everyone* has a story, we are most interested in stories from familiar people or those who give us information or inspiration to help us on our life journey.

If you're interested in writing your life story for friends and family, I would urge you to do so. There are several books available to help you, including Jeffrey Mason's *Tell Your Own Life Story.* Your children and grandchildren may find the story of your life fascinating. Best of all, *you* may find the process of writing your story a rewarding experience.

**Quote of the Week**

"As an editor and publisher, I frequently heard that an editor's job was to help the writer realize his intentions. That is true except for the fact that many writers have inappropriate intentions. The four most common I've heard are "I am expressing myself"; "I have something to say"; "I want to be loved by readers"; and "I need money." Those are all occasional outcomes of the correct intention, which is to **provide the reader with an experience that is superior to the experiences the reader encounters in everyday life.** —Sol Stein, *Solutions for Writers.*

If you're writing to save the world, preach a sermon, become famous, or clear your conscience, you're writing from the wrong motivation. Whether you're writing **fiction** or **nonfiction,** your goal should be reader-centered, not self-centered. Never forget that.

**Fiction or Nonfiction? Which Should You Write?**

Before we can answer that question, we need to understand the difference between the two genres. Some people might take paragraphs to answer that question, but the difference is simple:

**Nonfiction conveys information.**

**Fiction involves the reader's emotions.**

Many writers flock to fiction because best-selling novelists are better known than best-selling nonfiction writers, and because fiction is fun. But nonfiction need not be the dry recitation of facts. The best nonfiction freely employs fiction techniques to emotionally move the reader.

I started writing with nonfiction—I wrote magazine articles and did dozens of interviews with people ranging from the U.S. surgeon general to gospel singers. I learned along the way, and at one point I realized that by using fiction techniques in my printed interviews made my subjects come to life.

When I moved to fiction, I learned that writing fiction is more complicated—there is more to describe, and you are responsible for the emotional condition of many characters —but what I learned by writing fiction applies to nonfiction as well. The joy of finding that perfect phrase or metaphor is the same.

The fiction writer needs to know how to write nonfiction —and the nonfiction writer needs to know how to use fiction techniques to make his nonfiction become visual and alive.

Let's say your local paper asks you to write a story about the homeless people living in the downtown area. You could go to the downtown shelter and ask how many people sleep there on cold nights. You could go to your local paper and search the archives for facts and figures about homeless in your county and state. You could interview the woman who runs a soup kitchen and the priest who hands out blankets on chilly nights.

But your article will not be all it could be unless you speak to someone in your town who is homeless.

Your article could begin like this:

*The Homeless Leadership Alliance of Pinellas County, one of the most densely populated counties in Florida, served 1,511 people during December 2024. Sixteen hundred seventy-two persons were given permanent supportive housing . . .*

**OR like this:**

*On a chilly night in December 2024, more than 1500 people in lovely Pinellas County, Florida, only two hours from Disney World, "the happiest place on earth", sought emergency shelter from the cold and wind.*

**OR like this:**

*Greg Lawson, a tall, red-haired man of "about forty," used to be an executive for a leading furniture company, he tells me, his voice raspy from a cold. But tonight Greg, his wife, and his six-year-old son are huddled together on a cot at one of Pinellas County's emergency housing centers. Not a vestige of the executive remains.*

All three paragraphs offer the truth (well, for this newsletter I invented Greg Lawson), but which approach is the most emotionally involving for the reader? Which approach would work best if your goal for the article was to persuade people to donate time and money to the Homeless Leadership Alliance?

"But I'm writing fiction," you're saying. "Why are you telling me this?"

**Because you shouldn't say that you are a fiction writer or a nonfiction writer. A skilled writer confidently writes both.**

When you've finished a novel, you're going to have to write back cover copy, marketing copy, blog pieces, and letters to agents and editors. If you're invited to speak to a library about your new book, you're going to have to write a speech.

If you write a nonfiction book, you should use fictional techniques to portray your interviews with clients or experts. Every word you write should still be true—don't say Greg Lawrence has red hair if he's bald—but use all your writing tools to write nonfiction that paints a (true!) picture and moves your reader to tears, laughter, or action.

It takes time to master those tools. Chaucer, who wrote in the Middle Ages, said this about writing:

*The lyf so short, the craft so long to learn, Th' assay so hard, so sharp the conquering.*

If it's been a while since you've read Chaucer's English, he's saying that life is short, the [writing] craft takes a long time to learn, the work is hard—but the joy of conquering it is delightfully sharp.

Sol Stein says learning to write is like learning to ride a bicycle. At first, someone can tell you how to do it—how to hold the handlebars, apply the brakes, keep your balance, pedal fast, and turn. They can tell you when you need to lower your leg and how slow you can go before gravity takes over—but none of those things really clicks until you get on the bike and experience bike riding for yourself.

People can teach you all kinds of principles about writing, but it's not until you actually begin to do it that those principles make sense. And just as musicians and artists and photographers and surgeons have to master their skills before achieving quality, writers must practice writing.

But practice must be purposeful. You can't simply sit and write; you have to write and evaluate and correct what needs correcting. You have to write, set the work aside, and then look at your work with an editorial eye—and that's what you're learning to do by studying this newsletter.

So don't be discouraged if your early efforts to sell aren't immediately snapped up by a publisher or magazine—I'd be surprised if they were. Mine certainly weren't. But I had editors who were patient with me, and I kept writing and reading and studying and learning. And, as Chaucer implies, I'll be learning for the rest of my life. So should you.

So whether you are writing fiction or nonfiction, keep gathering and sharpening your tools. Read voraciously. Study and dissect. And feed your soul so you have something to say.

# ON QUERIES, CONSTRUCTION, AND CONTESTS.

**Write Well:** #60

**Word of the Week: querulous (QUER-uh-lus)**
Complaining, fault-finding, irritable, and petulant. *The teacher dreaded his monthly meeting with the principal, who asked questions in a querulous tone.* From the Latin *queri, to complain.*

*Query,* which can be a noun or a verb, comes from a different Latin root and means *to question.* There is no negative connotation with the word *query. When approaching a magazine or book publisher, the savvy writer first composes a succinct query letter outlining his idea and his publishing experience.*

## Q&A
**Question:** Which pays more—traditional publishers or self-publishing operations?

**Answer:** Which pays more? Hard to say, since the comparison is apples and oranges. You can earn a 70 percent royalty self-publishing, but you will probably sell far fewer copies than with a traditional publisher. You will also have to do all the work of publishing (editing, marketing, distributing, advertising, cover design, interior design, etc.) A traditional publisher may pay a royalty ranging from 10 to 20 percent, but you may earn far more because they have better distribution, they sell to brick-and-mortar bookstores, and they do the hard work that comes *after* you've finished writing. So you can't directly compare .

One thing is certain—it is harder to place a book with a traditional publisher because competition is keen. Your book must be exceptionally well-written and appeal to a large audience—but those qualities should be evident in a self-published book, too. In the end, it's your call, so make it wisely.

**Quote of the Week**

When he moved to California in 1964, Harrison Ford noticed that all the other young actors were in a hurry —they wanted to become stars, and they wanted those starring roles as quickly as possible. So Ford decided to settle in for the long haul. To support himself, he became a carpenter, and ended up working for a few stars—Francis Ford Coppola, James Caan, and Richard Dreyfus, for example.

In the early seventies, Ford was building a portico at the entrance to a building where George Lucas was holding readings for *Star Wars*. He asked Ford if he'd mind coming in and reading with some folks who were auditioning—he'd be feeding them their lines. Ford did. "I read with about 300 actors and weeks later, they asked me if I wanted to play Han Solo," he said. "By doing carpentry, I was able to wait it out. And as the years went by, the attrition rate eliminated many of those people from the competition pool until finally, there were only a few of us left on the bus from that entering class. I always saw life that way—you just have to find a way to stick it out, to prevail." (From Billy Oppenheimer's Six at Six on Sunday). https://billyoppenheimer.com

I feel like I say this all the time, but I'll say it again—there's a lot to be learned by **writing small things first**. Write—and get paid for—magazine articles, blog pieces, contributions to a novella collection. Writing a book is a huge undertaking requiring considerable skill, so make sure your skills are sharp before you jump in. You don't have to become a carpenter, but you will have to pay some dues, so you might as well be paid while you're paying them.

### Contests

I'm a writer today, at least in part, because I entered and won a contest. I had been writing magazine articles and small pieces for years—still learning, studying, and trying to improve—and I saw an ad for "unpublished children's picture book writers" in the back of *Writer's Digest Magazine*. Since I was unpublished in *any* kind of book form, I was eligible.

The contest, which required a picture book manuscript and three sketches, was being sponsored by Abingdon Press to honor one of their authors, Lorna Balian.

I knew I had to do three things: 1) learn how to write a picture book 2) learn everything I could about Lorna Balian and 3) find someone to draw three sketches.

So I went to the library and found a book on how to write picture books. Every kind of writing has a blueprint, and I discovered that picture books are usually 32 pages long, they eschew adjectives (because the art does the describing), and they're designed to be read *to* children, not *by* children. I also read some of Ms. Balian's books.

Though Abingdon was a Christian press, Ms. Balian's books were not overtly religious, which gave me a clue about what sort of approach to take. Clearly, they weren't looking for Bible story books.

Then I went to my local college, where a talented local artist had painted several murals. I contacted her, explained the contest, and was thrilled when she agreed to do the three sketches. Then she packaged our submission and off it went. Several weeks later we discovered that we'd won the contest, and the prize was publication *and* an advance.

Why am I telling you this story? Because today it can be difficult to get feedback on your work, and entering a contest is a good way to do it. Just check to see *how the works are judged*—if they are **read and judged** by publishers, readers, and/or other authors, great. Beware of any contest that can be voted on by people who haven't even read the book. That's a popularity contest, and it's not useful.

**American Christian Fiction Writers** has two contests, one for published authors (The Carol Awards) and one for unpublished authors (The Genesis Contest), in which entries are judged and judges' comments are provided to the entrants. Writer's Digest holds an annual writing competition and offers cash prizes. Romance Writers of America offers several contests for writers of romance. In fact, you can Google "writing contests" and find dozens of contests to enter.

**Beware of any contest in which you win a "publishing package" where you pay to have your work published. That's not a contest, it's a scam.**

Paying a contest entry fee is not unusual (because there *are* expenses in running a good contest), but you shouldn't be required to pay anything if you win. And don't bankrupt yourself by paying lots of contest fees.

When considering a contest, first do some research. Does this contest have a reputation for excellence? Who are some of the past winners? Reputable authors? Is a national organization affiliated with this contest? If not, you might want to pass. Does the contest offer feedback from judges? Even if you don't win, solid feedback can be worth the cost of the entry fee. Who are the judges—other writers or readers? What criteria do the judges use in evaluating an entry?

Contests can be a great way to test your skills and get feedback on your writing. But don't waste your money on useless contests, and remember that not all feedback will be useful. You might catch a grumpy judge on a bad day, so take the feedback that's valid and forget the rest. Life's too short to obsess over hurtful comments.

Your homework this week: Check out some contests, polish off some of your work, and enter something! You never know what will happen.

# ON DABBLING, BEST-SELLERS, AND STARTING YOUR STORY.

**Write Well:** #61

**Word of the Week: dilettante (DILL-uh-tahnt)**

Someone who dabbles in various arts. The original meaning pertains to someone who enjoys and appreciates the arts as opposed to someone who makes an effort to master an art. The contemporary meaning has a negative connotation, meaning someone who dabbles somewhat pretentiously. *Mr. Jones is quite the dilettante—he knows a lot about art until you ask about a specific artist.*

From the Latin *delectare*, to *delight*. Related words: *delectable, delectation.*

**Q&A**

**Question:** When a book is a best-seller, does that mean it is the best-seller of the year, of all time, or what?

**Answer:** It means that a title has appeared on a specific platform's best-sellers' list at one point. It may never appear on that list again, but once is enough to call a book an "XYZ best-seller." An author who has had a book appear on the prestigious *New York Times* best-seller list, for instance, may refer to himself as a "*New York Times* best-selling author." An author who's had a book appear on an Amazon best-seller list (and Amazon has dozens) may say, for instance, "An Amazon Cowboy Romance best-selling author."

### Quote of the Week

"Words can be like X-rays if you use them properly – they'll go through anything. You read and you're pierced."
— **Aldous Huxley,** *Brave New World*

### The All-Important Beginning

Seems like I am always talking about the importance of the beginning of your work—whatever it is—so let me allow **Sol Stein** to take over for a few minutes:

"Some years ago I was involved in an informal study of the behavior of lunch-hour browsers in mid-Manhattan bookstores. In the fiction section, the most common pattern was for the browser to read the front flap of the book's jacket and then go to page one. No browser went beyond page three before either taking the book to the cashier or putting the book down and picking up another to sample.

"Thereafter, whenever an author told me that his novel really got going on page ten or twenty or thirty, I had to pass on the news that his book in all likelihood was doomed...

"Readers have not grown more patient since that bit of research was conducted. Today, first sentences and first paragraphs of any writing are increasingly important for arousing the restless reader." (Sol Stein, *Solutions for Writers*, p. 15).

Stein wrote those words years ago. Today, I believe, you have only one page, even *one line*, to snag a reader's attention. In this era of texts and instant messages and social media ads, everyone needs to know how to hook a reader instantly.

So whether you're writing fiction or nonfiction, don't waste your first sentence.

Stein says that the **first paragraph** should do three things:

1. Excite the reader's curiosity, preferably about a character or relationship.
2. Introduce a setting.
3. Lend resonance to the story or subject (for nonfiction).

I would add that the **first sentence** should do two things:

1. Introduce a being—preferably a person, but it could be an animal or even a sentient robot...
2. Introduce a provocative situation or question.

*Ross Wakeman succeeded the first time he tried to kill himself, but not the second or the third.* That's from Jodi Picoult, and it's my favorite first line ever.

What works—or doesn't work—in the following first lines? **What question is raised in your mind after reading these first lines?** Would you keep reading?

- *Scarlett O'Hara was not beautiful, but men seldom realized it when as caught by her charms as the Tarleton twins were.*
- *There was no possibility of taking a walk that day.*
- *In the beginning, God created the heavens and the earth.*
- *In my seventh year, as the waters of the inundation rose to cover our fields, I noticed a subtle change in my mother.*
- *My mother is dead and I can't seem to feel the least bit sad about it.*
- *Silence, as heavy as doom, wraps itself around me as two guards lead me into the lower-level judgment hall.*
- *"I am going to kill a man."*
- *"Well, sir, I should have been sitting pretty, just about as pretty as a man could sit."*

Now look at the first line of your work(s) in progress, whether fiction or nonfiction. Is there a person in that line? What question is raised by the words?

Note: opening with a quote from a character can be passé unless the quote is startling and provocative. You are handicapped from the beginning because we don't know who's speaking, we don't know who is being addressed, and we don't know the situation. But the two quotation first lines above are intriguing because they are startling. In the first instance we wonder why the speaker wants to kill a man, and in the second, we want to know why he isn't "sitting pretty" though the speaker certainly should be.

Writing a winning first line isn't easy—I wish I could say that all my efforts are five-star, but some are better than others. What matters is *hooking your reader*. If you do that with the first line, and then follow up with more hooks, you'll have a reader who can't put your book down.

Susan Bell (*The Artful Edit*) says that "many writers don't find the first sentence to their book until they edit, because only then, on reading their draft, do they discover that the beginning is hiding on page three or four."

You may have succumbed to the temptation to clutter your beginning with material that is best omitted, and your best first line may be on the next page or even in the next chapter. Try removing the first scene of your book and beginning at the next scene—does the story read as well? Is it more gripping without that introductory material?

One more thing about your opening—your first chapter establishes a contract with your reader. As the reader reads, he or she intuitively understands 1) the genre, 2) the point of view, 3) the author's voice, 4) the time and place of the novel, and 4) the point of view character, which is usually the protagonist. Though some novels open in the point of view of a secondary character, it's always jarring to read the following chapter and realize that the guy in chapter one wasn't the protagonist at all.

So write so that your reader can gather this information effortlessly. If you are going to feature several POV characters, you might want to use at least two in your opening chapter so the reader will expect to enter the POV of other characters as well.

Our goal as storytellers is to establish what John

Gardner called "the fictive dream," and we don't want to break that dream by doing something that jars the reader.

That's your homework for this week: work on your first line, your first scene, and your first chapter until it is the best it can be.

# ON WRITING ROOMS, WEBSITES, AND CHARACTER IMPERFECTION.

**Write Well:** #62

## Word of the Week: apparatchik (ah-pah-RAHt-chik)

Historically, the word referred to a member of the Communist party. Currently the word has a negative connotation and refers to any member of a large political organization. *Don't mind him, he's an apparatchik of the labor unions . . .* From the Russian *apparat,* the administrative system of the communist party.

## Quote of the Week

In *Conversations with Joan Didion,* the writer said she never felt confident heading to her writing desk every day. Instead, she had "blind faith that if you go in and work every day it will get better. Three days will go by and you will be in that office and you will think every day is terrible. But on the fourth day, if you do go in, if you don't go into town or out in the garden, something usually will break through."

When the interviewer asked how she felt in the hours before heading to her writing desk, Didion replied, "Oh, I don't want to go in there at all. It's low dread, every morning. That dread goes away after you've been in there an hour. I keep saying 'in there' as if it's some kind of chamber, a different atmosphere. It is, in a way. There's almost a psychic wall. The air changes. I mean you don't want to go through that door. But once you're in there, you're there, and it's hard to go out."

As she spoke about putting in time on the job every day, regardless of her mood, the interviewer recalled Didion once mentioning that, unlike most, she used her good silverware at the table every day instead of saving it for special occasions. "Well," Didion replied, "every day is all there is."

From Billy Oppenheimer, 2/9/25

## Q&A

**Question:** Is having a personal website necessary for writers to sell their books?

**Answer:** Yes and no. I daresay most writers don't want to mess with the hassle of storing and mailing book orders, so they use their websites to link to their books on the sites of major online retailers (Amazon, B&N, etc.). If you *do* want to sell books direct, then yes, having a website will be crucial, but how are you going to drive people to your site?

I would say that the major benefit of having a website is to foster connection between writer and reader. If people hear about you, or read your book and want to know more, they can visit your website to read your bio, see what else you have written, and get a general sense of who you are. That kind of connection is invaluable. The same kind of connection can be fostered through a professional Facebook page or Instagram account.

## The Secret to Compelling Heroes, Villains, and Antiheroes

If you're human, you're imperfect (surprise!). We all are, so our characters should be a mix of virtues and flaws. But in a novel, sometimes you need an outright villain, someone who acts in his own interests, thus endangering others. Yet too many writers create villains that have no redeeming characteristics whatsoever, and unless you're creating an over-the-top weirdo villain like the Joker, you need to give your villain a virtue or two.

In the same way, avoid creating perfectly perfect heroes/protagonists. Even Superman has kryptonite as a weakness, and even a saintly person can be tempted if the circumstances are right. So let your protagonist slip and fall, then let him realize his mistake and atone for it. Your story will be stronger.

When I was a teenager, my mother gave me books by a popular Christian writer. I enjoyed reading them, but they were so obvious— the "bad" girls were always identified by their red nail polish. The heroines were squeaky clean, and went around whistling out of an overflow of good nature. Those books served their purpose, but today they seem hopelessly out of touch.

Perhaps it's the time we're living in, but lately I've noticed a pronounced rise in anti-heroes —the hero with a "flexible" moral code. *The Day of the Jackal* is about a hired assassin who kills people, but we find ourselves rooting for him because the people he kills are evil. *The Godfather* is about a mafia don, but we root for him because his crime family

refuses to sell drugs to children. *Dexter* is a psychopathic serial killer, but we root for him because he only kills murderers who have escaped justice. *Yellowstone* is the mafia set in Montana, but we root for the murderous Dutton family because the people out to get them are more evil and ruthless than they are.

When our society is such that we root for the lesser of heinous evils . . . well, I don't need to launch into a tirade about how deeply sin has permeated our world. But here's my point: when you live in such a world, writing perfectly perfect heroes and completely evil villains strikes the reader as absurd and unrealistic.

Yet our readers crave goodness. We *want* to read about someone who struggles against the tide of selfishness and corruption that pervades our society. Your reader wants someone to admire and emulate, so don't be afraid to give them such a protagonist, just be honest about that character's weaknesses, temptations, and yes, his failures. Then bolster him with courage, resolve, and spiritual strength. Give him (or her) a noble goal and the tenacity to persevere and reach that goal despite all the forces working against him.

Give both your hero and your villain someone or something to passionately love. In *The Day of the Jackal*, the killer loved his wife and baby. Godfather Don Corleone loved his family above all. Dexter, a psychopath, actually loved his sister. And John Dutton of Yellowstone loved *his* father, to whom he made a promise: he would protect the ranch at all costs. If you're writing an antihero, at some point the thing your protagonist loves must be threatened by the opposition.

Give your admirable heroes something to love, too, and let the reader see that love on display. Most people love their families—spouses and children—more than anything else. Some characters—the martyrs, for instance—love God more than anything, and would face death rather than denounce Him. Some characters risk their lives for their countries, their friends, or their cause. So no matter what your protagonist's life situation, give him (or her) something to love passionately, show his love for that person, cause, or institution, and then bring forward an adversary to threaten the thing your protagonist loves.

Note: you don't have to spend time/word count on giving *secondary* or minor characters flaws and virtues— they're only supporting the story, so let them play their supporting roles without delving into their psyches. Your focus should be on your major characters, on the complex inner working of their minds.

Incidentally, let's review the difference between **villain** and **antagonist**. Every villain is an antagonist (who stands in the way of the protagonist's goal), but not every antagonist is a villain. Any character—the protagonist's friend, mother, sister, or a stranger—can stand in the way of the main character's goal for the entire story or only for a scene. You don't have to deeply develop the psyche of an antagonist who's only blocking the protagonist for a scene or two, but their reason for blocking the main character should make sense.

Next week, we'll talk more about villains. Not every story has or needs one, but if you do, make sure he's not *completely* evil.

# ON HOMOPHONES, RETIREMENT, AND VILLAINS.

**Write Well:** #63

**Word of the Week: immanent, emanate, eminent, and imminent.**

**Immanent,** from the Latin *immaneon,* **to remain near.** If something is immanent, it is indwelling, present, or abiding in. *The writer had an immanent talent for creating drama.* Synonym: inherent.

**Emanate,** pronounced EM-en-nate, from the Latin *emanat,* **to flow out from.** *Thankfully, a great deal of warmth emanated from the small fire.*

Write Well is a reader-supported publication. To receive new posts and support my work, consider becoming a free or paid subscriber.

**Eminent,** from the Latin *eminent,* **jutting or projecting.** Eminent means outstanding in a particular field, as one can be *an eminent researcher* or a man can have *an eminent talent for oration.*

**Imminent**, from the Latin *imminent*, **overhanging or impending**. About to happen, as in: *Some say that California is in imminent danger of falling into the Pacific.*

## Q&A

Question: Why do authors retire from writing? And what do they do for a living after they retire?

Answer: Why would an author retire from writing? I've known writers who retired because they wanted more time to spend with family, but there is no reason why writers *have* to retire. Theoretically, a writer can write until the day he or she dies. What do they do for a living after retirement? They live on their retirement income—if they have been wise enough to save for those days. If can't support themselves on retirement funds, I suspect they will keep busy by writing, teaching, editing, or some combination of all three.

## Quote of the Week

"I'll tell you what I was most surprised to discover about my writing process, and that is that I never know what I'm doing." —Sharon Cameron

## Types of Villains

Are you writing a thriller, a murder mystery, or science fiction? Not every novel requires a villain, but many of them do. Here's a handy dandy guide for fashioning your villain, adapted from something I read in *Writer's Digest* decades ago.

I. **The Accidental Villain** (that'd be a good title for a novel): this is the normal guy who doesn't intend to do wrong. But he has an uncontrollable weakness for something, and his weakness gets him into deeper and deeper into trouble—the drug addict who agrees to hold his dealer's stash for a few days and ends up on the run from the dealer's supplier. The faithful husband who has a one-night stand and ends up haunted by an obsessed pregnant woman as in *Fatal Attraction*. The woman who tells one little lie and ends up getting another woman killed by a jealous husband.

That first misstep may be small, but it results in huge consequences. To write this character, reveal the fatal flaw early, in the first scene, and keep it small—otherwise, this character is a moral person. Write scenes in the character's point of view so can we see he's not diabolical. But after his mistake, results begin to pile up and we see his reaction to his own sin.

2. **The Examined Villain:** the character who weighs the odds and *intends* to do wrong. He or she plans the crime carefully and carries it

through. To write this character, tell the story in his or her point of view. Show us what drove her to this crime. Give her quirks and personality. Keep the story rooted in reality. And finally, make sure what she's doing makes sense to her. This character is not crazy; she's motivated to commit evil for a reason.

3. **The Surprise Villain:** this character is introduced sympathetically and we don't see his or her evil until well into the story. Don't make him or her a point of view character. Plant hints that all is not as it seems, but keep them subtle. Make sure the character is plausible both before and after the revelation of his/her evil.
Example: *Rebecca*.

4. **The Over-the Top Weirdo Villain:** an exaggerated character (The Joker in **Batman**, the mad bomber in **Speed**). The appeal of this villain is not realism, but novelty. Make him an original.

Hints for writing this character: give him big beliefs—that humans are alien products, that the president is an android, or that society is a computer matrix. Match the villain's evil to the hero's weakness. If your hero is a doctor, make the villain an evil medical researcher. And because this villain is so exaggerated, surround him with factual details. Keep the science and surroundings as real as possible.

5. **Mundane, standard villains:** they are ordinary people who are evil because they are stupid or weak or selfish. They steal because they're lazy. They destroy because they're jealous.

Hints to write this villain: deepen the stereotypes with unexpected twists. Use lots of sensory details so we can see, hear, and smell this character. He or she lives in a dreary moral vacuum.

6. **The Anti-hero:** we talked a little about this type last week. If you recall that conversation, you'll see that the protagonists of many movies and books these days are actually anti-heroes. These are not people you'd welcome into your family because their moral code is based on doing what's best for them and their cause. But they are the heroes of their stories because the people they are fighting *are worse than they are.* Our society holds situational ethics. Anti-heroes are a reflection of our time.

If your story needs a villain, make sure he or she is so well-developed that you could tell the story from his perspective instead of the hero's.

Years ago I learned something from reading *How to Win Friends and Influence People* that has stayed with me: **people can always justify the wrong they do.** For instance, if a car thief steals your car, he'll blame *you* for being dumb enough to leave the keys inside or for parking in a high crime neighborhood. Make sure your villain convinces himself that doing evil is the logically correct thing to do.

Last night my husband and I watched *Mr. Bates Versus the Post Office* (it's streaming on the PBS app for a short while). It's an excellent David v. Goliath story, and it illustrates the following point:

Make sure your villain's resources and strength equals or surpasses the protagonist's in most of the story. The villain should be winning the battle for the greater part of the novel, pitting his/her enormous resources against the protagonists' few. It should appear impossible for protagonist to triumph and achieve his or her goal. (We love to root for an underdog.)

But at the bleakest moment—relying on *immanent* strength and virtue—the protagonist foils the villain. For your reader, the protagonist's victory should be in doubt through most of the story. Your reader will keep turning those pages to see how your protagonist foils that villain.

# ON PEAKS AND VALLEYS, FINDING TIME, AND REACTIVE PROTAGONISTS

**Write Well: #64**

**Words of the Week: nadir (NAY-dur) and zenith (ZEE-nith):**

Nadir: The lowest point of anything, the deepest depression or loss. **Zenith:** the highest point.

I've been mispronouncing *nadir* all my life. I've always said nay-DEER, but it's NAY-der. Fortunately, it's a word I *see* more often than I *say*, so I will hitherto attempt to pronounce it correctly. From an Arabic word, *nadir*, the opposite of *zenith*. So if the nadir is the lowest point of a graph, a mood, or a movement, the zenith is the highest. You may also refer to the highest point of a thing as the *apogee* (AP-ah-jee), *pinnacle, apex,* or *vertex.*

*Her love for him reached its zenith the day he brought her flowers. It reached its nadir the next morning when he forgot her birthday.*

**Q&A**

**Question:** What is the process for obtaining permission to use someone's artwork in a publication?

**Answer:** Contact the artist or the artist's agent and buy a license. (If you are using a stock photo service like deposit-photos.com, they are acting as the artist's agent.) That will give you permission to use the artwork for a certain amount of time or a certain number of copies, depending upon the terms of the license. Kudos to you for realizing that every photo, illustration, or copy of art you see on the internet is NOT available for free use.

### Quote of the Week

"One of the most difficult things [to write] is the first paragraph. I have spent many months on a first paragraph and once I get it, the rest just comes out very easily. In the first paragraph you solve most of the problems with your book. The theme is defined, the style, the tone. At least in my case, the first paragraph is a kind of sample of what the rest of the book is going to be."

"Ultimately literature is nothing but carpentry. Both are very hard work. Writing something is almost as hard as making a table. With both you are working with reality, a material just as hard as wood. Both are full of tricks and techniques. Basically very little magic and a lot of hard work involved." —Gabriel García Márquez

*Quote is from **The Paris Review** interview conducted by Peter H. Stone. García Márquez's sons translated his answers into English.*

### How Do You Find Time to Write?

I hear this question all the time, even from established writers. How can you write a book and finish it in a timely fashion? Here are some tips:

1. If you don't have a deadline, give yourself one. Just make sure it's realistic.

2. Print out a calendar from your computer. If it has your personal appointments and such on it, great —you'll need to work around those, right? Now draw an X over the days you know you won't be able to write: travel days, family birthdays (if you need time to prepare, etc.), Sabbaths, etc. Now count the days with no X—those are your writing days.

3. Know your pace—how many words can you comfortably write in your available hours per day in a *first* draft? How many pages can you edit in a day for *subsequent* drafts? Figure how many days you will need for each draft—for me, fifteen days per draft at five drafts usually results in a finished novel, but I'm a full-time writer (though I rarely actually write more than four or five hours a day). Be realistic—we all know *life takes time*. There are appointments to make, laundry to do, spouses to care for, children with needs, pets that need walking, etc.

4. On your paper calendar, pencil in your daily "assignment" for each day. Draft one days should have "Write 1-3,000 words" (or whatever your daily quota is. You know your pace). Give yourself a couple of spare days in that first draft, because Life Happens. (And remember—it's okay for that first draft to be horrible. Most are.) For drafts 2 through 5 (for instance), just write "Draft 2" on however many days you think you'll need. You can fill in the page numbers once you reach that stage. No way to know them in the planning stage.

5. Work through your schedule and don't go to bed until your daily quota is done. If a life emergency strikes and your schedule gets messed up, print out another calendar and start again. You'd be surprised how you can make up for lost time by doing an extra page a day, or working Sunday afternoons.

6. Between drafts, reserve a couple of days for triage. These are days for "big picture" fixes of the draft you've just finished before you jump back into the line by line edit. They also serve as emergency days if you've lost a day because of illness, hurricane, family emergencies, etc.

7. Your last draft—whichever it is—should be a quick review. I like to divide the manuscript into large chunks. I print out a paper copy and sit at my desk following along while the computer reads the polished manuscript to me. My ear will catch things my eyes have missed, and you may find that the story hangs together better when you hear it in three or four sessions—as a reader

would read it. After that—it's off to the editor or agent!

### The Reactive Protagonist

I've been writing historical fiction with biblical characters for the last several years, and I always find myself facing a particular challenge when I sit down to plot—but same problem is often evident when I examine many beginners' ' proposals. The problem? A protagonist who doesn't *act*, she *reacts* to whatever life throws her way. The women of ancient times didn't have the luxury of deciding their fates —their fathers arranged their marriages and their husbands arranged their lives. Rarely does the Bible tell us about a woman who acted with free agency, so I usually end up inventing a situation that's logical, but extra-biblical.

But remember the WAGS concept of what should be in a novel? A different WORLD, plus an ACTIVE protagonist with GOALS and high STAKES.

I was on a plane once when they showed the movie THE PURSUIT OF HAPPYNESS, with Will Smith. I didn't like the movie. Maybe because I was squished into my seat, but mostly, I think, because Will Smith's character experienced *bad* thing after *bad* thing after *bad* thing. He eventually set goals and overcame all his misfortune, but the pacing of that plot was off. In the plot skeleton, the ribs are *curved*, meaning that after a bad complication, you have to give the protagonist some grace—a little recovery time so he can experience something positive.

I've seen too many plot synopses where the protagonist suffers bad thing after bad thing after bad thing . . . but never does she set a goal, grit her teeth in determination, and go for her goal. We read books and watch movies to see the protagonist suffer, grow, and learn. A plot where the protagonist merely reacts turns out to be a plot about the main character's suffering and that's a bummer of a plot.

So make sure (I'm also talking to myself here) that right after the inciting incident, you give your protagonist a difficult, film-able goal—something we can *see* her win or reject. Throughout the struggle, she will learn a lesson that will benefit not only her own life, but the lives of all who read her story.

Make your protagonist act, not merely react. That's one of the keys to strong fiction.

# ON MOVING IN CIRCLES, HABITS, AND CHASING TIME.

**Write Well: #65**

**Word of the Week: circumlocution (sir-cum-low-cue-shun).**

A roundabout way of talking, or using more words than necessary. It is not the same thing as **verbosity** (general wordiness), but Charles Riker says, "circumlocution means wandering all around an idea as if it were hot and you were afraid to touch it." For instance, if someone has died and you don't want to bluntly say so in front of a child, you might shroud your meaning in **circumlocution**.

From the Latin *circum* (around) and *loqui* (to speak). From *circum* we get **circumcise, circumambulate, circumference, circumnavigate, circumscribe, circumspection,** and many others. From *loqui*, we get the useful word **loquacious**. Take a guess at what these words mean, then use a dictionary to check your answers. And remember —the best way to remember these words is to use them in your writing *today*!

## Q&A

**Question:** If a person has limited time to work on their writing, what are the benefits to having a fixed time to write?

**Answer:** Anything you do 30 or so times consecutively becomes a habit, and the habit of writing leads to completion. I write every workday, and I've done it for so many years that it is a habit. When I wanted to earn a doctorate, I dedicated every Sunday afternoon to that enterprise. It worked so well I earned *two* doctorates by reading and writing for my schoolwork every Sunday afternoon.

One of my friends wrote her first novel by getting up an hour earlier each morning, writing for an hour, and then going to her day job.

So if you want to write something—be it a book or a doctoral thesis or whatever—dedicate a certain time each day or each week and stick to your goal.

## Quote of the Week

John McPhee has published more than twenty-five books, even though he rarely writes more than 500 words a day. He once tried tying himself to a chair to force himself to write more, but it didn't work. He said, "People say to me, 'Oh, you're so prolific.' It doesn't feel like it—nothing like it. But, you know, you put an ounce in a bucket each day, you get a quart."

From Garrison Keillor's THE WRITER'S ALMANAC, March 8, 2025.

## Tame the Interruptions

I usually schedule all my appoints (doctor, dentist, etc.) in the morning so I can have uninterrupted afternoons to write. You might not think that a quick trip to the grocery store can ruin a writing session, but it can. When I was writing nonfiction, it was easy to drop a project, run an errand, and come back to my work. But in fiction, it takes time to get back into that fictional story world, to say hello to the characters, to immerse yourself back into a scene or a situation.

Billy Oppenheimer's newsletter recently included a quote from Brandon Sanderson: "One thing that people don't generally understand about writing—for most writers, it takes time to get into it."

Sanderson writes in four-hour blocks. "For me," he says, "the first hour is like 200 words, as I'm warming up and getting into it. Then in the second and third hours, I write about 1,000 words. And by the fourth hour, I'm starting to run out of steam, and it's just a couple hundred words . . . . The brain circuits that turn on first are of the stress system . . . . The agitation and stress that you feel at the beginning of something—when you're trying to lean into it and you can't focus: you feel agitated, your mind's jumping all over the place—that is just a gate. You have to pass through that gate to get to the focus component."

"So," Sanderson continues, "if I get interrupted for fifteen minutes—after I've spent 45 minutes really getting it going—what it does is it resets me back to the beginning . . . So a five-to-fifteen-minute interruption is really more like a 45-minute delay in me getting back to that zone where the writing is really working."

In addition to restarting the process of getting to the focus component, allowing yourself to be distracted triggers a psychological effect known as "attention residue." If you've stopped writing to check emails, when you return to writing, some part of your brain is still mulling over those emails.

So set aside your writing time and don't allow yourself to be distracted . . . except, of course, in case of emergency.

**Finding Time to Write**

How do you eat a cow? One bite at a time. The same principle applies to writing a book.

Many people are overwhelmed by the mere idea of writing a book. But it's not difficult when you think of it as writing a page a day. If you began today, a year from now you'd have 365 pages, a virtual tome. If even that seems overwhelming, ask yourself what you'll have a year from now if you *don't* do anything to begin your project.

There's more to writing than a page a day, however, because you will need time for research and preparation. You'll also have days where you're in the groove and you'll write five pages, or even ten. Or maybe you'll get a delicious three-day weekend and have an entire day to yourself—you may write three chapters!

I'm like most of you—busy. I have a family with children and grandchildren, I have three dogs who can be demanding, I manage two Airbnb units at my home, serve at my messianic synagogue, lead a book club, travel and teach, and spend time with my husband. You undoubtedly have a busy schedule, too.

But over the years, I've learned that we find time to do the things we really want to do. And if you really want to write *anything*, you can find the time.

Here's how.

Go to your computer and open your calendar program. Print out copies of the next few months. With the printed pages before you, put a slash through all the days you know you absolutely cannot work on your book. (Like travel days, Saturdays, and some holidays.)

Now look at the remaining days—where you can find a block of two or three free hours? Weeknights? Sunday afternoons? Saturday mornings?

Look for your open blocks of time, and block them out. Consider them sacrosanct appointments with your writing project. Now, on that printed calendar, give yourself a goal for each block of time. It can be as simple as "research" or "write five pages" or "edit pages 4-13." If you're just starting the work, though, you'll want to pencil in days for plotting, character development, interviews, and research.

If you habitually struggle with finding time for *anything*, I have a few tips that might prove helpful—they've certainly helped me.

1. Realize that you don't have to answer the phone. If the call is important, the caller can leave a message.

2. Learn to say no. Scarlett O'Hara had a little speech memorized for occasions when men proposed to her. It

went something like, "Kind sir, I am not unaware of the honor you have bestowed upon me by asking me to be your wife, but I cannot in good conscience accept your offer . . ." You can come up with a similar speech when you're asked to head a charity drive or take an extra week for carpool or bake four dozen cookies for the bake sale. If the request interferes with your writing time, you should say, "Dear friend, I am not unaware of the honor you have bestowed upon me by asking me to participate in your endeavor . . ." Well, you get the idea. Feel free to *accept* the things that will fill your life. Deny the things that will *drain* your life.

3. Tame the television. Trust me, even with 500 channels, television isn't so compelling that you must watch it every night. Pick out the shows you really enjoy and watch those, but turn the thing off during your writing time.

4. Capture stolen moments. When you find yourself waiting at the doctor's office, sitting in the carpool line, or standing in the queue at Starbucks, pull out the book you're reading for research or pop in your ear buds to listen to an audio book. Either option is a good way to redeem time. This is when an e-book reader is invaluable.

5. Have a particular place to write. You'll save time if you don't have to "set up" your desk, computer, dictionary, music, whatever you use to get in the flow.

6. Remember this principle: your lifetime consists of a finite succession of moments. Wasting time is literally wasting your life.

7. Harness the power of the carrot. Yep, you're the toiling donkey, so what will you use to reward yourself at the end of your writing time? A cold Diet Coke? A nap? Playtime with the puppy?

8. Remember that multi-tasking is a myth. When most people say they are multi-tasking, they are actually switch-

tasking, shifting from one task to another. This is not an effective way to do anything.

In the 1740s, Lord Chesterfield offered the following advice to his son: **"There is time enough for everything in the course of the day if you do but one thing at once, but there is not time enough in the year if you will do two things at a time."**

So when you're writing, focus on the writing alone.

# ON RESOURCES, STYLE, AND BEING CLAY.

**Write Well: On resources, style, and sticky words**
    #66

**Word of the Week: rubicund (ROO-buh-cund).**

Red, or inclined to redness, ruddy. *He was a darling boy, with rubicund cheeks.*

From the Latin *rubicundus*, meaning *red*. This one should be easy—what color is a RUBY? Red. Related words: *rubidium*, a metal whose emission spectrum is red; *rubiginous*, meaning *rust-colored*; and *ruby*.

## Q&A

**Question:** How many books should a person publish through KDP before they will earn a decent income?

**Answer:** Impossible to say because we don't know the quality of your books, and we don't know how you define "decent income."

But I can offer this bit of information: According to a 2023 poll from the Author's Guild, the median book income for all authors (including those who write part-time) who completed the survey (80 percent of whom consider themselves professional writers, but of whom only 35 percent considered themselves full time), was just $2,000 for 2022, and the median total writing-related income was $5,000.

If you are just asking an AI program to churn out books for you, I doubt you will earn more than the minimum cited above.

**Quote of the Week:**

The writer Jorge Luis Borges said, "A writer—and, I believe, generally all persons—must think that whatever happens to him or her is a resource. All things have been given to us for a purpose . . . All that happens to us, including our humiliations, our misfortunes, our embarrassments, all is given to us as raw material, as clay, so that we may shape our art." —From Six at Six on Sunday.

He's right. I can't tell you how many times I have gone through something tough, and I immediately reach for a notebook to record what I am thinking and feeling. Why? Because some day one of my characters will go through something similar, and I want to get the reactions and feelings right.

**Choose the Right Writing Style**

Fiction, unless you're aiming for a literary novel, should be written in a conversational tone, with variations depending on the POV character. (Your educated character will speak better than the high school drop-out character.) Doctoral theses will have a far different tone and a far different audience.

So when you are writing, think about your reader above all. Don't try to imitate someone else, simply write your story using your own voice and your own words. If you're using a grammar checker, see if it has a setting—some can be set to "formal" or "informal."

That advice also holds true for nonfiction. I was once hired to take a man's doctoral thesis and turn it into a nonfiction book. It was dense and heavy with footnotes taken from the year he did his research. When I sat down to write, I asked myself who would buy this book—ordinary people. So I resolved to make it as easy and exciting to read as a magazine at the grocery checkout line. He had traveled to an exotic land to do research, so I portrayed him as a character, truthfully describing the things he saw, smelled, and experienced while he was overseas. I also updated the footnotes and quoted from current newspaper articles.

When he read the draft, he said, "You've made me sound like Indiana Jones!"

Bingo.

The academic material was still there—but the book was written in a conversational style anyone could read and enjoy. Because the topic was timely, the publisher rushed it to press and it came out six weeks after I'd handed it in . . . and it sold a gazillion copies.

Another time I was reading fiction chapters for critique. I'd been told that one of them had been written by a teenage girl, and I identified it in no time. Not by her name, but by her style. "I don't know this girl," I told my roommate, "but I can tell she comes from a home with no television—and she's probably homeschooled."

How could I tell? Because though the girl was a good writer, I felt as though I were reading something from one of the Bronte sisters. The language wasn't modern and neither was the narrative. I was pretty sure she read classic novels for pleasure. Nothing wrong with that, but today's writers have to communicate with a *modern* audience.

I have nothing against homeschooling—I did that myself for a while—and while much of today's television is insipid, to reach our world, you have to *live* in our world. You have to be aware of how people speak, act, and think. You have to know at least a few things about the culture. Otherwise, your writing will miss the mark.

Good writing is tight writing, without unnecessary words. Kill most of your adverbs and limit your adjectives. Turn passive words into active verbs. Instead of writing "I felt my breath catch in my throat," write, "My breath caught in my throat." Having too many words is like having too many unnecessary parts in your car's engine. Beware of the filter words like *felt, saw, heard* because they TELL us that a character is feeling, seeing, hearing instead of just allowing them to experience, see, and hear.

But don't cut the lovely details from your romance—for instance, romance readers love active descriptions of the hero and heroine. *Do* cut excess description in your thriller or mystery, especially if geared to men. Study other books in your genre (nonfiction, too) and see what tone is most often used. See how much description is typically utilized.

I know I'm talking generalities here, and you can always find exceptions. But the best thing you can do is read other books in the genre, note how the story flows, and write your story with the same tone.

You be you. A polished, practiced, practical you.

# ON CRAZY LYRICS, FIRST DRAFTING, AND AUTHOR WEBSITES.

**Write Well: #67**

**Word of the Week: mondegreen (MON-duh-green).**

I don't know how useful this word will be in your writing, but it will be great for improving casual conversations. Here's the backstory: In the seventeenth century, a 17th-century Scottish ballad went like this: "They have slain the Earl o' Moray / And layd him on the green." But when the song was sung, people thought the singers were saying that nameless persons had slain the Earl o'Moray and *Lady Mondegreen.*

In an episode of Friends, Phoebe was singing "Tiny Dancer" by Elton John, but instead of singing "Hold me closer, tiny dancer," she sang, "*Hold me closer, Tony Danza.*"

When we were first married, I heard my husband singing "You're So Vain," by Carly Simon. Instead of singing, "some underworld spy or the wife of a close friend," my beloved husband sang, "*or the wife of a clothes pin . . .*"

How funny it is when our ears supply another interpretation to popular songs. So if you hear that happening—or if you invent your own lyrics—you're encountering a mondegreen!

## Q&A

**Question:** What makes a fantasy hero's sacrifice meaningful if he doesn't achieve his goal?

**Answer:** Lots of heroes—fantasy or not—refuse their goals even after a great deal of strife because they have discovered something better. I once wrote a novel about a woman's quest for vengeance—but when finally offered the chance to take revenge on the woman who had harmed her, she refused, having found that a life of peace with God and man was better.

In the case of a sacrificial hero, I would assume that the sacrifice was made so someone else or a cause could be saved . . . and in that lies the hero's meaning and purpose. Self-sacrifice is one of the most noble and courageous acts a hero can perform because it is done for the love of others.

## Quote of the Week

"Anyone who wishes to become a good writer should endeavour, before he allows himself to be tempted by the more showy qualities, to be direct, simple, brief, vigorous, and lucid.

"Prefer the familiar word to the far-fetched. Prefer the concrete word to the abstract. Prefer the single word to the circumlocution. Prefer the short word to the long. Prefer the Saxon word to the Romance." —Henry Watson Fowler

## Amazon's KDP Program update

Amazon has just announced changes for books in its

Kindle Direct Publishing program. But they've sweetened the deal a bit for those who publish books in color.

**Royalty rates for hardcover and paperback books are changing:**

On June 10, 2025 Amazon will reduce the royalty rate for print books from 60% to 50% for books priced below: 9.99 USD. Books with list prices at or above the amounts listed will continue to earn a 60% royalty rate.

If you make updates to book details or content after June 10, 2025, you will be required to update your list price to reflect the new minimum list price.

**Printing costs for paperback books:**

On June 10, 2025 Amazon will reduce printing costs for:

- All regular and large trim size paperbacks printed in standard color and purchased from Amazon.com.
- All regular and large trim size paperbacks printed in premium color and purchased from Amazon.co.uk, Amazon.de, Amazon.fr, Amazon.es, Amazon.it, and Amazon.nl.

**Tip of the Week**

I was reading an article about the science of (metaphorical) choking under pressure, when I realized that some of the advice applied to writers. Psychologist Roy Baumeister proposed that when under pressure, people realize that it is important to perform well so their consciousness attempts to monitor their performance. But the skill does not lie in a person's consciousness, so the success of the performance is reduced.

For instance, most of us have learned to type. After

hours of practice, we can type without looking at the keys or thinking about where the keys are. But if we are told to *think* about our typing, we slow down because the knowledge of typing isn't in our consciousness, it's in our subconsciousness and muscle memory. We are not *thinking* about hitting the *a,* the *b,* the *d,* etc.

The same principle applies when we are first-drafting and forming a story. If you are busy thinking about adverbs and adjectives while you are creating, you could be stifling your performance. Fashioning a story or an article requires a different part of the brain than editing, so keep your mind focused on *creation*, not on perfecting your output. In fiction, let the story flow from your fingers into the computer (or recorder, if that's what you use). In nonfiction, let your thoughts about your topic stream forth.

Later, in the second or even third draft, you can switch into editorial mode and fine tune the words. But do yourself a favor and let go of the pressure to "get it right" while you're creating. You can always finesse what you've put on the page.

**Your Writer's Website**

### When do you need one? What should be on it?

If you are just starting out, I don't think you need a website. Publishers always urge new writers to have a platform (a readership), and that's easier to garner through social media than a website. Start with your Facebook page and your Instagram accounts. Talk about your writing journey and your work-in-progress. Join Facebook groups of readers and writers of like mind. You will begin to develop followers and friends, and they will rejoice with you when you finally publish your first book. *That's* when you need to get a website.

The **purpose** of a website is to provide information for readers and the press. The home page of most author websites includes a **header** with the author's name, photo, and tagline. This should set a certain tone and indicate the sort of books you write.

After the home page, you will want pages to **display your books** (one book per page), your **bio**, and a **contact (message) box**.

Your **book pages** should feature links where your book can be purchased. Some shoppers prefer one online store over another, so include several purchase links. You should also include a jpeg of your **book cover,** and a brief description of what the book is about: your back cover copy usually works well on this page. If you've received excellent reviews, you might want to include two or three on this page.

Make sure your **bio** is written in third person, not first, so it can easily be copied and pasted into a program or an article. Make sure the first paragraph or two contains the most important information so it can be copied easily. Include less important details about your hobbies, interests, and pets at the end.

Somewhere—in the footer or sidebar of every page—

you will want a box where readers can **sign up for your email list** to receive updates and news about upcoming releases. Your publisher will want to know how many people you have on your email list, so you might want to encourage people to sign up by offering a "reader magnet" —a free e-book, a deleted scene, or a short story as an incentive.

Many writers have **blogs** on their websites—I used to have one, but ran out of things to say. I've discovered that I'd rather talk to my readers on Facebook than in a blog, because Facebook is where they are.

Finally, your author website should have a **contact box** that automatically forwards to your email, so people can contact you. You don't want to put your email address on your website—or you'll be forever deleting spam emails.

Your website should be clean, uncluttered, and easy to navigate. You can build a nice, free website on Wix.com to get started. I am not an expert on computer codes, but you don't have to be—many websites can be built with drag and drop methods. I built a site for my husband's ministry on Wix in a couple of hours. But be sure to check out this article for information about web hosting on a budget. https://www.authormedia.com/web-hosting-for-frugal-authors/

Do you need a website for each book you publish? No. Your website should feature *you*, and your books will have individual pages on your site. Or dedicate a page to a series, and put all associated books on that page. Your goal is to make it easy for readers to find your books without a lot of clicking.

For more information about what makes good website design, watch this video from my friend Thomas Umstattd of Novel Marketing. He "graded" several websites from published authors to see what works and what doesn't. I learned a lot from watching it, and I'm sure it will be helpful for you. Also visit this link to learn even more about author websites. https://www.authormedia.com/platform/#websites

## SPECIAL EDITION: MAKE THE WORDS DO THE WORK.

The photo? That's me dancing with my daddy at my 1975 debutante ball. Being Baptists, I'm afraid we didn't do much more than step on each other's feet out on the dance floor, but it was still a night to remember.

If I were a beginning writer, I might write the following as a caption for that image:

**The night was a beginning and an end!! A farewell to childhood, a welcoming of new horizons!! An occasion to put on my best, practice formal manners, and learn how to curtsey!! If I'd been a little less giddy, I might have appreciated these things!!!**

What's wrong with the above? You guessed it—nothing

marks a beginning writer faster than an overdose exclamation points. Take them out and the caption is improved 100 percent.

Consider exclamation points as analogous to a president's ability to launch an air strike—you should use exclamation marks with the same amount of deliberation and reserve, and you'd better be sure the effect will be worth the big guns. *Words* are supposed to do the work of evoking emotion, not punctuation, capital letters, or colored fonts.

And when you choose words, choose hunky nouns and adjectives—don't opt for spindly verbs that require an adverb to prop them up. You might need an adverb on occasion, but they should be, like calling in the military, a reluctantly-used option.

In one of my favorite *Seinfeld* episodes, Elaine is dating and editing an author named Jake Jarmel. When he takes a phone message about a friend having a baby and doesn't use an exclamation point, Elaine is peeved because apparently he doesn't appreciate how important the baby is . . . well, to women everywhere. To demonstrate her displeasure, she peppers his manuscript with exclamation points, bombing the thing to smithereens. Ker-pow! Ka-boom! Ka-blewy!

Her boss is less than amused. So is Jake Jarmel.

So do yourself a favor. Go through your work in progress and eliminate almost every exclamation point you can find. Unless, of course, it is an appropriate target. Your manuscript, and your editor, will thank you.

# ON FORGETTING,
# SERIES, AND CHOICES.

**Write Well:** #68

**Words of the Week: frenetic and lethologica.**

Frenetic (freh-neh-dic): frantic or violently agitated. From the Greek *phrenitis*, "disease of the mind." *Phren* is the root referring to mind, and *itis* usually refers to inflammation. From *phren* plus *ology* (to study) we get also get *phrenology*, the once-popular belief that we could deduce a person's mental capabilities by studying the shape and size of their skull.

Here's a fun word—I'm not sure how useful it will be in your writing, but I'm sure you have experienced *lethologica* (LEE-tho-logic-ah). From the Greek *lethe* (forgetfulness) and *logos* (word), lethologica is when you forget a word that hovers on the "tip of your tongue." The older we get, apparently, the more often we experience this annoying condition.

*Lethe*, according to the Greeks, was a river in Hades where one could drink and forget the past. *Lethan* refers to the river, so it's capitalized, and is used to speak of something that causes forgetfulness, and *lethargy* is a lack of energy and determination.

## Q&A

**Question:** What impact does writing a series, instead of a standalone book, have on a writer's career trajectory?

**Answer:** If a series is centered on a protagonist, a family, or a place the reader wants to visit again and again, it will do very well. Readers enjoy knowing what to expect.

Many writers plot stories that are resolved in each book, but a story arc continues through several books. For instance, in the TV series **Downtown Abby**, the overarching dramatic question was introduced in the first episode: when the heir to the estate drowns with the sinking of the *Titanic*, how will the estate survive? All the subsequent episodes, while occupied with the affairs of the staff and the nobility, dealt with smaller issues while working out the larger question about the estate's survival.

In the same way, a well-conceived series can keep readers coming back for similar adventures and pursue a story arc that runs through all the books. That sort of plan is good for any writer who wants readers to return for more books.

## Writing Lessons from the Front

If you're looking for help with a specific topic, check out Writing Lessons from the Front. These are brief lessons, chock full of examples and instruction, with no unnecessary filler. Topics covered? Plotting, characterization, showing and telling, beginning and ending, evoking emotion, the business of writing, and much more! Sixteen books and counting . . .

**Creating Tension in Your Story**

One of the best ways to keep your reader turning pages is to create tension in your story. By tension, I'm not talking about a fight scene or an argument. I'm talking about the pull a reader feels **to know what happens next**—does the hero choose the good girl or the bad? Does he follow the criminal or the schoolteacher? Does he kill his enemy or go home for supper?

So let's do an exercise. One of the best ways to create tension is to have your protagonist *want something.* Your protagonist probably already has a goal: Dorothy wants to go home to Kansas, Sarah Conner wants to escape the Terminator, Lars wants to have a relationship with a real girl. What is your protagonist's goal in your work in progress? Say it out loud—I can't hear you, but I want you to participate, so say it.

Thank you.

Now—we all know that one way to increase tension is to **stall the protagonist's achievement of that goal.** So we create complications that distract him, weaken him, dissuade him, discourage him, hamper him, handicap him . . . you get the picture. While he's working on that Big Goal, we give him other issues to deal with so he can keep moving forward.

But another powerful way to increase tension is to give your protagonist **two desires.** You've already said what your story protagonist wants . . . what *else* can he or she want? Perhaps your protagonist wants this other thing *almost* as badly as the primary goal.

So . . . what *else* does he or she want?

Perhaps Kevin wants to be promoted in his company. Perhaps he also wants a raise.

Yet we're not going to find much tension in that combination, are we? Most people automatically get a raise if they're promoted to a higher position. So let's up the ante—**what secondary desire can Kevin have that is the complete *opposite* of his first goal?** Perhaps he wants to be promoted . . . but he also wants to marry Kristen, his secretary, with whom he's secretly in love. If he's promoted, he'll have to move to Pittsburgh, and there's *no way* Kristen would ever move to Pittsburgh. Forcing Kevin to choose between love and position increases story tension and keeps readers reading to learn what Kevin will do.

The best example of this conundrum I've found was in *Twilight*, the young adult vampire story by Stephenie Meyer. Edward, the noble vampire who only killed animals and bad guys, loved Bella with all his vampiric heart, but he also had a fierce yearning to drink her blood because it smelled more intoxicating than anyone else's. He wanted to be near her, but he couldn't risk his compulsion to drain her of the liquid that gives life. Tough situation (which conveniently disappeared in the second book).

Bella had the same problem. She thought Edward was cute and cool and mysterious, *and* he had saved her life once, but she didn't want to *die* in order to date him.

In *The Hunger Games*, Katniss Everdeen wants to survive the winner-kills-all game, but she also wants to maintain her moral values and protect innocents like Rue and Peeta. She wouldn't kill them, but the rules of the game demand that she kills or she'll be killed. What's a heroine to do?

In *Frozen*, Elsa isolates herself because she's afraid she might harm others with her unpredictable icy powers, but she also yearns for connection, especially with her sister, Anna. How can she have both?

In *The Little Mermaid*, Ariel wants to remain with her beloved under-the-sea family, but she also wants to experience love with the above-water prince.

And let's not forget the Apostle Paul, who wrote "But if to live on in the body means fruit from my work, what shall I choose? I don't know. I am torn between the two—having a desire to leave and be with Messiah, which is far better; yet for your sake, to remain in the body is more necessary" (Phil. 1:22-24).

So—with those situations in mind, **what can your protagonist want that is the complete opposite of his or her story goal?** I'm thinking about my own WIP as I write this—Rebekah wants to keep Jacob near her, but in order to save him from Esau, she has to send him away . . . ah. That works.

One more note, because it came up in a chat discussion this week: **when you create a complication for tension (not the overarching goal), try to resolve it within four or five scenes.** Otherwise its importance becomes exaggerated, and you might have readers impatiently skipping ahead to find out what happened. Before I wrote in Scrivener, I used to create an Excel sheet that had one row for each scene. I had two columns: one was for "dramatic question raised" and the other for "dramatic question answered." These "dramatic questions were complications to the main story goal, and I tried to resolve/answer/settle them within a few scenes. I color-coded them, so I could see at a glance how the complications and resolutions matched up.

| Chapter | POV | Date/Time | Place | Action | Weather | Mood | Others present | Dramatic Question Asked | Question Answered |
|---|---|---|---|---|---|---|---|---|---|
| 1 | Miryam | AD 19, Aug. 14 | Prison, judgment hall | She stands before a judge (?) and begins to tell her in cell | hot | calm | the scribe, a tribune?, a Roman guard | What value? Why death? | Who she is - Mary M. |
| 3 | Miryam | AD 30, June 8, TH morning | Magdala, market | She is working in her market stall with her daughter and family | hot sunny | modest | Rabbi, Roman women | Where's going with Benjamin? | |
| 3 | Attticus | AD ??, Aug. 12 | Outside judgment hall | Atticus arrives late, is listening to the woman tell hers | hot | curious | the scribe, scribe, etc. | Why is she his enemy? Was a she? | |
| 4 | Miryam | AD 30, June 8, afternoon | by Sea of Galilee | Miryam takes baby and goes to visit her husband hot sunny | excited | | Yaakov, Avram, Benyam | Why won't they talk about Benyamin? | |
| | Miryam | AD 30, June 8, afternoon | on street of Magdala | overhears her son, sees him insult a Roman-son hot sunny | dread | | Avram, Romans, etc. | Why didn't the Roman react? | |
| | Miryam | AD 30, June 8, afternoon | her home | Hadassah, Judith's 16 year old daughter, comes over, | scary child | Loves this girl, reminds her of baby lost | | |
| 5 | Miryam | AD 30, June 8, evening | her home | She fusses at Avram for insulting the Roman | hot, still | angry | Avram, Hanzi, Yaakov | | |
| | Miryam | AD 30, June 8, evening | the Inn of Magdala | She goes to deliver the silk and get the money | hot, still | anger/fear | Lady Carina, her slaves. What has happened at home? | | The Roman swipes |
| | Miryam | AD 30, June 8, evening | her home | She comes home to find family dead, house but hot, No | pains | Uriah and Judith, her neighbors | | The house is burning |
| 6 | Atticus | AD ??, Aug. 12 | Prison, judgment hall | He remembers the night the woman speaks of. If hot, still | memory | is Journey, men of the city | What is Oath? | |

Tension—the push and pull between two strong forces, two strong yearnings. Make the most of that power in your story today.

## ON DEDICATION PAGES, LOVE SCENES, AND CHARTS.

**Write Well:** #69

**Word of the Week: aggrandize (ah-GRAN-dize).**

To increase, exalt, make greater (in wealth or power), often at another's expense. The word has a negative connotation. From the Latin *aggrandire*, from *grandire*, "to make larger." *The self-proclaimed philanthropist took a mission trip to Africa, but spent most of her time with a photographer, determined to aggrandize her reputation as a caring person.*

Related words: *grandiose* (excessively grand or ambitious), *grandiosity*, *grandiloquent* (*grandire* plus *loqui*, which has to do with words)—excessively overblown language intended to impress, *grandiflora* (really big flowers).

**Q&A**

**Question:** Is it possible for a book's dedication page to simply say, "This book is dedicated?"

**Answer:** I wouldn't advise doing that. People will assume the dedication is incomplete or an error. Better to just skip the dedication entirely if you don't want to dedicate a book to a person or a group.

I've been skipping dedications in my novels for years because they don't do anything for the reader. (It's all about them, remember?) Instead, I insert an *epigraph*—a verse or a profound saying that states the theme of the novel. This leaves a subtle impression on the reader—at least, that's the idea. It's a foretaste of what's to come, and I believe it's far better for the book than a dedication.

But as the author, using a dedication or not is your choice.

### Quote of the Week

George Saunders, who's been teaching in the creative writing program at Syracuse University for over twenty years, says the dividing line between those who go on to publish and those who don't is that the first group "overturns the tyranny of the first draft," realizing that the first draft doesn't need to be good, it just needs *to be.*

So give yourself permission to write a horrible first draft. It's like birthing a baby—once that kid is on the table, it doesn't matter what it looks like. You can always clean it up, teach it some manners, and send it to finishing school. Time enough for that later. :-)

### Writing Love Scenes and Fight Scenes

I wish I could take credit for this little exercise, but I got it from Donald Maass. And it works—even for more than love scenes and fight scenes. It could work for a car crash or a gun going off. It works for *any scene with strong emotion and physical action.*

Here's the problem: when we set out to write one of these scenes, we typically focus on the emotion OR the action, when we need to have both . . . plus a few little extra tidbits tossed in.

So create yourself a chart with three columns and four rows. Here are your column headers:

1. **Physical action 2. Stuff outside the frame. 3. POV character thoughts**

Now, what's your scene about? A man kissing his girl-friend for the first time? Two guys having a bar fight? A man falling from a ten-story building?

Now create four or five ROWS. **Under "physical action," write the physical things** that are happening. For instance: 1). The hero sucker-punches the drunk at the bar. 2). He pulls the bar stool out from under a woman 3) He kicks the drunk and 4) He swings at the bartender and misses.

Just because you're writing down these physical actions doesn't mean you have to USE them. You're compiling a list of possibilities.

Now move to column two: **sounds, smells, sights outside the action frame** your POV character could observe, hear, and smell. 1) the "Miller Time" clock on the wall. 2) The blonde babe who's entirely TOO into this fight 3) the $100 bill on the counter 4) the smell of spilled beer on the floor

Now move to column 3: **what is your POV character feeling? You don't want to write that he's very, very angry.** No. Use internal monologue to write thoughts that wouldn't be obvious to the reader. 1). He's angry because the guy insulted his wife. 2) He's wondering if the wife knows this guy—maybe too well? 3). He's concerned that his opponent might be related to his boss and 4). What if he has to call his kid to get him out of jail? He'll be humiliated.

Now that you have twelve or more elements to write this scene, write it, using items from each of your three columns. You don't have to use all the elements, but do use things that make the scene more than kiss, kiss, kiss, punch, punch, punch, or I'm passing floors nine, eight, seven, six . . .

I used a chart like this to write the scene below (from my novel, *The Face*.) See if you can pick out the elements I put in my chart to write this bit where a bad guy shoots my heroine (who is going to donate her face to Sarah, her niece who was born without a face and has been hidden away for years):

*I rub my aching jaw and smile. "My life isn't yours."*

*"But I can take it."*

*"Not really. You can kill my body, but you can't touch my soul." I squint at him in amusement. "I wish that were original, but someone else said it first."*

*"You think I am kidding, woman?"*

*"No . . . in fact, I'm hoping you're not. I'm counting on it."*

*Espinosa's hand swings to his belt, and for the first time I notice the oversized bull's head buckle. Compensation, no doubt, for the stature he will never achieve. He wraps his hand around the weapon, withdrawing it, and with pulse-pounding certainty I realize that my faceless life is finished.*

*Yet God is good. He will redeem the life I've wasted.*

*Across the room, plastic creaks as one of the men lifts a monitor, but my eyes are filled with Espinosa and the circular barrel of his pistol. How like a toy it is! In my peripheral vision, one of the goons turns his head, probably to escape a spray of gore, and my hand, pale now and forever because I will never take that beach vacation, swings up and catches the gun.*

*Espinosa's eyes widen. He probably thinks I intend to wrestle the weapon away from him, but instead I lift the barrel, pulling against his superior strength, until the muzzle is aimed not toward my chest, but toward my forehead. For Sarah's sake, my heart must keep pumping.*

*Espinosa's finger bends, pulls the trigger. The flash blends with the odor of burning and a sudden surge of light that fills the room, and I am free, ready to fly toward the Savior I have come to love without ever seeing his face.*

*Before departing, I swoop down and study my features—they are calm, almost serene, the lips curved in a slight smile. Aside from a small nick near the right eye, the face is undamaged.*

*Satisfied, I stretch gossamer arms toward the heavens and ascend to the Light of Love*

Cool trick, huh? Things like the belt buckle, the computer creak, the unexpected thoughts about her missed beach vacation, her humor in the face of death, the smell of gunpowder, the flash and light and freedom ...

Using these details makes the scene come to life for your readers. So find a scene in your work in progress that could use a little love, and chart it out! (Now I'm off to do the same thing!)

# ON CHIMERAS, COPYRIGHTS, AND HIDDEN NEEDS.

**Write Well:** #70

**Word of the Week: chimerical (ki-MER-ih-cul).**

Fantastic, imaginary, wildly fanciful. Greek mythology had a monster called chimaera: the body of a goat, the head of a lion, and the tail of a serpent. In English, the word chimerical refers to anything that is unrelated to reality—but modern science has revealed the existence of *chimeras*, and I have even written a novel about the situation (*When Darkness Comes*).

So the word not only means something that is beyond reality, but it can also refer to an organism combined of two genetically different creatures—something out of the ordinary.

*A human who contains the body of an undeveloped twin could be a chimera.*

*Science has successfully created mouse-rat and sheep-goat chimeras.*

Related words: chimerism. **Unrelated words:** *chimenea* (a bulbous freestanding chimney, and pronounced with the *ch* sound, not the hard *k*) or *chimichanga* (a deep-fried tortilla, also pronounced with the *ch*).

**Q&A**

**Question:** Do you think it is unusual that the publishing industry has been predicated on the idea of acquiring copyrights rather than the idea of servicing?

**Answer:** Your assumption is incorrect. Most publishers don't acquire the copyright, which should remain in the name of the creator/author. What publishers acquire is a license for permission to print the work in a certain area (worldwide, or English-speaking countries, whatever the contract stipulates) for a certain period of time (for a set number of years, or until sales slow to a given point, etc.). When the terms of the contract's termination are met, or the publisher goes out of business, the right to publish returns to the author. The copyright should remain with the author the entire time.

The only time a copyright should transfer to the publisher is in the case of a work for hire, where a writer is hired to write an article, book, or publication for a specified fee. This should be agreed upon in a written contract before publication.

## Quote of the Week

Once stretched by a new idea, man's mind never regains its original dimension. —Oliver Wendell Holmes

## Your Protagonist's Inner Journey

If you're familiar with the plot skeleton—and you should be, by now—you know that in the first act, your job is to reveal your protagonist's obvious problem (something active to hook the reader), his admirable qualities (to bond the reader to your character), and his hidden need (the quality that will change by the end of the novel). At the end of the first act, after the inciting incident, the protagonist establishes his story goal—to save the world, win the girl, or whatever.

But this article is about the hidden need.

Coming up with a suitable hidden need can be tricky—it is usually something emotional, something deep, and something born out of a wound in your character's backstory. It can't be trivial—it needs to be significant.

**So how do we determine this hidden need—the need that will be met as a result of your protagonist's inner journey?**

Sometimes it helps to ask yourself how your protagonist will be different at the end of his adventure. What major change do you want to see in him at the story's end?

Think about your protagonist's past—what event or situation or longing in his or her past causes pain now? How has this scarred him? What is a logical result of that scarring? This is likely the hidden need or flaw.

As your **character** to fill in the blank for this statement:

"I am fully committed to achieving my goal of _____, just don't ask me to _____, because _____." How significant and important is the action in that **second** blank?

Ask M'Lynn of *Steel Magnolias*: "I'm committed to saving Shelby's life, but don't ask me to let her die because my life is wrapped up in hers."

Ask Lars of *Lars and the Real Girl*: "I'm committed to finding love with a real girl, but don't ask me to talk to one because I'm terrified of intimacy."

Ask Rocky of *Rocky I*: "I'm committed to fighting Apollo Creed, but don't ask me to believe in myself because I know I'm a bum."

Ask Sheriff Brody in *Jaws*: "I'm committed to being a good police chief, but don't ask me to go out on the water because water terrifies me."

Ask Red in *Shawshank Redemption*: "I'm committed to serving my time in prison, but don't ask me to have hope, because it's just too painful."

Ask Walt Kolwaski in *Gran Torino*: "I'm committed to minding my own business, but don't ask me to get involved with my Asian neighbors because it reminds me of my painful war experiences."

As your story unfolds, it's your job to *ask your protagonist to do the thing* he can't do at the beginning of your story. He will take small steps toward it even as he works to reach his outer, more obvious goal.

Your character's **outer** journey—the attainment of his film-able story goal—is visible. It's obvious: Brody wants to kill the shark, M'Lynn wants to save Shelby's life, Walt Kolwaski wants to be left alone.

Your character's **inner** journey is invisible, but it must be present, written between the lines, demonstrated in your character's actions and reactions. Together, the inner and outer journey make a circle . . . and complete your story.

The resolution of your story, the last scene or two, lets the reader *see your new and improved protagonist doing the thing* he was unable to do before your story events unfolded.

Walt Kolwaski lays down his life for the Hmong boy he's learned to care for.

Rocky Balboa doesn't win the fight, but he goes the distances and realizes he's not a bum.

M'Lynn realizes that Shelby has died, but her life continues in her grandchild and her friends.

Lars finds the courage to bury his imaginary girlfriend and ask a real girl to take a walk.

Sheriff Brody goes to sea and not only survives, but he kills the great white shark that had terrorized his town and his livelihood.

And Red, though he's terrified by the freedom that comes from his parole, rejects suicide and travels to Mexico to build a new life with his friend.

Does your protagonist have a hidden need as memorable as these? Have you quietly revealed it in the first act and clearly shown how the need has been met in the final scene?

It's in that final scene, when the hidden need has been met, that we see a character's self-ridicule turning to self-confidence, hate turning to love, and fear turning to courage.

What is your protagonist's progression?

If you're writing fiction, that's your project for this week. Come up with an emotional, significant, memorable hidden need for your protagonist. This extra work is worth the effort!

# ON POTENTATES, ADVERBS, AND PITCHES.

**Write Well:** #71

## Word of the Week: potentate (PO-ten-tate).

A person having great political power; a ruler or person in authority. From the Latin *potentatus*, political power or supremacy. *Gladys Hartford ruled the school like the iron-fisted potentate she was.*

Related words having to do with *power*: *potency, potent, potential, potentiality, impotence.*

## Quote of the Week:

Failure to hit the bullseye is never the fault of the target. To improve your aim, improve yourself.

If your work is not being acquired by editors or agents or publishers—keep working to improve your work. Writing is the one profession in which we can never learn everything!

## Q&A

**Question:** How often do good writers use adverbs?

**Answer:** Not as often as unpublished writers.

An adverb, by definition, supports a verb. Good writers choose strong verbs that don't need supporting.

And novelists shun adverbs in speech attributions. "Don't go there," she said angrily.

Yuck! Anything is better than using an adverb in that case.

*She slammed the book down. "Don't go there."*

*She glared at him. "Don't go there."*

*"Don't go there," she said, her words as cool as ice.*

Try this: after you finish a first draft, have your computer search for every "ly" and replace them with "LY" in capital letters. Then on your second draft, your adverbs will stand out, so see if you can improve on that sentence. I'm betting you'll be able to.

## Perfect Your Pitch

Do you have perfect pitch? I don't, but I know people who do. Lowell, who used to travel with me in the Re'Generation, used to joke that his electric razor's hum was a B flat. My friend Oliver was a prodigy in junior high. He could hear a song—any song—and then play it on the piano, complete with bass riffs and other things I don't know how to name. He not only knew what the notes were, he could replicate them all!

You have to be born with perfect pitch. But some musicians develop relative pitch—they spend so much time in the music room that they can usually pick a given note out of thin air because they hear it in their heads. Gary, the guy who leads worship at my messianic synagogue, usually sits in front of me during the service. After the final blessing, the gal at the sound board always plays the same song—and before she hits the play button, Gary and I like to see if we can pull that note out of the air. We usually can because we've heard it so many times it's firmly in our heads.

When it comes to writing, however, *pitch* has nothing to do with music, and everything to do with how you present your proposed book or series to an agent or editor. So if you're planning to put a proposal together soon, or if you'll be traveling to a writer's conference this year, you need to spend some time perfecting your pitch.

An effective pitch (often called an elevator pitch, in case you only have a couple of minutes) is short, complete, and provocative—in other words, it hooks the agent's or editor's attention. To lay the groundwork for your **novel's** pitch, jot down the following:

1. Your book's working title.
2. Your book's genre and category
3. Your protagonist—who is he or she? What is his or her profession? What makes your protagonist unique?
4. What is the main problem facing your

protagonist? Why is this problem different for her than for other people like her?

5. What is your main character's inner conflict (hidden need)?

6. Is there an unexpected twist or details about this story that makes it different from any similar stories?

7. Finally, in the last sentence of your pitch, use one of these magic words: *love, heart, dream, journey, fortune,* or *destiny.* These words resonate with readers.

Okay—now that you've established your particulars, write three to five lines to present **most** of those elements—and don't forget to add at least one of the magic words in the last line!

Some of the elements will be obvious—for instance, if I mention Abraham and Sarah, most folks will know I'm talking about biblical historical fiction, so I don't have to mention that. Keep it simple and brief.

For example:

*The Chicken Who Loved Books, a picture book for ages three through eight, features Little Red—a gutsy, smart little hen, who loves books and the boy Henry, who brings books to the coop every day. But trouble arises when Henry stops bringing books to the coop and instead brings a video game. Little Red must use all her creativity—and the help of the other chickens—to convince Henry that books, not video games, are the key to keeping the chickens happy and fulfilling their dreams.*

Or

*The Tale of Three Trees, a picture book for all ages, features three trees on a mountaintop. Each tree cherishes a dream—of holding treasure, sailing mighty waters, and pointing to God—*

*even when woodcutters chop them down. When the three trees end up as a feed box, a small fishing boat, and ordinary beams, they despair . . . until they realize their lives have been touched by One who can make even the most unexpected dreams come true.*

Or

*In **Righteous Heart: The Story of Rebekah**, the heroine's journey begins with a fateful choice. When offered the hand of Isaac—heir to wealthy and well-respected Abraham, her kinsman—she leaves behind the only world she has known and ventures into the sunbaked lands of Canaan. In Abraham's household, Rebekah finds not only a husband, but knowledge of a God unlike any other—the mysterious Adonai whose favor has showered Abraham's family with abundance. Spurred by memories of her own childhood, she makes a sacred promise: when blessed with children, she will love all of them equally, without prejudice or condition. But as her sons grow into men, Rebekah finds herself torn between her solemn promise and undeniable truths. In a household guided by divine destiny, how can a mother's love remain impartial in the light of God's sacred covenant?*

Isn't this exercise fun? Spend some quality time developing your pitch—and here's the bonus: This copy works beautifully for your book's back cover and advertising copy! If you are self-publishing, this is the copy for the back of your book and your website sales page.

Note: this copy is *not* a synopsis. It's not telling the reader what happens in the story, and it does not include spoilers. This is a teaser, or advertising copy, so it's *not* what your editor wants to see in a proposal. In a proposal, the (usually) one-page synopsis demonstrates that you have developed the beginning, middle, and end of your story, so those elements need to be *revealed*, not teased.

When I submit a finished manuscript, however, I usually put whatever I've written as "pitch copy" on the title page, under the heading, "Suggested back cover copy." The marketing folks always want to take a stab at that task— after all, it's their job—but I do try to give them a head start. After all, no one knows our manuscripts better than we do, right? Marketing folks rarely have the time to read the novels they are working on, so any help we can give them should be appreciated.

For a **nonfiction** pitch, jot down your book's working title, the genre, and the intended audience. Then write *what your reader will receive from your book* . . . and *how you can convince prospective readers that they need what you have to offer.* You might want to mention a similar existing book, but explain how your book will go farther and do more to meet the reader's need. Finally, choose one of those magic words (*love, heart, dream, journey, fortune, or destiny*) and include it —along with your reader—in your closing sentence. Example: *In short, **The Adoption Option** will provide prospective adoptive parents with all the tools they need to make their dreams of family a reality.*

That's your assignment for this week—perfect the pitch for your work in progress, whether it's fiction or nonfiction.

## SPECIAL EDITION:
## CLASSY AUTHORS.

Do you know the difference between classy authors and working writers?

Classy authors never show their toes in public. Writers go barefoot as often as they can.

Classy authors are always dressed up. Writers don't comb their hair before lunch and wear sweat suits while they're working if no one is coming over. Because I live in Florida, I'm usually in shorts with bare feet. Or in my jammies.

Classy authors never yell. Writers get excited and scream when their kids are pounding on the door, the printer won't print, or the power goes off unexpectedly. We used to live in a rural area where our power transformers were mounted atop high telephone poles. I can't tell you how many times

I've been hard at work, heard a large *kaboom*, and stepped outside to discover that a squirrel had committed suicide atop my telephone pole. Being a dedicated *female* writer, naturally I went back into the house, called Florida Power, and went shopping.

Classy Christian authors only read newspapers, the Bible, and *My Utmost for His Highest*. Working writers read those things, too. But we also read the comics first thing in the morning and wistfully peek at Best Seller lists. We read other authors and gleefully note grammatical errors in the margins.

Classy authors don't eat except at banquets where they're always the speaker and guest of honor. Writers snack all the time and consequently gain two pounds per book—unless they learn to chew sugarless gum instead.

Classy authors have housekeepers who cook for their families. Writers make tons of spaghetti and memorize the phone number for any pizza place that will deliver.

In 1983, when I started writing, I wanted to be a classy author. I'd dream about people standing in three-mile lines for my book signings and people stopping me on the street and saying, "Aren't you--"

But *five years later*, I actually wrote a book that a publisher wanted to buy. And the night after I got "the call," I lay awake thinking that the time had come to get serious, I would soon be writing things that didn't get tossed into the waste bin when they'd finished. And my books might change their lives in the way some books had changed mine. And that God had just given me a weighty responsibility . . .

A couple of summers ago I went with my husband's youth group to a camp that offered horseback riding. I mounted a hot, sweaty mare and leaned forward to brush horseflies from her face. "What's this horse's name?" I asked the trail guide.

"Classy," he said.

I grinned. I knew that was as close to classy as I would ever be.

# ON VACUUMS, SLOW GROWTH, AND STORY WORLDS.

**Write Well:** #72

**Word of the Week: vacuous (VAH-cue-us).**
Empty, blank, void. A lack of ideas or intelligence. Not quite the same as *empty*, which implies that something might have once existed in that space, **vacuous** indicates a permanent state of nothing. Example: *Dumb blonde jokes usually portrayed blondes as vacuous.* Or *His vacuity made it impossible for anyone to converse with him.* From the Latin *vacuus*, meaning *empty*. Related words: *vacuity, vacuum* (which empties a space of something).

**Q&A**

**Question:** Before computers, how did writers write and edit their books? Did they write in a notebook and draw lines and edits all over it?

**Answer:** As a writer who vividly remembers buying her first computer, I know what we did. We used typewriters, and we edited on typing paper, then we typed the manuscript again. And again. And again after each draft.

Which is probably why so many of us are excellent typists. :-)

**Quote of the Week**

If you play it safe in life, you've decided you don't want to grow anymore. —Anonymous

In *The Secret Wisdom of Nature*, Peter Wohleben explains that while trees require sunlight to grow, the strongest and longest-living trees don't get much sunlight during their early years. Instead, they spend their first few decades waiting patiently in their mothers' shade. Limited sunlight leads to slow growth. Slow growth leads to the development of dense, long-lasting wood.

Youngsters without any shade, on the other hand, grow fast and therefore develop wood that is airy and susceptible to fungi, yeasts, molds, and mildews. "A tree that grows quickly rots quickly and therefore never has a chance to grow old," Wohlleben writes. A tree that develops a strong trunk must struggle for every ray of sunlight.

The struggle in one realm is compensated for in another, but what is gained in growing quickly is paid for by getting destroyed easily. From Billy Oppenheimer, 4/28/25.

We've all seen people who achieved success quickly . . . and we've seen others who worked years to become "overnight successes." I've been writing forty-two years now, and I've seen people come and go . . . and I've seen people stay and stick. **Don't fret if it takes you a while to achieve your writing goals. If you're learning and working, you're growing stronger.**

### Creating A Story World

If you write contemporary novels, you may not think much about creating a story world—after all, you're writing in the same world your reader lives in, so you don't have to reveal things your reader already knows.

But if you're writing a contemporary novel in a communist country, or if your character is in prison, or if your character is autistic, the story world you create will be vastly different from your reader's world—and that's a good thing. Remember WAGS? Taking our readers to a different world is one of the earmarks of a good story idea.

If you write fantasy, science fiction, or historical novels, you will have to set up and illustrate the world of your novel —and you have to reveal it without a ton of **telling**. You already know that you're supposed to **show** it. So how do you do that?

Here are some prompts that should help you create and reveal your story world. Take a moment to jot down brief answers to each of these questions.

**The Physical World:**

· What does it look like? What makes it different from any other place? Flora and fauna? What do people see when they look around?

· Where do people live? Tents? Igloos? Mud brick homes or skyscrapers?

· Any strange creatures around? Dangerous creatures? What sort of wildlife exists in the area?

· Do people have pets? Why or why not?

· What is the climate? Does it vary from season to season? What are the extremes?

· Food? What do your story people eat, and when and how do they eat it?

· Are there sacred places? Forbidden places? Historical places?

**Your story's emotional world:**

· Do people express emotions here? Are they reserved or are they compelled to show every feeling?

· Is it a culture of fear or intimidation?

· What are the society's virtues?

· What are society's crimes?

· What are families like? Do people live with their parents? Do people *have* parents?

· How do people fall in love, if they do?

· What is the greatest joy?

· What is the greatest fear?

**The socio/political world**

· Can people vote or govern themselves?

· Who is in power? Why? How did this come to be?

· What jobs are most important?

· What are the key laws that shape society?

· What is the attitude about family? Love? Sex?

· How do people pay for things?

· Are children prized or devalued?

Who are the workers? Who are the bosses?

**Your story's spiritual world**

Do your story people worship one god or many?

What is the origin story of your people group?

What is the most common belief about life after death?

Do your story people pray? If so, to whom do they pray?

Describe your society's god—who is he/she, and what are his/her powers?

What happens to people who refuse to follow or obey this god?

What are the "Ten Commandments" of your story world?

**Ready to add some zest to your story? Take one element from each of those categories—physical world, emotional world, socio/political world, and spiritual world—and combine them to create a plot or a complication for your work in progress.**

For instance: I recently wrote a book about Rebekah and Isaac. As I pondered this situation, I decided to take the goats from her physical world, posit that she had not yet fallen in love with her new husband (arranged marriage), reveal that she was expected to have children with this man, and add that the Lord God had promised that Isaac would be a father to millions. Considering those four elements, I could write a scene in which Isaac teaches Rebekah how to milk a goat, and he makes it fun, they laugh, they kiss, and they fall in love and finally consummate their marriage, thus making it possible for them to one day produce those children.

My story world wasn't that unique, but yours may be! So let your imagination wander, consider all the possibilities, and let your story world help you craft a story that is unlike any other. Perhaps your story people live in a world without oxygen (so everyone wears a space suit), and it's forbidden to fall in love, but your hero and heroine are assigned to guard a boundary to a neighboring space station inhabited by face-eating zombies, but the female is captured so the male must rescue her despite the commandment that says, "You shall not cross into Alien lands..."

You get the picture. I once read that **writers get stuck, plot-wise, only when they don't understand their story or their characters well enough.** That is true. If you thoroughly create and understand your story world, you will never hit a wall—you'll have too many options to explore.

So have fun investigating your story world!

# ON PETTY COMPLAINTS, BLANK PAGES, AND SYNOPSES.

**Write Well:** #73

### Word of the Week: cavil (KAV-ul)

Rhymes with *ravel*. To make petty and unnecessary complaints. *If you ever want to hear people cavil, attend a meeting of a local HOA. If someone cavils, a kerfuffle is likely to follow.* From the Latin *cavillaire*, to censure and *cavilla*, mockery. Related words: *caviler* (someone who cavils), *cavalier* (showing a lack of proper concern). Notice the difference between those last two words—it's like the difference between *Calvary* (the place of crucifixion) and *cavalry* (the mounted horsemen of a fighting force.) Spelling matters.

### Q&A

**Question:** Why do publishers sometimes ignore authors' suggestions for book covers, even though they ask for input?

**Answer:** Because the publisher's artists and marketing departments believe they know best when it comes to designing your book . . . and they are usually right. They ask for input, and then they do what is best, taking into consideration genre, what's currently selling in the marketplace, how your cover will look as a tiny thumbnail, etc. They are more experienced than the author and they want your book to sell. Occasionally they miss the mark, but not often.

### Quote of the Week

"You may not write well every day, but you can always edit a bad page. You can't edit a blank page." —Jodi Picoult.

### How to Write a Synopsis . . . and why it's the most important part of your proposal

I'll be honest—writing the synopsis of a novel or nonfiction book (and I still do them with every proposal) is my least favorite part of the entire writing process. Why? Because to write a proper synopsis, you have to pretty much have the entire book in your head. You have to know the beginning, middle, and ending.

In **nonfiction**, you usually submit an outline with a suggested table of contents, listing your chapters and briefly noting the topics covered in each. An attractive nonfiction proposal attracts an editor by showing that you've thought the subject through and you have considered how to hook the reader, how to feed his appetite for new information, and how to wrap up so that he has a great reading experience.

**Fiction** is a little more complicated, but the first and most important thing you need to convey is **the desire that drives your protagonist throughout the story.**

I was recently given several proposals to evaluate. Each had a synopsis, but not one even indicated that the protagonist *had* a driving desire or goal.

A proper fiction synopsis shows the editor that you have

come up with a strong opening, a strong driving goal, complications to stall the achievement of that goal, a bleakest moment, an epiphany, and a resolution that shows how the character has been changed.

Hint: SPELL OUT what the protagonist's driving desire or goal is. Editors are speed readers. You need to **define that goal.** Don't write it in a blink line or just assume that the editor will pick it up subconsciously.

Susan wants to win the race, marry Tom Smith, or become the CEO of her company. Tom wants to pay off the mortgage or save his child from a kidnapper or stop the man who wants to murder a spoiled movie star. DON'T let the goal be something vague, like "Tom wants to be a better man." Nope. Give us something we can SEE him achieve on the page.

A proper synopsis is NOT catalog copy that poses questions: *Will Polly Purebred meet the love of her dreams? Will she settle in California or follow her handsome hunk to Piscataway?*

A synopsis is NOT a list of the bad things that happen to pitiful protagonist: *Sweet Sally is orphaned, then she loses her job, then she gets kicked out of her apartment, then she hits her head, then she's kidnapped, then she's . . .* My eyes glaze over when reading proposals like that. Yours would, too.

A synopsis is NOT centered on all the other characters in your novel: *Polly gets a job working at the grocery, where she meets Kit, who is desperate to become a concert pianist, but her piano burned down, so George offers to help Kit replace the piano, but Charlie is a bad influence on George, so Kit probably won't be able to help Polly . . .*

Never forget: a novel is ONE person's story. You can briefly mention the name of the love interest or a chief antagonist, but don't describe anything that doesn't relate to how the other characters affect your protagonist.

A synopsis is NOT a list of things that happen: *And then war breaks out, so all the people run into the woods, and Anne, who happens to be the protagonist, loses her dog, but then she finds him, but then the dog drowns, so Anne has to get a job, and then she falls in love, but the guy turns out to be a jerk, and then they go to Mount Rushmore, and then another war breaks out . . .*

Here's how you write **a simple, one-page synopsis:** 1.) Work through the plot skeleton for your story, assigning an event to each of the "story bones." If you've forgotten, either read this previous newsletter or get the lesson.

(Example: obvious problem: her house is on fire. Hidden need: to know that her mother loved her. Admirable qualities: she's likable, self-deprecating, she loves animals, inciting incident: she meets Joe; goal: to marry Joe, complication #1: Joe's allergic to her cat, etc.).

2.) Once you have identified all the story "bones," simply turn those things into paragraphs and write the synopsis. Highly compressed example:

- *A Burning Love* opens when Jane Smith discovers that her house is on fire. She rushes into save her cat, Whiskers, and in the follow up at the fire department, she meets Joe, an attractive single guy who seems to like her—when he's not sneezing because he's allergic to cats. They fall in love and Jane wants to marry **him**, but how can she choose between Joe and Whiskers? Then Joe discovers Sneeze-No-More, a decongestant, and Jane can hear wedding bells.
- But other complications arise: Joe loses his job and his apartment, Jane has already lost her house, and the debt collectors make life complicated for the duo. At the bleakest moment,

when Joe disappears and Jane wonders if love was ever meant for her—because her mother certainly never loved her—she finds a charred box one of the fireman saved from the fire. It contains a note from her mother, explaining why her mother had to leave when Jane was three years old. Her departure had nothing to do with Jane, but with the mad scientist who was determined to use her rare blood in his unholy experiments. Jane weeps with joy and compassion for her mother, and goes to thank the fireman who saved the box, only to discover that it was Joe—who has *not* left town because he loves her and he's just been given a promotion, so now they can afford to rent the cute little house Jane has been dreaming of. They kiss, they marry, and all is well.

Okay—that is highly compressed and quite tongue-in-cheek, but do you see how the elements of the plot skeleton are included? The opening in the story world, the inciting incident—meeting Joe, the goal—to marry him, the

complications (and you don't have to list them ALL, just the major ones), and how they swing from negative to positive, then the bleakest moment, the meeting of the hidden need, the lesson learned, the decision made (to marry Joe), and the ending.

An editor reading a proposal like that will see that you have a beginning, a middle, and an ending—but more important, he or she will see that you know how to tell a story. And that's what editors are looking for.

Have you written a synopsis for your novel-in-progress? It might be a good idea to do a rough draft of a synopsis and adjust it as you work on the manuscript. Keep it to one page —editors are busy people—but keep it focused on the plot elements, the "bones" of the story. You will be glad you did.

# ON BIRTHING, CIVILITY, AND WRITING RULES.

**Write Well:** #74

### Word of the Week: nascent (NAY-sent)

Coming into being, being born and beginning to display signs of future maturity . *I looked at the puppy, befuddled by nascent feelings of love.* From the Latin *nascent.* Related words: *natal* (relating to time or place of one's birth), *natalism* (advocacy of childbearing), *native* (a person born in a place), and *nativity* (the occasion of a person's birth).

### Quote of the Week

**Rosellen Brown** takes pleasure in the fact she sustained a writing career while bringing up two daughters, and she still relies on some of the routines she developed when her kids were small.

"I start every day by reading a little something," she told *TriQuarterly.* "I've always done that in order to change the cadence of what I've been listening to, especially with children around. You know, you start the day saying, 'Yes, there is a matching sock somewhere,' or, you know, 'Hurry up, you'll miss the school bus.'

And then I ... had to sit down and try to get into a very different place by reading something. But what that ends up doing to me within a few pages is [it] makes me terribly envious, jealous — makes me want to do it myself."

—from Garrison Keillor's THE WRITER'S ALMANAC, May 12.

## Q&A

**Question:** Is it common for authors to be rude when asked to sign their books?

**Answer:** Not if you ask at an official book signing. But if someone is, for instance, eating dinner and someone shoves a book under a writer's nose, I think he or she might be excused for refusing to sign. If that is rude, well, so is interrupting while someone is trying to eat dinner . . . or have a private conversation . . . or catch a plane. As in all things, civility requires that we consider the feelings of others.

**P.S.** You didn't ask, but just so you know—it is considered quite rude to shove your manuscript beneath the door of a bathroom stall when an editor is inside.

## Rules! Huh! What are they good for? (Absolutely Nothin' . . .)

Excuse the riff on the Edwin Starr song about **War** . . . it just felt appropriate.

I once taught eleventh and twelfth grade English at a private school where the kids knew all the rules—no drinking, no cussing, no fighting, no short skirts, etc. Lots of rules.

And after my students graduated, I heard story after story about how some of those same students had gotten themselves into trouble of various sorts. Apparently they threw the rule book out the window after graduation.

Writing rules are the same—once we learn them, we follow them assiduously when we're starting out, but if we don't sell right away, we throw them out the window and say rules are for suckers. Writing is about personal freedom and creativity, right? Writing is about self-expression, dude. It's about being ME. It's about doing my own thing.

Well . . . not really. Oh, you can write whatever you want on your Substack or your Facebook page or in your journal, and you can even self-publish a book of your liberated scribblings. Some of your stuff might be good. Most of it probably isn't.

You know why? Because the rules don't exist to rein you in—*they exist to teach you principles that create good writing.* They exist to remind you that writing is a communication tool, and to communicate, you need a reader. And if you want to reach that reader, you have to consider his or her thoughts, feelings, and desires. **You have to write for others, not yourself.**

Back to my example: Those kids at that private school—not all of them, thank heaven—hadn't internalized the *principles* behind the rules. There was a rule about drinking because Scripture says we're not to be drunk with wine and it's easy for teenagers to overdo. There was a rule against vulgar language because Scripture says our speech is supposed to be beneficial, not crude or vulgar. There was a rule against short skirts because Scripture says believers are supposed to be modest.

The "rules" were training wheels. The *principles* are what mattered.

The same thing is true of writing rules.

We're told to "show, don't tell" because the reader wants to experience the story vicariously, not have someone tell it to her. We're told to open with action because the reader doesn't want to be bored on the first page. We're told to use active verbs, not passive ones, because otherwise we'd need twenty words to do the work of one.

We don't despise adverbs because we have a personal vendetta against LY, but because nine times out of ten, cutting an adverb and using a stronger verb will result in cleaner, tighter writing. We use one point of view character per scene because continually hopping in and out of characters' heads confuses readers. Writers didn't observe that rule back in Dickens' day because he wrote in omniscient point of view. Even then, he took pains to be sure his reader knew which character was speaking, acting, and thinking.

When you understand the principles, *you can break the rules if and when your intended effect is greater than the result of following the rules.*

The rules are constantly changing because culture is constantly changing. Used to be that whenever a new character entered a scene, the writer took an entire paragraph to describe that character, from his head down to his boots. We don't do that today because block paragraphs of description stop the action, and we were raised on film and video; we don't tolerate inaction for long.

Used to be that a character's thoughts were italicized and switched into first person (in a third person POV scene). We don't do that anymore, either, because we're mostly writing in deep point of view. In deep POV, what you write is what the character is thinking, so there's no need to change the tense and the font just to indicate a thought.

I am currently finishing up a book on the biblical Rebekah, age 14 to 133. And you can bet there's a lot of *telling* in this book. There's a lot of *showing*, too, but there's no way I could *show* everything in every pivotal scene because the book would be 1,000 pages long. The trick is to keep the telling *visual*, so your reader can *see* the things you are detailing.

So yes, learn the rules and the principles behind them, *then* trust the voice inside you. If you're unsure of your inner voice, read some modern authors, because writing styles *do* change. Read analytically and notice techniques. Read a book or article twice, if necessary—once for content, once for technique. Once you've grasped a writing principle, *then* you can trust your voice. Your unique voice is the ingredient an editor is looking for, and it's something only you can provide

Every writing "rule" I've ever described in this newsletter can be broken . . . if you can explain to an editor why it should be. That's news you can use.

# ON ARBITRATION, SHOOTING HOOPS, AND CO-WRITING.

**Write Well:** #75

**Word of the Week: arbiter (AR-bih-ter).**

A person who settles a dispute or has authority in a matter. A judge. From the Latin *ad* "to" and *bitere*, "to go to, or witness." *The rose and the lily had an argument as to whose blossoms were the most beautiful, so they asked a butterfly to be their arbiter.* Related words: *Arbitrate, arbiter elegantirum* (a judge of artistic taste and etiquette), *arbitrary* (based on your own judgment).

## Q&A

**Question:** Is it realistic to have talking animal characters in children's stories? If not, why do people write talking animals in stories for children?

**Answer:** While I would love to debate the matter of if animals talk (my dogs communicate quite well), I think you are asking if it's realistic for animals to speak in words as they do in children's books.

Writers use talking animals in their books as substitutes for people, to provide safe emotional distance for their young readers. Beatrix Potter didn't write a story about a young *boy* whose father ended up murdered in Mr. McGregor's garden, she wrote about a young *rabbit* whose father who ended up in Mr. McGregor's stew. Using animals as characters helps children learn about life while maintaining an emotional "safe zone." Peter Rabbit is a stand-in for the young reader, and the lesson for boy and rabbit alike is "bad things could happen to you if you don't listen to your mother."

Children understand this intuitively.

**Quote of the Week**

When Kobe Bryant was twelve, he played a twenty-five-game basketball season without scoring a single point. Not one.

"I was terrible," he said. "Awful."

Asked if that season was when he began to develop his legendary work ethic, Kobe said, "No. I think that's when the idea of taking a long-term view became important." "I wasn't the most athletic," he explained. "So I had to look long term. Because I wasn't going to give up on the game, I said, 'Ok, this year I'm going to get better at *this*. Next year, *that*.' . . . And I got better . . . piece by piece. . . . You do that over a long period of time—three, four, five, six, seven, eight, nine, ten years—you get to where you want to go." —Kobe Bryant quoted in Billy Oppenheimer's Six at Six on Sunday.

Writing is much the same . . . but when you miss a basket or a free throw, you *know* you've missed it. In writing, when something misses the target, you don't always know. That's why you need an editor or a good critique partner when you're starting out. You need someone who will tell you when what you've written misses the mark.

**That's why I urge you to start writing smaller things— articles, blog pieces—something you can SELL.** When you sell it, you know you've scored. If it doesn't sell—provided you've offered it in the right market—you know you need to keep working.

Way too many writers are tossing words around with no way of knowing if they've scored. Spend your time and your efforts wisely. Write something that can be judged—*arbitrated*—so you'll know what you're doing well and what you need to change. If Kobe Bryant had never had a basket to aim for, he never would have become the *legendary* Kobe Bryant. :-)

**Writing with a Partner**

Sometimes two heads are better than one. Sometimes one head is better than two.

I've co-written several books, ranging from simple ghostwriting (which I don't do any more) to nonfiction collaborations where I helped someone (usually a celebrity) tell his or her story.

I enjoy "true life" **collaborations**—the key to writing a

good one is to use novel structure to tell the person's story. For instance, my editor once emailed to ask if I'd be interested in collaborating with the wife of Brett Farve, the football player. Since I don't watch football, I called out to my husband, "Have you ever heard of Brett Fav-ray?" He quickly corrected my pronunciation and said, yes, everyone but me had heard of Brett Farve.

In short, Brett's wife, Deanna, had developed breast cancer, and my publisher wanted to tell her inspirational story. So I traveled to the Favres' home for a couple of days, talked to her, made lots of notes, and came home to write. When you're writing one of these stories, you aren't writing the person's *entire* life story, of course—you're usually writing about a pivotal event in his or her life. So you can use the handy-dandy plot skeleton to structure your story— there's an ordinary world, an inciting incident (when Deanna discovered she had cancer), the setting of a goal (to survive), complications, a bleakest moment, a lesson learned, a decision made, and a resolution. I wrote up the story, Deanna and I did some back-and-forth for her to make corrections and additions, and we produced a book that landed on the New York Times Best Seller List. Not because of me, I assure you, but because of Deanna and Brett Farve.

I've also co-written fiction in different ways—some I would recommend, and some I wouldn't.

My first co-writing venture was with a nonfiction prophecy author—to be frank, a publisher wanted to copy the success of Tim LaHaye and Jerry Jenkins' **Left Behind** series, so they hired me to be the novelist and the late Grant Jeffrey to be the prophecy expert. I enjoyed working with Grant—he was knowledgeable, pleasant, and he and his wife graciously hosted me a few days while we put our heads together. I think we wrote some great books, one of which won a Christy Award.

*(Life lesson learned: books intended to ride the coattails of another book's success rarely come close to the success of the original book.)*

But I did not enjoy the publisher's set up, which I entered with eyes wide open. The royalty and advance split was not even, and the first two books were work-for-hire, so I don't even own the copyright. If the books had earned millions of dollars I wouldn't have felt the pinch, but they didn't, so I did. In the end, I began to resent working really hard for less money than my partner, and that's on me. While I enjoyed working with Grant, I did not enjoy the publisher's business arrangement. I have done this more than once, and regret *every single time.* **Anyone can have an idea,** you see—but not everyone can turn ideas into good novels. I don't mind doing nonfiction books with non-writers, but writing fiction is more difficult.

On the other hand, some of my other co-writing experiences have been delightful. I once had an idea to write a novella about a couple's first year of marriage—about all the adjustments and how men and women have to realize that they don't—*can't*—think like the other person. I asked my writing friend Bill Myers if he wanted to join me, and he did, so Bill wrote the groom's POV chapters, and I wrote the bride's. The resulting novella, *Then Comes Marriage,*is, I think, a charming and realistic novella.

My friend Lori Copeland and I put our heads together to write a whimsical fictional series about a little town. I'd been writing a lot of "heavy" stories, and Lori was known for her humor, so we invented an island with seven houses, set it off the coast of Maine, and invented a backstory about how each house was guarded by a guardian angel. We wrote five books, and to keep our stories straight, in each book we each took one house (and its occupants), and wrote a story about those people. We limited the time span of each story to one month. Then Lori emailed me her story and I cut and pasted the two stories together chronologically. Then—and this was the fun part— either I would go to Lori's house or she'd come to mine, and we'd work through the book together, adding little bits of humor and insight as we went along. *Synergy*—the cooperation of two agents to produce a greater effect than one could alone— was in full effect as we edited. The **Heavenly Daze** series was delightful, even spawning an online community of ladies who bonded over those stories of life, love, and faith.

So if you are considering co-writing **fiction**, here are a few tips you might want to consider:

- Make sure the workload is spelled out in a written agreement. If one of you is writing *and* editing while the other is only writing, make the royalty or advance split 60/40, not 50/50.
- Make sure your written agreement spells out how expenses, if any, will be handled. Will you need to hire an editor? Cover designer? Interior designer? Publicist? What about travel expenses?
- Make sure all parties understand the meaning of —and share a commitment to—the *deadline*.
- Make sure the copyright is listed in both names. Decide how the names will be listed on the cover. Or will you create a pen name to represent the two of you?
- Determine your approach to publication: will you try for a traditional publisher first? An agent?

Or self-publish right away? If self-publishing, how will you share the marketing responsibilities and expenses?
- Don't assume anything.

If you are considering collaboration on a **nonfiction** project:

- Make sure the workload is spelled out in the written agreement. One of you may be relating a life story while the other writes, or both of you may be writing on a topic. Detail the work in your agreement.
- Determine how to split the expenses. Usually, they are shared (if co-written) or paid by the person whose story is being told. If the book is already under contract, sometimes the publisher will pay the expenses.
- If this is to be a work-for-hire project, the writer should be paid half upon signing the contract, and half upon completion of the manuscript. The copyright will be in the employer's name, and the employer will decide on the route to publication.
- If you will first prepare a **proposal** to shop to agents and publishers, the writer should be paid for the proposal.

This is far from an exhaustive list of considerations, but I did want to give you some tips in case you're seriously thinking of co-writing. Sometimes people get so caught up in the joy of an idea that they don't consider the nitty-gritty of shared work, so consider these points before making your decision.

You can find a sample co-writing agreement here. https://www.allianceindependentauthors.org/wordpress/ wp-content/uploads/2020/01/Sample-Coauthor-Agreemen t.pdf

Whew! This was a long one. I hope it's helpful!

# ON SANDWICHES,
# HAM, AND HAMILTON.

**Write Well:** #76

**Word of the Week: fey (fay).**

Giving an impression of magical powers or otherworldliness, sometimes in an affected way, or having supernatural powers or knowledge. *The painting includes a number of fey creatures—elves, gnomes, witches, and goblins. She is a fey writer of romance novels.* Related words: feyly, feyness.

## Q&A

**Question:** How can you politely give constructive criticism to a writer about their book and advise them not to publish it yet?

**Answer:** Use the sandwich method—praise what is praiseworthy, then offer the constructive criticism with concrete examples, and then praise the writer for what he or she has accomplished thus far. If, after that, they persist in thinking that their book is ready for publication, ask if they want to be remembered for something good or something *great*. That should be enough to send them back to work. (At least, I hope it is.)

The "sandwich method," by the way, also works well if you're a member of a critique group.

### Quote of the Week

Have you seen *Hamilton*? Whether you've seen the play or the video, I'm sure you were impressed by the unique approach to American history. But perhaps you didn't know this—

Lin-Manuel Miranda wrote the first song, "Alexander Hamilton" in 2009. He finished the second song, "My Shot," in 2011, the same year he performed "My Shot" in front of a few people at an event. Everyone loved the song, and at a post-show party, Tommy Kail went up to Lin-Manuel and suggested that he hurry up and finish the musical. "So let's pick a date," Kail said, "six months from now, and just write two songs a month and let's just see what happens."

Flush from the success of that night, Lin-Manuel said, "I can do that!"

"I know you can," Kail said. And he did, proving the truth of the quote, "If it weren't for deadlines, nothing would get done."

So if you are working on your project without a deadline, give yourself a realistic one . . . and meet it!

### CGD: Critique Group Dependency

Should you join a critique group? Yes, if you find a good one. But don't develop **critique group dependence** or you may dilute the voice that makes you unique.

Years ago, I read an anecdote in *Reader's Digest* that went something like this: A young husband watched his wife cook a ham, but was mystified when she cut off both ends before placing it in the oven. When he asked why she did it, she said, "Because my mother did." So they called Mom, asked her the same question, and got the same answer: "Because *my* mother did."

So the newlyweds called Grandmom and asked why she always cut off both ends of the ham before baking. "Simple," she said. "Because my baking dish was too small for the whole ham!"

Ah, gotta love that. Sometimes the rules we adopt defy logic.

Critique groups can be helpful, beneficial, and fun. But in the past, I've noticed an epidemic raging among would-be novelists—I call it **CGD**, or critique group dependency. I've seen firsthand how CGD can stifle a writer's voice and fill his/her head with nonsense.

I know crit groups have been around forever, but many aspiring novelists have picked up a set of writing rules that are too much like Grandma's undersized baking pan. Critique groups can be adamant about what should and should not be done, and too often they're the blind leading the blind.

CGD tends to stifle creativity. At one conference where I

taught, I worked through a stack of manuscripts and kept reading comments like "My critique group feels this is too (insert adjective.) But I think (insert comment.)"

Why would you let a critique group wield that kind of influence? If they offer a suggestion and you are persuaded by their logic, fine; they've been helpful. But if they offer a suggestion and it goes against everything in your gut, skip it. The people across the table are probably not editors. They have no purchasing power. They may not have anything but self-publishing experience behind their opinions. Or their experience may be based on the way things were done years ago.

At one writers' conference, I reviewed a stack of fiction proposals. Several of them contained mini book reports on other novelists' works that read something like this: "My book is a little like Karen Kingsbury's (insert title here) except that my book features a (insert noun) and she works in a (place) instead of a (Kingsbury place).

*What?* Later I asked my class where this had come from (since I'd only seen it in that particular region), and they said they'd been told to do it like that. Someone heard that advice at a conference and came back and told their critique group . . . and hello, Grandma's too-small pan.

(I'm pretty sure the original advice was that your proposal should mention **comparative titles** on the market —so your publisher could market your book to those readers. They don't want book reports, they simply want to know who your ideal reader is. They also want to know your book will offer something at least a little bit different.)

I've seen manuscripts where the author second-guessed every other line based on feedback from her critique group, but a writer's voice has to be confident. At some point you have to trust yourself and not listen to anyone else. Writing is a science *and* an art, and at certain times the art overrules the science. Yes, there are rules and you should know them, but sometimes the rules can be broken. If you break them, break them with aplomb.

Critique groups have their own jargon. They talk about RUE and SDT as casually as chefs talk about spices. (*Resist the Urge to Explain* and *Show, Don't Tell*). I've been in many a session where I had to ask the writer to please interpret the jargon they were using. That's okay—what I call a *bleakest moment* may be your *dark night of the soul*, but they're the same thing.

CGD can result in over-exposing the book that's dear to your heart. If you're not careful, you can talk the magic and enthusiasm right out of your work. Others can pick at it until your amazing idea looks like a pampered Persian left out in the rain.

Critique groups can be helpful. If you've found a good one, count your blessings. But you may find that having a good critique *partner*—one matched to your skill level and experience—is better for you. Fewer voices in your head can equal more confidence in your heart.

So be aware of CGD and its symptoms. You don't want to throw out good material because it just doesn't fit in Grandma's pan.

# SPECIAL EDITION: PROCRASTINATION MADE PERFECT

A few years ago I read an Associated Press article about the dangers of procrastination—dangers with which self-employed writers are well-acquainted. In order to pace myself and meet an impending deadline, I usually give myself a daily assignment . . . and then I fritter the morning away with email, housecleaning, and Spider Solitaire. When it becomes apparent that I'll be up late unless I get to work, I open my computer and begin to write.

University of Calgary professor Piers Steel, a Canadian industrial psychologist, completed a study on procrastination and its effects. The ten-year-study—which, interestingly enough, was supposed to be completed in *five* years--discovered that procrastination makes people poorer, fatter, and unhappier.

A more recent study revealed sixteen health outcomes as a result of procrastination: symptoms of depression, anxiety, and stress, disabling pain, unhealthy lifestyle behaviors (poor sleep quality, physical inactivity, tobacco use, cannabis use, alcohol use, and breakfast skipping), psychosocial health factors (loneliness and economic difficulties), and a decline in general health.

Professor Steel's thirty-page report, published by the American Psychological Association, found that only 5 percent of the American public thought of themselves as procrastinators in 1978 while today the figure is closer to 26 percent. Why the surge in dedicated delayers? For one thing, we have more distractions than we did in '78: instead of working, Americans can watch TV, surf the Internet, talk on our cell phones, play video games, listen to podcasts, and text our friends.

Steel estimates that the U.S. gross national product might rise by fifty billion dollars if our computers lost the icon that appears at the bottom of our screens when new email arrives. I didn't intend to test Mr. Steel's theory, but once during a major computer malfunction, my mail icon *also* malfunctioned, so I wasn't aware when new emails came in. The result? I wasn't thinner, richer, or happier. In fact, I probably wasted more time than usual because I kept manually checking my inbox.

A wise person knows better than to procrastinate in certain situations—if you are sick, you should go to the doctor. If you spot a leak, call a plumber. If you notice raging flames, dial 911. Delay only compounds obvious problems.

Yet procrastination has undeniable benefits. Creativity often needs time to flex its muscles, so if you hit a wall while working on a perplexing problem, stop. Take a walk, play a video game, file a fingernail. The more mindless the alternate activity, the more brain cells available to aid your subconscious. And deep within those cellular recesses is where your answer is often found.

Procrastination can be an ally when dealing with emotional situations. Problems that looked insurmountable at six p.m. often assume manageable proportions after a good night's sleep. Raging tempers can cool when left unattended. Even grief eases a degree when life settles back into a daily rhythm, which is probably why people who have lost a spouse are encouraged to wait a year before making drastic life changes. Adjustment takes time.

Even the intellect can be aided by procrastination. Gems of knowledge are often unappreciated until we are able to put them in the proper setting. I didn't enjoy the study of history as a high school student; now I am fascinated by people of the past. Why do college professors routinely praise continuing education students? Because adult students drink deeply at the fountain of knowledge while most younger students only gargle.

In his *Confessions*, St. Augustine admitted that even his prayers were laced with procrastination: "Da mihi castitatem et continetiam, sed noli modo," he prayed, or, in words that would probably make Professor Steel shudder, "give me chastity and continence, but not yet."

So evaluate your to-do list and deadlines carefully. Do what you must when you should, but allow time for your subconscious to percolate. That is procrastination made perfect.

# ON ILLUSTRATIONS, BRAHMS, AND MYERS-BRIGGS.

**Write Well:** #77

**Word of the Week: martinet (MAR-tih-net).**

A super strict disciplinarian. The word comes from the name of Jean Martinet, a French general who built up the first regular army in Europe during the reign of Louis XIV. His contribution to military knowledge? How to drill and drill and drill. *In **The Caine Mutiny**, Captain Queeg was a paranoid martinet.*

**Q&A**

**Question:** Is it necessary to have experience in writing children's books in order to illustrate one?

**Answer:** No, but in the case of picture books, it certainly helps to at least know the basics. I have hired inexperienced artists and realized that they didn't understand how the gutter works—that space between two double page spreads that is caught up in the fold of the book. The illustrator must be careful that no important elements (faces, text, hands or fingers) are hidden in the gutter or in margins that can be cut off during the printing process.

Likewise, the *writer* needs to know that he or she doesn't need to use adjectives to reveal what the pictures will clearly show—that Billy is wearing a blue jacket, for instance. It's also the writer's job to plan the text so that each page or double page spread shows *one specific action* or aspect of the story.

I would recommend that writers *and* artists read a good book on how to write picture books before attempting to write or illustrate one. My Book

## Anecdote of the Week

In his old age Brahms announced to his friends that he was going to stop composing music and enjoy the time left to him. Several months went by and Brahms didn't write a single note.

But then a new Brahms composition made its debut. "I thought you weren't going to write anymore," a friend reminded him.

"I wasn't," said the composer, "but after a few days away from it, I was so happy at the thought of no more writing that the music came to me without effort."

We often hear that we should write every day . . . but the mind needs a rest, too. Take it when you need it . . . and consider a regular Sabbath.

"Take rest; a field that has rested gives a bountiful crop." —Ovid, "The Art of Love"

## A Tool for Quick Character Development

No matter what your business, you may have been intro-duced to the **Myers-Briggs** (MBTI) type indicator. If you haven't, you can take a quick, free test online. Take a moment to take the test now, then we'll move on. https://www.16personalities.com/free-personality-test

**Building Your Character**

The Myers-Briggs Personality Indicator assigns each person four letters: I or E, S or N, T or F, and J or P. For instance, I am an INTJ married to an ESFP. Opposites do attract.

Let me briefly explain the differences between the letters. Once you understand how the profile works, you can define the characters in your story by simply asking four questions.

1. **Is your character an extravert or introvert?** These words aren't defined in the usual way. In Myers-Briggs parlance, an extravert is someone to goes to a party to be energized. An introvert is someone who goes to a quiet room to recharge. Which are you? Which is your character?

2. **Is your character an iNtuiter or Sensor?** Intuiters make decisions by going with their gut feelings. Sensors make decisions after

evaluating external data. What does your character do? What about you?

3. **Is your character a thinker or a feeler?** This doesn't mean that thinkers never feel or feelers never think—the difference has to do with a person's dominant response. If tragedy strikes, will your character apply his reason to make himself feel better, or will he take time to live in his emotional response?

4. **Finally, is your character a Judger (a filer) or a Perceiver (a piler)?** Is his desk covered with little piles of to-do projects, or is everything neatly filed away? If you ask him to lunch on the spur of the moment, will he have to consult his schedule (filer) or will he drop everything and live in the moment (piler)?

To see how this system works, let's analyze a character most of us know: Jesus/Yeshua. Was He an extravert or an introvert? When He needed to recharge, did He go to the party, or to a quiet place? Answer: He routinely sought solitude. He's an I, for introvert.

Was Jesus—who *did* have a personality—an intuiter or a sensor? I think we can agree that He made decisions based on his gut instinct—He didn't need to evaluate with his senses, because He *knew*. So He's an N, for iNtuiter.

Was Jesus a thinker or a feeler? This one's a little tricky, considering He had the omniscient mind of God, but what does the Scripture tell us over and over again? When He looked out over the crowds, he was . . . *moved with compassion* on them. Let's call him an F, for Feeler.

Finally, was He a judger or perceiver? Neat and organized or impulsive? When I consider the feeding of the five thousand, I'm struck by how He had his disciples pick up the leftovers . . . and there were neat baskets of food taken up, all nicely counted. I'd give him a J for Judger, a filer. God appreciates order.

So for Jesus/Yeshua, we have **INFJ**. So all I have to do is Google INFJ, and I will find dozens of descriptions of this personality, with details about what an INFJ would wear, what kind of car he would drive (if he had one), what sort of house he would favor, etc.

I would find this: **Often referred to as "the Advocate" or "the Idealist," INFJs are known for their compassion, idealism, and ability to form deep connections with others.** I would actually find a lot more description online and in books about the MBTI . . . and yes, INFJ fits Jesus.

So when you are developing your character, ask yourself those four questions, then look up the result and see if that profile fits the character you have in mind. If it doesn't sound quite right, try shifting a letter to see if that result better suits your story.

You will still have to write your character's history and define his quirks, but using the MBTI will give you a head start on your character's core personality. Should you do this for all your characters? Not all, but certainly your major players—protagonist, antagonist, and love interest, if there is one.

The character profiles may even spur ideas about plot development. Yes, opposites attract, but they can also result in friction because people with opposite personalities will not always agree. An INTJ woman—a thinker—may find it difficult to find women friends because she's fundamentally different from most women (most have a predominant *feeling* aspect). An INFJ man—who would have been a sensitive adolescent—may find himself bullied and consequently develop an overly-tough facade because he's more tender-hearted than his peers.

Study your character profiles and develop their personalities so that they will be real and absolutely human on your pages. The Myers-Briggs tool can be a *great* asset.

Your homework? If you're working on fiction, analyze the personalities of your leading story characters. Now come up with some plot developments that stem from their character qualities. To deepen your characters is to deepen your story.

# ON LIFE EXPERIENCES, MBTI, AND AI TOOLS

**Write Well: #78**

**Word of the Week: incontinent (in-CON-tih-nent)**

*Incontinent* is the word I always use when referring to my elderly dog. I also hear it in relation to adult diapers. But the word means so much more—it means *unrestrained, unchaste, with no control of one's passions or appetites.* One might say that much of society today is *incontinent*—we want what we want, and we want it now. You might write a character with an *incontinent* desire for risk or danger—an adrenaline junkie.

## Q&A

**Question:** How can someone find an author's email address? Is it common for authors to share this information?

**Answer:** If an author wants to hear from readers (and most are delighted to, as long as you're not taking them to task for something), visit their website. It will usually have a "contact" link through which you can send an email. If you want to send them a letter through the U.S. mail, send it to them in care of their publisher.

By the way—don't send another writer your manuscript unless he or she has asked for it. Writers don't want to leave themselves open to possible charges that they "stole" your idea. When I receive what looks like an unrequested manuscript, I return it unopened.

## Quote of the Week

"To become a professional writer you don't have to live a particularly eventful life. Average living experiences are enough. You don't have to be a former elephant hunter, a reformed drunk, a confessed child molester writing his memoirs. You need only learn how to transpose the sensations and perceptions you have actually experienced into the lives of your characters.

"Two irreplaceable abilities the writer must continually use are: 1.) to be in touch with his own feelings (past and present) and learn how to transpose them into an invented character and 2.) to develop a sense of unrestrained invention. Fiction is invention, not interpretation or the reporting of real-life events and people.

"The sense of invention creates the situation. The writer's ability to transpose personal feelings into invented characters fill the content with dramatic authenticity." — Leonard Bishop, *Dare to Be a Great Writer*

## ChatGPT and Myers-Briggs

Last week we talked about how to find the Myers-Briggs personality for your main characters. My work-in-progress features the biblical matriarchs Rachel and Leah. As I write this, I'm in the planning stages, making notes and working on the plot.

But one of the first things I did was to establish the Myers-Briggs type for Rachel and Leah, based on things we know about them from Scripture and other historical documents. I decided Rachel was an ESFP (extraverted, sensor, feeler, and perceiver) while Leah was an INFJ (introverted, intuiter, feeler, judger).

Then I went to the free ChatGPT and simply asked for summaries of each type in the light of those biblical characters—and I got more than I asked for. I got this:

🪦 **Leah's INFJ Summary**

🕊 **Core Traits:**

- **Introverted (I):** Draws strength from solitude and reflection; reserved but emotionally deep.

- **Intuitive (N):** Future-focused, seeks meaning beneath surface details.
- **Feeling (F):** Driven by empathy, inner values, and a desire to heal others.
- **Judging (J):** Organized, decisive, values structure and long-term purpose.

### INFJ Strengths in Leah:

- **Empathic Depth:** Leah feels the emotions of others keenly—especially Rachel's and Jacob's—even when they wound her.
- **Resilient Idealism:** She quietly bears humiliation and neglect, yet longs for transcendent meaning (e.g., naming her sons with hope-filled declarations).
- **Protective Love:** As eldest, she may feel **responsible** for Rachel's emotional world—even as they compete.
- **Spiritual Yearning:** Likely to have a private, profound connection to the divine, marked by longing for inner wholeness and recognition.

### INFJ Struggles in Leah:

- **Feeling Invisible:** INFJs ache to be seen for their true selves. Leah's sense of being unloved is not just romantic—it's **existential**.
- **Internalizing Pain:** She hides suffering behind calm or duty, but it festers.
- **Conflict Avoidance:** She may defer, appease, or withdraw instead of confronting Rachel or Jacob —until the pressure breaks.

### 🌿 Leah as Twin to ESFP Rachel:

Leah is the **moon to Rachel's sun**—a figure of mystery, quiet devotion, and soul-deep longing.

- **Rachel speaks to crowds; Leah listens to hearts.**
- **Rachel captivates instantly; Leah endures quietly.**
- Their bond is fraught with mirrored jealousy: Leah envies Rachel's attention, Rachel envies Leah's fruitfulness.
- Their twinship can be a source of **pain and prophetic poetry**—two halves of a shattered whole.

### 🌿 Rachel the ESFP in Ancient Haran:

### 🔥 1. Romance with Jacob: "Love at First Sight"

**ESFP Trait:** Charismatic, emotionally expressive, and physically attuned.

- Rachel likely had a **captivating presence** at the well—not just because of her beauty, but due to her *vivacious spirit*. ESFPs draw people in with warmth and charm.
- Her interaction with Jacob could have been **playful, bold, and emotionally intense**. She might have met his gaze directly, offered a teasing word, or laughed easily—things that would feel electrifying in a world of arranged and duty-bound marriages.
- ESFPs live in the moment, so Rachel's quick, deep emotional bond with Jacob makes sense. She may have **romanticized their connection**, dreaming vividly of what their life could be.

### 🕯️ 2. Rivalry with Leah: The Spotlight Struggle
**ESFP Trait:** Sensitive to social comparison and emotional exclusion.

- Rachel thrives on **being seen, loved, and appreciated.** The shock of waking up to find Leah married to Jacob in her place may have felt not only like betrayal, but a **loss of identity.**
- Her rivalry with Leah could be framed as a **struggle for emotional validation**, not just status or children. ESFPs fear being overlooked. Rachel's bitterness might stem from feeling *eclipsed*—in beauty, in love, and eventually in motherhood.
- She might show **emotional volatility**—weeping, confronting, withdrawing, then returning with intense affection. This would give her complexity and vulnerability.

### 🕊️ 3. Longing for Children: An Emotional Epicenter
**ESFP Trait:** Deep empathy, need for emotional fulfillment, reactive to unmet desires.

- "Give me children, or I'll die!" is an iconic ESFP moment—**emotion-driven, dramatic, and raw.** She's not manipulating—she's living her pain fully and externally.
- Rather than quietly bearing infertility, Rachel might throw herself into rituals, remedies, and emotional appeals—expressive and visible. ESFPs act when they feel.
- Her giving of Bilhah as a surrogate may come less

from calculation and more from **emotional desperation and action in the moment.**

🐾 **Emotional Tapestry in Storytelling: Interactions to Highlight:**

- **With Jacob:** playful flirtation, intense loyalty, sensual gestures, spontaneous laughter, or tears.
- **With Leah:** moments of jealousy, hurt, sarcasm, perhaps even an attempt at reconciliation—then withdrawing when it fails.
- **With God:** maybe she's not a theological thinker like Rebekah, but her prayers are *visceral*, almost childlike in their directness.

**Rachel's Core ESFP Conflict:**
**"If I am not adored, am I still worthy?"**

Her inner journey could be one of realizing she is not only loved for her beauty or fertility—but for her full self, even when unseen.

I also got the following chart—after simply telling ChatGPT that my next novel would be about ESFP Rachel and INFJ Leah:

**Side-by-Side Emotional Arcs of Leah (INFJ) and Rachel (ESFP)**

*A tale of two sisters, two hearts, and one God who sees them both.*

**Side-by-Side Emotional Arcs of Leah (INFJ) and Rachel (ESFP)**

*A tale of two sisters, two hearts, and one God who sees them both.*

| Stage | Leah (INFJ) | Rachel (ESFP) |
|---|---|---|
| **1. The Dream/Desire/Hearts** | Longs to be chosen for who she is. Craves emotional security, a life that bites compassion. Feels deeply but hides it. | Shines effortlessly. Enjoys attention, knows she's desirable. Beautiful's comrade—passionate love story. Assumes life will reward her charm. |
| **2. The Disruption/...with arrives/** | Begins to hope—perhaps Jacob might see her. Then is swept into Laban's scheme. Feels used and unseen. | Immediately wanted. Jacob chooses her. Her a swept up in the display of romantic desire. Leah's presence is an afterthought. |
| **3. The Fallout/The wedding & afterwards** | Betrayed and shamed. Jacob's rejection wounds her to the soul. Feels invisible, like a shadow in her own marriage. | Feels violated by the deception. Her spotlight stolen. Angry, passionate, and even more threatened to keep Jacob's love. |
| **4. Striving for Love/Childbearing years** | Bears son after son. Each is a plea: "See me." She internalizes rejection, stays dutiful, prays alone. | Barren and desperate. Begins to realize beauty and love do not secure everything. Envies Leah's fertility. Makes impulsive choices to gain sons (e.g. giving Bilhah). |
| **5. Emotional Breaking Point** | With Judah's birth, she pivots inward: "This time, I will praise the Lord." She begins detaching from Jacob's validation. | Cracks under pressure. Her rivalry with Leah intensifies. She demands children from Jacob. Her confidence falters—"Give me children or I die." (Gen. 30:1) |
| **6. The Quiet Rise** | Becomes spiritually grounded. Prays less to be loved, more to be whole. Finds dignity in the role of matriarch, not exactly wife. | Finally hints Joseph. A moment of triumph—but it doesn't last. Her deeper ache: Her want to be the center of affection remains. |
| **7. Loss & Legacy/Rachel's death** | Outlives Rachel silently. Steps into a quiet leadership role. Others outspoken to Rachel's sons. | Dies in childbirth. Her story ends on the road, unfinished. Symbols of her pursuit of love that always moved just ahead. |
| **8. The Eternal Contrast/...end & legacy** | Buried beside Jacob in the Cave of Machpelah. Her lineage becomes the line of Judah, David, and Messiah. Vindicated in legacy. | Buried alone by the roadside. Beloved in life, but her legacy passes through her overlooked sister. |

Pretty cool, huh? I don't *have* to follow this information, of course, but since most of it is extrapolated from Scripture, I might. But consider how useful this information will be when I start filling in the "bones" of the plot skeleton—the goals, the complications, the bleakest moments (one for each of them) the lesson learned, and the resolution.

Don't let ChatGPT write your book—we've previously discussed how bad chatGPT writing can be. But *do* use the tools that are available to you as a starting point. You can always take what you've been given and make it your own.

I hope you'll give this a try with your work in progress. Analyze your main two or three characters, then go to ChatGPT and "introduce" them. Since ChatGPT won't know the plot of your story, you may have to say something like, "Sam Jones, an INTJ, is a detective trying to solve a murder in 1965 Boston. The villain is Alex Troublesome, an ESTJ who is determined to murder everyone who turned down his mortgage application. Can you help me develop their character arcs?"

Let me know how it works for you!

# ON LATENCY,
# DONATED BOOKS,
# AND TELLING DETAILS.

**Write Well:** #79

**Word of the Week: latent (LAY-tent).**

Hidden, unawakened, or dormant. Something is present, but not visible. From the Latin *latere*, to lie hidden. *I have seen horror movies involving latent alien seed pods. I love discovering latent talent.* "*What we want is not more little books about Christianity, but more little books by Christians on other subjects —with their Christianity latent*" —C.S. Lewis.

Related words: *lateral* (appearing from the side), *lateral thinking* (the solving of problems by a new and creative approach), *latent period* (the time between exposure to a virus or other agent and the appearance of symptoms).

## Q&A

**Question:** Do authors still receive royalties when their books are used in prisons?

**Answer:** Many books are donated to prisons, and authors don't receive royalties on books that are given away to prisons or other ministries. As a writer, I'm delighted that my books are given to prisons and other outreach programs. Books that are not donated may be offered at discount pricing, for which the author may receive a discounted royalty. For details, check your contract—the terms are usually spelled out.

## Quote of the Week

"Either write something worth reading or do something worth writing."
–**Benjamin Franklin**

## Reputable Book Awards

One way to promote your book is to announce that it has won an award—but the feat is not so impressive if no one's ever heard of the award. Here is a list of 30 reputable awards programs for traditionally and self-published books—and books that haven't been published yet! Be sure to check it out, but keep an eye on those submission fees—you don't want to blow your budget with fees. https://insights.bookbub.com/book-awards/

## Powerful Description

Too often our descriptions of characters are limited to what they look like on the surface—hair color, eye color, build, etc. But *truly* powerful description often ignores the surface and tells us so much more.

To quickly establish character, find **one telling detail** about someone and relate that:

From BEGINNER'S GREEK, a novel by James Collins:

**Peter entered and the woman quickly rose to greet him. She was full-figured and in her fifties, with brassy red hair, black eyebrows, and one discolored front tooth. She made every utterance with great enthusiasm.**

The woman described above is an office secretary. James Collins doesn't give us an entire paragraph of description, only two sentences, and one of those is about the woman's action, not her appearance. But Collins has given us a few details that tell us a great deal about this woman. From what we read above, we know her education level—probably high school graduate. We also know her income level—she makes very little money at this job, because she can't afford to have her tooth fixed or her hair properly dyed. The woman is energetic and trying hard to please, but she'd never be hired to work in a swanky corporate office.

Am I making assumptions? Of course, that's why this works. The novelist chooses a detail about which the average person assumes certain things, and thereby paints a picture with very few words. In real life, this wouldn't be fair, but this is fiction.

In the same book, I found the following description. Peter, the protagonist, is sitting on a plane, and describes the passenger who sits next to him:

**The young woman sat down. As well as he could, while pretending to idly look around the cabin, Peter studied her. She appeared to be Peter's age, and she had long reddish blond hair that fell over her shoulders. She wore a thin, white cardigan and blue jeans. What Peter first noticed in her profile was the soft bow of her jaw and how the line turned back at her rounded chin. It reminded Peter of an ideal curve that might be displayed in an old painting manual. His eye traveled back along the jaw, returning to the girl's ear. It was a small ear, beige in color, that appeared almost edible, like a biscuit.**

There's more than one detail in the above description, but I'm sharing it not because of what it tells us about this young woman—she could have been almost any twenty-something—but because of *what this passage tells us about Peter.*

What is Peter's educational level? He knows about old painting manuals, so he has probably graduated from a liberal arts college—he might have been a humanities major. He notices the fine details of her profile much as he would admire a fine sculpture. And finally, and most important, how does Peter feel about this woman? He is attracted to her—so attracted, in fact, that he'd like to nibble on her ear.

This story is told in first person, but the latter description is told in deep third person point of view, meaning that the thoughts are coming directly from Peter's head (without italics or change of tense), allowing the reader direct access to Peter's thoughts, impressions, and vocabulary. This is the power of deep point of view. You wouldn't want to write the entire book like this, but it certainly works to reveal (show) Peter's attraction without being obvious about it.

The description of the secretary is not as deep—Peter is simply describing—telling—us what he sees, and we are left to decipher the information ourselves. But the description of the attractive young woman delves into Peter's thoughts, memories of that painting manual, and his actions, his eye traveling from the woman's jaw to her ear. He's caressing her with his eyes, of course, and he certainly didn't do that with the office secretary.

I've just reached into the TBR stack on my nightstand and come up with another description in THE BOYFRIEND, by Freida McFadden:

**I stop thinking about all the weight on my shoulders, and instead, my eyes are drawn to her neck again. She is so slim that I can see her carotid pulse perfectly. I even notice the way it speeds up as she waits to see how I'll respond to her confession.**

Not having read this book yet, I can only assume the narrator is either a med student or a vampire. Again, it's a safe bet that he's attracted to her, and apparently she's either attracted to him or keenly interested in his response. Not a word here about hair color or eye color—we only know that she is slim and has a visible carotid pulse.

If I tell you that a knight is in prison and a sag-bellied rat scurries across the floor, what does the room look like? What color is it? Is it warm or cold? Dry or wet?

In writing description, you don't have to describe everything—let the reader's imagination fill in the scene based on the telling details that you reveal. Save most of your words for the *story*. As long as your reader is generally familiar with a prison, they can supply the visuals.

The exception to this rule is if you're writing about something your reader has never experienced—in a fantasy world, for instance, or in a historical setting that no longer exists. Then you may have to paint the scene a little more thoroughly, but it's always better to do that through *action* than through static description. Show your character moving *through* that unfamiliar terrain, handling that unusual stone, using that futuristic equipment.

Your homework this week is to look at your description —in fiction *and* nonfiction—and determine if it's all surface or if you have delved a little deeper to find the telling details that really matter. Those details will save you a lot of words.

# ON CHOCOLATE CAKE, FANTASY, AND PROPOSALS

**Write Well:** #80

**Word of the Week: compunction (com-PUNK-shun)**

Remorse, the prick or sting of conscience; regret for wrongdoing. Though similar to *remorse*, compunction is less severe—it's more of a momentary, even fleeting regret. *I feel remorse when I sin. I feel compunction when I eat a piece of chocolate cake.*

From the Latin *compunctio*, remorse. I used to confuse *compunction* with *compulsion*, being forced to behave in a certain way. Perhaps it's because I often feel *compelled* to eat chocolate cake, and thus feel *compunction*.

## Q&A

**Question:** What are some tips for writing a query letter that will get the attention of an agent or editor? How long should the letter be, and what information should it contain?

**Answer:** I've seen *books* written on this topic, but here's the bottom line: A query letter to an agent or publisher should be about **a specific project**—a fiction or nonfiction book, or a series. Query letters don't need to be more than **one page long,** as editors are busy people.

In the letter, **introduce your project in one paragraph,** explaining what it is, what genre it is, and include a hook that will make the editor want to ask for your proposal.

In a second paragraph, **detail your writing experience** —previous publications, books, or articles. If any of these were self-published, say so. If you have developed a following on social media, this would also be a good place to mention it. If you have a TV or radio program that would enable you to sell your book, mention that as well.

But do **keep your query letter brief and to the point.** For a book, offer to send a proposal, not the entire manuscript. For an article, you'll offer to send the entire article.

For a book, you have a three-part job: 1.) Write a query that will make the editor ask for your work 2.) Write a proposal that will make the editor ask for the entire manuscript, and 3.) Write a manuscript that will compel the editor to offer a contract.

Easier said than done, but people do it successfully every day. **Be one of those people.** If today's not your day, aim for tomorrow.

### Quote of the Week

J.R.R. Tolkien probably would not have finished writing *The Lord of the Rings* if not for the encouragement of his friend C.S. Lewis. Why? Because, Colin Duriez explains in *Tolkien and C.S. Lewis: The Gift of Friendship,* "In the 1920s, there was no adult readership for fantasy, or literature in which the story element was predominant."

In the 1920s, Tolkien was a professor at the University of

Oxford, and among his peers, fantasy wasn't considered serious literature. To write fantasy was to stoop to writing less-than-worthy literature.

In his 1956 *New York Times* review of *The Return of the King*, the poet W.H. Auden wrote, "I rarely remember a book about which I have had such violent arguments. Nobody *seems* to have a moderate opinion: either, like myself, people find it a masterpiece of its genre or they cannot abide it, and among the hostile there are some, I must confess, for whose literary judgment I have great respect." Auden explains that most of the objection was due to the fact that, at the time, most "people object to Heroic Quests and Imaginary Worlds on principle; such, they feel, cannot be anything but light 'escapist' reading. That a man like Mr. Tolkien, the English philologist who teaches at Oxford, should lavish such incredible pains upon a genre which is, for them, trifling by definition, is, therefore, very shocking."

After his books went on to sell more than 600 million copies, Tolkien would eventually be called the "father of high fantasy."

Fantasy isn't the only genre often considered sub-par. Though romance is the best-selling genre, much of the literary world disdains it. Christian fiction is another genre routinely criticized by those who haven't read it. Westerns, Amish stories—they have all been routinely dissed, but those who read these books are voracious readers. And frankly, I'd rather feed a hungry reader than write a high-brow novel that few people will ever enjoy.

Write what you want to write, because you'll bring your passion to your work. And no matter what genre it is, write with excellence and make every word shine. That's what Tolkien did.

**Speaking of Proposals . . .**

How do you create a proposal for an editor or agent?

Before I answer that question, I know some of you are thinking, "I'm going to self-publish, so I don't need to know this."

Unless you have a book idea that a traditional publisher absolutely would NOT be interested in (niche market or local interest only), opting *first* for self-publishing is like a baseball player saying he only wants to play in the minor leagues. A lot of ball players *do* play in the minors, especially when they're starting out, but they accept the lower pay, smaller crowds, and rougher conditions so they can *eventually get to the majors.*

So—back to those proposals for fiction and nonfiction books or series. First, as mentioned above, you write a winning query letter to an agent or editor (and to get through the door of some big publishers, you have to have an agent, so you might as well start with them). Once an agent or editor says, "Yes, send me a proposal," here's what you do.

1.) **Write another winning letter.** Mention that you were asked to send the enclosed proposal, summarize it in a sentence so the editor or agent will recall the gist, and thank them for their time and consideration. Be polished, be professional, and be confident, not cocky. Don't write that your story is going to be a best-seller, don't say that God told you to write this book, and don't say that the editor has never read *anything* as good as your enclosed proposal.

2.) **Next is the outline (for nonfiction) or the synopsis (for fiction).**

The outline: list all your chapters, and briefly describe the material covered in each chapter. At the end, be sure to mention any extras you are planning: a list of resources, footnotes, diagrams, index, maps, whatever you need to fully cover your topic.

The synopsis: We covered how to write a synopsis in an earlier newsletter. (July 15th). Keep it to one page, and be sure it spells out your story's beginning, middle, and ending.

3.) **The Marketing Overview:** this is where you demonstrate that you're willing to help sell this book.

- What similar titles (on the same topic) have already been published? How will your book differ yet appeal to the same audience?
- Explain why you are passionate about this story or topic. What makes this project personal for you?
- Who is your ideal reader? Don't say "everyone." Men? Women? Professional people? Parents? Single Parents? Grandparents? People who love history, baking, archery, etc.?
- Do you have a platform or audience who will jump to buy this book? How many followers on social media? Do you have a TV show or radio program? Would your ministry or group buy thousands of copies to distribute? Do you have dedicated readers of a blog? Are you in a position of leadership? Bottom line, how can you help market this book?

4.) **Previous publishing credits and any relevant reviews** from *Publishers' Weekly, Kirkus, Library Journal, Bookstore Journal,* etc. If you don't have previous credits or reviews, ignore this.

5.) Finally, include **three sample chapters**—preferably the first three. This will help the editor see your writing style.

I have heard of people who hire editors to polish their chapters before submitting them, and I think that's dishonest. The editor and agent want to see how *you* write, so polish your work to the best of your ability and send it out. If you hire an editor, you'll be selling HIS or HER style, not yours, and if the editor requests the entire manuscript, they may wonder why the rest of your manuscript doesn't match the quality of your proposal.

Always be honest. Always be prepared. And always submit your most excellent work.

I love what David says in 2 Samuel 24:24: "I will not offer to the Lord that which costs me nothing." Pay the price, put in the time, and do the work.

Put your proposal in a **single Word document** file, label it with your name, and email it (with a cover email) to the editor or agent IF they have said they will accept an emailed submission. If they don't, send it snail mail with a self-addressed, stamped envelope.

By the way, make sure your document is **formatted correctly**—double spaced, 1" margin on all sides but 1.5" at the top, title halfway down the first page, your name and address in the top left corner. Use a generic font like Garamond or Times New Roman, size 11 or 12. Page numbers in the upper right corner with your surname. Make it easy for your reader.

# SPECIAL EDITION: SENTIMENT VS. SENTIMENTALITY

I used to be confused by those two terms, which is unfortunate because *sentiment* in a novel is a Good Thing, while *sentimentality* is not. Then I heard the difference explained this way: sentimentality almost always goes for the "expected" thing, the quick option, often to the point of cliché. A depiction of true *sentiment* covers new territory and deepens characterization in a unique way.

I don't watch much TV, but I have always been an *Alias* addict. Didn't watch it on TV, but I rented the DVDs and was enthralled by the writing. Never a dull moment, never a plot thread tied off without another one being woven into the story. Sydney Bristow, the CIA-spy-protagonist, has more conflicts in her personal and professional lives than any human could realistically endure, yet she carries on with style and a smile.

Anyway, in season two CIA agent Vaughn and super spy Sydney are attracted to each other. You *know* Vaughn wants to declare his feelings, but is he going to do it in a sentimental way? Of course not.

They're together in their clandestine meeting place (spies can never meet in public, you know) and he points to his watch. "You see this watch?" he says. "My dad gave it to me. He said you could set your heart by this watch."

Sydney looks at him, waiting.

Vaughn continues: "The thing is, this watch stopped on October first. That's the day we met."

Their respective beepers go off, reminding them that duty comes before pleasure. Then, with tears in her eyes, Sydney looks at him, smiles, and says, "Me, too."

And I want to swoon. Why? Because they didn't go for the easy reaction, saying "I love you" and blubbering all over the place. Instead, the writers rely on subtext, i.e., *unspoken* dialogue. Vaughn is saying that his heart stopped the day he met Sydney. Aw . . .

Why is this great writing? Because it's unexpected and not "on the nose." It's not tit for tat. Sydney responds to what Vaughn is thinking, (*I think I love you*), not what he's saying.

Best of all, Vaughn's watch keeps showing up throughout the series, and every time it does, it's laden with emotional meaning. The writers don't have to say anything, because devoted viewers know what the watch means to Vaughn and what it represents between him and Sydney.

I saw another great exchange the other day. Sydney and Vaughn are sitting on a bench eating ice cream cones, and Syd confesses that she lied to Vaughn about a co-worker. She says she pretty much grew up alone, so she's not used to being accountable to someone, and she's sorry she lied.

Vaughn cocks a brow and we're not sure if he's going to be angry or forgiving or hurt or irritated . . . and he offers Syd a bite of his ice cream, then he stands and extends his hand.

*Invisible* dialogue, pure sentiment, not gushy sentimentality. He's offering forgiveness and acceptance in those simple gestures.

Most of us have a little writer inside who is constantly predicting what a character will say--and in a lot of movies and TV shows, I find myself able to parrot dialogue along with the characters because the setup and following lines are predictable. I've never been able to do that with *Alias*. And that's a delight.

If you're writing a scene and you want to show that your hero loves your heroine, the *sentimental* thing is to have him send—what? Yep, red roses. Chocolates. Typical, boring stuff.

But to show real sentiment, back in chapter three, plant a conversation where your heroine confesses that she spent the best summer of her life on the sugar sand of Clearwater Beach. In chapter twenty, your hero, to demonstrate his feelings, calls a friend in Clearwater, has him scoop up some white sand, Fed Ex it to the hero, then he puts the sand in a toy bucket with a little shovel and leaves it on the heroine's doorstep, with a plane ticket to Clearwater, FL. You show him working hard, spending money, sacrificing to fulfill her unspoken wish, and when she finds that bucket, she knows what the hero feels for her: true sacrificial love.

Does depicting true sentiment require more work and more thought? You bet. Is it worth it?

Ask any *Alias* fan.

# ON TEMPORALITY, SELF-EDITING, AND COFFEE.

**Write Well: #81**

**Word of the Week: temporal (TEM-por-ul).**

Worldly, earthly, and temporary, as opposed to things that are heavenly or spiritual. *Most of us spend far too much time focusing on temporal treasures.* From the Latin *tempus, time.* Related words: *temporary*, a *temp* (in an office, for instance), *tempest* (a storm from a season, hence related to time), *tempo*(the time or speed of music), *temporality* (existing within time), and *temporize*(to avoid making a decision in order to gain time).

### Quote of the Week

"A good science fiction story is a story with a human problem, and a human solution, which would not have happened without its science content." —Theodore Sturgeon

"All you need to write a ghost story is put a ghost in it. For a detective story you need a plot." —P.D. James

## Q&A

Question: Are there any rules or guidelines about how long a novel should be?

Answer: Though there are always exceptions, an adult novel usually ranges from 80,000–100,000 words. A novella is usually between 25,000–30,000. Gift books are usually around 25,000 words, and short novels, such as some series romances, clock in around 50,000 words.

There are no rules, but the above are guidelines. A book that is overly long will cost more to produce, and some readers don't care for books—especially those in book clubs that read a book every month—that are overly long.

The important matter is that you tell a complete story with a satisfactory beginning, middle and end. How many pages will that take? Your story will tell you, but—if a scene or chapter does not move the plot forward or deepen character, it doesn't belong in the novel.

## Market Trends

I've just returned from the ACFW (American Christian Fiction Writers) national conference, where I sat in on a panel of industry editors and experts. They were asked about market trends, and they had this to say about the Christian market:

What is hot? Sweet reads with a touch of magic.

Present truth, but don't be preachy.

New imprints are promoting "clean reads"—for Christian or secular readers who want to read good stories without violence, sex, or bad language.

**Haven** is a new imprint featuring books written from a Christian worldview, but not an overt Christian message. You can read details here.

Writing for Love Inspired or Love Inspired Suspense

(Harlequin) is still the easiest way to break in. They are always looking for new writers, and the books are only 55,000 words. Get their writer's guidelines here and here.

When asked to describe the current state of the market in one word, the editors said: "transitioning," "grit," "evolving," "exciting," and "gorgeous."

The **smartest move** a new writer can make? These were their answers:

*innovate

*build a platform

*Learn to write articles, start blogging, get your name out there [Sound familiar? I preach this all the time!]

*Learn the business side of writing

*Write for Love Inspired and Love Inspired Suspense to get your foot in the door.

*Think about your reader.

**Self-Editing**

Since I am always harping on the subject of self-editing and stressing the importance of intentional practice, I thought I'd give you a specific assignment—an exercise, if you will.

Below you'll find a short story authored by ChatGPT. Your job is to edit it, so copy and paste or print and scribble. Next week, I will publish the story in an edited version so you can compare. And since it's important for you to know the genre, this is a romance.

**"Pumpkin Latte Love"**

*By A. Beginner*

Amber walked quickly down the sidewalk, leaves crunching under her brown ankle boots. Fall was finally here. Her favorite season. The air smelled like cinnamon and smoke and something else she couldn't name. She hugged her cardigan closer to her body and turned the corner to the café. She always got her pumpkin latte on the first day of October.

Inside, the little bell jingled above the door and the smell of coffee hit her right away. The place was kind of busy, but she didn't mind. The buzz made her feel alive. She got in line behind a tall guy with dark hair and a green flannel shirt. He turned slightly and smiled.

"Oh, sorry," he said, stepping forward. "Didn't mean to cut."

Amber shook her head. "No, I just got here."

He smiled again. He had a nice smile. Kind of lopsided, in a charming way. She looked away fast.

He ordered a regular coffee. No sugar, no cream. That surprised her.

"Amber," the barista said when she got to the counter. "Pumpkin spice latte?"

She laughed. "You know me too well."

The guy was still standing at the pickup counter when she joined him there. "Pumpkin spice," he said, nodding at her cup when it came up. "Should've guessed."

"What's that supposed to mean?" she teased.

He looked slightly embarrassed. "No, nothing bad. I just think girls like that stuff more."

She sipped. "That's a stereotype."

He laughed. "Guilty."

They stood there for a moment. Amber looked at him. He looked back. For once, she didn't feel awkward.

"I'm Josh," he said.

"Amber."

There was a pause.

"Hey, so . . . I was just going to sit and read for a while," he said, lifting a paperback book. "Want to join me? If you're not busy, I mean."

Amber hesitated. She didn't normally say yes to strangers. But something about him seemed . . . safe. Genuine.

"Sure," she said.

They sat by the window. The light was soft and golden, and they talked for an hour. About books and movies and why he didn't like pumpkin spice ("Too sweet," he said) and why she loved it ("It's not fall without it!"). Time passed too quickly.

"I should probably go," she said finally.

Josh stood too. "Yeah, me too. But this was nice."

"Yeah," she said, smiling.

He shifted his weight. "Can I get your number?"

She nodded and typed it into his phone. As she walked away, she felt strangely happy. Like something new had started.

### Three Weeks Later

Amber walked into the café again, this time looking around before ordering. She spotted Josh at their usual window seat. He stood up and gave her a quick hug.

"I got you the latte already," he said.

"You're learning," she joked.

They sat, knees almost touching under the table. Outside, leaves danced in the wind.

"So," he said, "I was thinking maybe next weekend we could go apple picking. Or something cheesily autumnal."

Amber laughed. "You're a secret romantic, aren't you?"

He pretended to be offended. "No comment."

She sipped her drink. "I'd love to."

Josh reached out, took her hand gently.

"I really like you, Amber," he said. "I'm glad I ran into you that day."

Her cheeks went warm. "I'm glad too."

Outside, someone started playing guitar. The song was slow and sweet.

Josh leaned in. "Can I kiss you?"

Amber nodded.

The kiss was soft, warm, and a little bit spicy from the drink.

It tasted like October.

**Ready? Set? Edit!**

# ON IMPUNITY, FORCED EDGES, AND SELF-EDITING.

**Write Well:** #82

## Word of the Week: impunity (im-PYOO-nih-tee)

Exemption from consequence or punishment for an action. *The impunity of the police chief's law-breaking son astounded the town's citizens.* From the Latin *impunitas, impune,* without punishment. Related words: *impudence*(someone who behaves as if they will not be punished).

## Quote of the Week:

Maybe you've felt the same way . . . I know I have.

**Poet Linda Pastan** once said: "I often write poems in my head to distract myself during hard times. . . . Years ago, after a car crash, while I lay waiting for the ambulance, I actually finished a poem I had been working on, determined not to die before I had it right." From Garrison Keillor's *Writer's Almanac.*

## Q&A

**Question:** Lately I've been seeing books with beautiful,

decorated edges—is it possible to achieve that effect (without spending a fortune or hand-painting each book) if you're self-publishing?

**Answer:** Yes! They are called *forced edges*, and they *are* beautiful. Vellum, the software that allows authors to professionally design and lay out their own books, now makes it possible for authors to add forced edges to their self-published books. I wouldn't use it for every book, but for a commemorative edition or a story collection, it might be just the thing.

If you think this would be a beautiful look for your book, first you will have to purchase the Vellum software. (For Mac computers only). It's easy to use and does make a book look professional. Second, you will have to acquire the artwork for your forced edge. After that, the Vellum help guide will help you create this beautiful look for your finished book. I haven't tried it yet, but perhaps soon!

**AI Scam Alert**

Along with most of my writing friends, I have recently noticed a flood of AI-generated emails in my inbox. These emails are surprisingly complimentary and detailed, like this one:

*Hi Angela,*

*Congratulations on your upcoming release, The Daughter of Rome! I was immediately drawn to how you bring to life Nero's Rome with such vivid detail and spiritual depth. The story of Calandra, torn between family loyalty, survival, and the faith of the early Christians, feels both timeless and profoundly moving.*

*Your ability to weave biblical history with human struggle makes The Daughter of Rome not just a historical novel, but a faith-filled journey that resonates deeply with readers seeking both truth and inspiration.*

*I believe The Daughter of Rome has incredible potential to reach . . . etc.*

After reading the letter, I realized there was nothing in this letter that couldn't be gleaned by reading the Amazon.com blurb.

Then I began to get four of five such emails a day, and all of them had two things in common—1) highly complimentary words about my book (supported by facts any AI engine could discover) and 2) The author was trying to sell me something.

Remember this—we all love to get emails and letters that praise our books. But if the writer is *also* trying to sell you something, **don't believe a word of it.** That's not praise, that's flattery offered with malicious motives. Delete those emails and never look back.

### Self-Editing Review

How did you do on the self-editing project? I don't expect any of your responses to match this revision word for word, but I do want you to see the principles involved. Pull out the copy you worked from—and if you didn't do the exercise, print out last week's newsletter and do it—and follow along:

#### Pumpkin Latte Love

*Revised for clarity, flow, and polish*

Amber crunched through crisp leaves on her walk to the café. October had arrived, wrapping the morning in cinnamon air and chimney smoke. Her cardigan wasn't quite warm enough, but she didn't mind. It was the perfect day for a pumpkin latte.

A bell chimed overhead as she stepped inside. The café buzzed with conversation and the rich scent of espresso. She joined the line, stopping just behind a tall guy in a green flannel shirt.

He glanced back with a crooked smile. "Did I cut in front of you?"

"Not at all," she said, noticing the way his eyes crinkled when he smiled.

He turned forward again.

"Amber," the barista called. "Pumpkin spice latte?"

She laughed. "You've got me memorized."

Flannel Guy—Josh, according to the name scribbled on his cup—was still waiting when she reached the pickup counter.

"Pumpkin spice." He nodded at her cup. "Very seasonal of you."

She raised a brow. "And what did you get—black coffee?"

He held it up like a defense. "No judgment. I like to taste the coffee."

"Says the man wearing a shirt the color of moss."

He laughed. "Fair."

They stood in companionable silence, then he pointed to the tables. "I was planning to sit and read a bit. Want to join me?"

Amber hesitated. She didn't usually say yes to strangers —but something about him felt solid. Easy.

"Sure."

They took a window seat. Sunlight spilled over the table,

warming the wooden surface. Josh pulled out a paperback. She sipped her latte.

"So," he said, "what's your favorite book?"

An hour passed—books, movies, hometowns, the great pumpkin spice debate. He teased. She teased back. And when it was time to go, neither of them moved right away.

"This was fun," he said.

She nodded. "It was."

He pulled out his phone. "Can I get your number?"

She typed it in, then stepped out into the golden afternoon with a smile.

Three weeks later, Amber spotted Josh waiting by the window, two drinks on the table.

"You ordered for me?" she asked, slipping into the seat.

"I live to serve," he said. "Besides, it's October. I had a fifty-fifty shot."

"Not bad."

They talked like always, but this time he reached for her hand. His thumb brushed over hers.

"I'm really glad I met you," he said.

She looked down at their hands, then up at him. "Me too."

He hesitated. "Can I kiss you?"

She nodded.

The kiss was soft and warm, with just a hint of cinnamon.

Outside, leaves danced along the sidewalk

✎ **Self-Editing Checklist: From First Draft to Polished Prose**

### 1. Trim Redundancy

- ☑ *Ask:* Am I repeating ideas or words unnecessarily?
- ✗ "She got in line behind a tall guy . . . He turned slightly and smiled . . . He smiled again."
- ✓ *Fix:* Combine or streamline actions that repeat ("He glanced back with a crooked smile").

### 2. Strengthen Dialogue

- ☑ *Ask:* Does the dialogue sound natural? Does it reveal character?
- ✗ "Girls like that stuff more."
- ✓ "Very seasonal of you." (*subtle, playful, in-character banter*)

### 3. Cut Filler Words

- ☑ *Ask:* Can I tighten sentences by removing "just," "kind of," "really," etc.?

- ✗ "Kind of busy," "just got here," "really like you"
- ✓ Use direct, confident phrasing: "The café buzzed with conversation" or "I'm glad I met you."

## 4. Show Emotion Through Action

- ☑ *Ask:* Am I *telling* the emotion, or *showing* it through behavior, setting, or reaction?
- ✗ "She felt strangely happy."
- ✓ "She stepped out into the golden afternoon with a smile."

## 5. Use Specific, Fresh Description

- ☑ *Ask:* Are my sensory details vivid and specific?
- ✗ "The air smelled like cinnamon and smoke and something else she couldn't name."
- ✓ "October had arrived, wrapping the morning in cinnamon air and chimney smoke."

## 6. Clarify Character Motivations

- ☑ *Ask:* Do my characters' choices make sense and feel earned?
- ✗ "She didn't usually say yes to strangers" → then she says yes without much reflection.
- ✓ Add one beat of hesitation: "She didn't usually say yes to strangers—but something about him felt solid. Easy."

## 7. Watch Pacing

- ☑️ *Ask:* Are scenes moving too slowly or quickly? Does each beat earn its place?
- ❌ Spending multiple lines on ordering drinks and standing in line.
- ✔️ Streamline the scene to focus on the spark and connection.

## 8. Use Transitional Phrasing

- ☑️ *Ask:* Are time jumps and scene breaks clear and elegant?
- ❌ "Three Weeks Later" just plopped at the top.
- ✔️ Embed subtly: "Three weeks later, Amber spotted Josh already waiting..."

## 9. Avoid On-the-Nose Narration

- ☑️ *Ask:* Am I trusting the reader to infer meaning?
- ❌ "She didn't feel awkward for once."
- ✔️ Let the lack of awkwardness *show* in her comfort with him: "They stood in companionable silence."

## 10. Tighten Endings

- ☑️ *Ask:* Does the final paragraph leave a lasting impression without over-explaining?
- ❌ "It tasted like October." (*on-the-nose cliché*)
- ✔️ "The kiss was soft and warm, with just a hint of cinnamon. Outside, leaves danced along the sidewalk." (imagery + mood)

ChatGPT made the above edits, but I deleted a couple of speech attributions, also a few adverbs, corrected the chronology of movements (ChatGPT had her notice his crinkling eyes when his back was to her), and fixed some punctuation.

How do your edits compare to this version? Don't make the mistake of thinking that *editing equals adding words*. Most of the time edits delete the clunky in favor of the smooth and substitute the precise for the nebulous.

One more thing: ChatGPT and other AI engines are not infallible. They frequently make mistakes. So take their advice carefully while staying true to your voice and your style.

# ON COMMAS, QUESTION MARKS, AND APOSTROPHES.

**Write Well: #83**

**Word of the Week: scion (SI-en, rhymes with *Zion*).**

1. A shoot/sprout/sucker off a plant.
2. A descendant from a notable or wealthy family. It didn't matter that he was poor—he was a scion, a Rockefeller.

No derivatives for this one—I'm including it because I heard it used in a YouTube video and thought it a useful word we all ought to know.

### Quote of the Week

With decades of experience and over 73 million books sold, Jerry Jenkins said he's eager to pass on what he's learned to the next generation. He now teaches thousands of aspiring writers online and offers this counterintuitive advice: don't start with a book.

"A book is not where you start, it's where you arrive," he

said. "Start with blogs, start with articles, start with short stuff. Learn to work with an editor. Learn the business. Get the quarter-million clichés out of your system. Take the process slow. You'll get there. But go through the steps and learn the business."

Now I ask—does this advice not sound familiar? Get yourself a copy of WRITER'S MARKET and start writing and selling small pieces. Get published by someone who pays for your work. Build credibility. Be edited by a professional. Establish a reputation. Learn the nuances. Know your audience.

It's a journey.

## Q&A

**Question:** Is being an author a difficult job, or does it depend on the type of writing?

**Answer:** Lots of people are **writers**—some write for the joy of it; others write as their occupation. Writing for joy is easy. Writing for work is harder because you have to meet a professional standard, meet deadlines, and delight a sometimes fickle audience. Plus, the competition is keen.

Some writing is more difficult because it requires more research and preparation; some is more difficult because it demands more of the writer's internal thoughts and feelings. But after being a professional writer for over thirty-five years, I can say that it's not easy . . . but it can be extremely satisfying, especially when you see hearts and lives changed through your words. The writing life is not always lucrative, either—we don't all achieve the success of John Grisham or Nora Roberts. But most of us don't write for money; we write because it is what we are made to do, and we work hard at polishing our craft. If we can make a living at it; great. If we can't, we usually have a second job.

## Search/Replace is Your Friend

One of the best tools for revision/self-editing is the search and replace feature. As I discuss in my lesson about Weasel Words, we all have pet words and phrases that we tend to overuse. So once you identify your pet words, do a search/replace through the entire manuscript and search for that word or phrase, then replace it in all capital letters. On your next pass, you'll see that capitalized phrase, and you'll know to fix it.

Look what I found on my fourth draft—don't read it, just look at the capitalized words. They jump out.

my embroidery but watching the interactions between our guest and my sister. The fifth night of Jacob's visit was much like the first, yet I FOUND MYSELF noticing details that had escaped me before.

Jacob sat cross-legged on a cushion, his face animated as he told another story from his many travels. "The merchant swore the camel could carry twice its weight," he was saying, his eyes twinkling with humor, "but when we loaded it with his precious carpets, the beast simply refused to move. No amount of coaxing could convince it to rise."

Rachel giggled and leaned closer to him. "What did you do?" she asked, her voice low though our entire household was listening.

"We had to unload half the cargo and find another camel," Jacob replied, more focused on Rachel than his story. "The merchant was furious, but the camel was quite willing to carry a reasonable load to Gerar."

I FOUND MYSELF enjoying the tale, as I had the others he had shared during our mealtimes together. Jacob was a natural storyteller, with a talent for bringing distant places and people to life through his words. He had traveled throughout Canaan, and he spoke of cities and peoples I could only dream of visiting.

Though he was skilled in conversation, I FOUND MYSELF drawn to his character. Each morning and evening, I had watched as he slipped out of the house and went into the fields to pray. He would face the land of Canaan, raise his hands

Ack! I FOUND MYSELF three times in one scene. You can be sure those will not be present in the fifth draft.

## Punctuation Primer

Sometimes your punctuation can give you away—I once watched a murder mystery with a supposed suicide. The detective established that the deceased could not have written the supposed suicide note because the note included a semi-colon, and the dead man wasn't educated enough to know how to use one.

But if you want to be a professional writer—and I think that's why you're here—you need to know how to use punctuation. Don't assume that the copy editor will make things right for you, because like that detective, the editor reviewing your manuscript will know if you've learned enough to be a good writer.

So here's a *brief* overview. If you want more information, click on the links.

**The comma:** I'll be honest. The comma rules I grew up with seem to have changed, because I've noticed that my copy editor has been removing many of them. For instance, I was taught that you always put a comma before *for, nor,* and *but*, but that rule seems to have changed. *I wanted to go to the store, but couldn't.* This reads right to me, but the rules have shifted.

The current rule is that **a comma is only needed when the conjunction (for, and, but, or) joins two independent clauses** (if each clause could stand as an independent sentence). If one of the clauses is dependent, the comma should be left out. So *I wanted to go to the store, but George had other plans* is correct because *George had other plans* is a sentence on its own. But in *I wanted to go to the store but couldn't*—the comma should not be there.

My friend Eric has a handy saying to help us remember: *A cat has claws at the end of its paws, but a comma's a pause at the end of a clause.*

There is one comma I will root for: the Oxford (or serial) comma. Without it, you get sentences like this:

*I'd like to thank my parents, the Pope and Mother Teresa.*

The serial comma is the last comma in a list of things. That sentence should be *I'd like to thank my parents, the Pope, and Mother Teresa.* Otherwise the Pope is in trouble.

And what if you'd written the headline below? I have it on good authority that this cover is fake, but it *is* still funny —in an embarrassing sort of way.

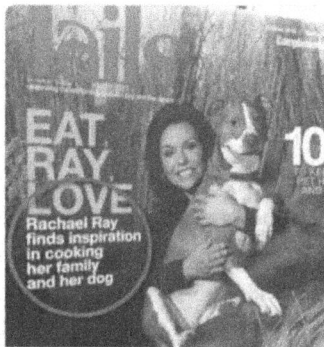

The only time you would not use a serial comma is if you are listing items that go in pairs: *I've set the table with plates, napkins, and salt and pepper shakers.* Salt and pepper shakers are considered one item, so no comma between them.

Another comma I'd insist on is the comma after direct address—when you address a person, put a comma afterward.

*Time to eat Grandma* versus *Time to eat, Grandma.*

Consider the difference a comma makes in the following:

*Woman, without her man, is nothing.*

Versus:

*Woman—without her, man is nothing.*

Punctuation matters.

**The em dash.** The em dash is so named because it takes up the same space as an M. It is used for abrupt halts, when character dialogue is interrupted, or for sudden shifts in thought. In more formal writing, when an em dash is used to indicate *note what follows*, you would opt for a **colon**.

**The colon** silently says *note what follows: I made the salad with various fruits: bananas, oranges, and apples.* In casual writing, you could substitute an em dash for the colon, but a colon would be preferred.

**The semicolon:** the semicolon is an actual comma on top of a period, and it symbolizes what it does. If you have two complete sentences, but they are closely affiliated that you don't want to stop the flow; use a semicolon. The previous sentence is two complete sentences, but they are affiliated. A semicolon is appropriate.

NOW—I have participated in writers' groups debates about whether or not a semicolon is appropriate in fiction. One camp says NEVER, my camp says SOMETIMES. I use semicolons in narrative and dialogue because my characters speak in long sentences that need semicolons. (Probably because that's how I talk.) And honestly? I have no idea if my semicolons make it into the final manuscript. My editor may be cutting them out, but I don't check.

But here's the thing—punctuation affects the *sound* of sentences and the rhythm of words, and I write dialogue and narrative as I hear it in my head. That's how I want my reader to hear it, so if my character has expressed a couple of thoughts in one exasperated breath, I'm going to join those sentences with a semicolon. You choose your own camp and write as you will. If I hear a comma—a slight pause—I will place a comma, because even the Chicago

Manual of Style allows for "author's preference" in some debatable cases.

**Ellipses:** The ellipsis is *space dot space dot space dot.* According to the Chicago Manual of Style, it is NOT three dots in a row, though some organizations use those (see link for more details). If you type dot dot dot, some writing programs may autocorrect with a group of three spaced dots, and that's okay, but you can't go wrong with *space dot space dot space dot.*

In nonfiction, an ellipsis is used to indicate missing words in a direct quote. In fiction, usually dialogue, an ellipsis is used to indicate that the character has paused or has drifted off in thought. "I used to live in Carolina . . . but I can't remember why we left."

**Parentheses:** These lowly punctuation marks rarely appear in fiction, but they are common in nonfiction. They are used for bits of parenthetical information. *"The designation BC is being replaced by BCE (Before the Common Era)."*

Note that the period and end quotation mark are placed AFTER the final parenthesis. *(There is an exception to this rule, of course: if the added information is a separate sentence, put the period inside the closing parenthesis.)*

How to punctuate Bible verses references: note where the period goes.

In the beginning, God created the heavens and the earth (Genesis 1:1).

Or you could write: In Genesis 1:1 we read: "In the beginning, God created the heavens and the earth."

In the USA, periods go *inside* the quotation marks. In Britain, they go outside. I have no idea why.

**The apostrophe:** You learned this in elementary school, but it's easy to slip up and a spell check usually doesn't catch this mistake.

Use an apostrophe with contractions: *You'll shoot your eye out!*

Use an apostrophe plus s with possessives: The purse is Alice's.

Put the apostrophe at the end of a plural possessive: Judas held the disciples' purse.

With the names *Jesus* and *Moses*, you need only an apostrophe: Jesus' face.

But with any other name that ends with S, you need the apostrophe plus s: *Judas's brothers formed the Maccabees. The Maccabees's reputation was fearsome.* Yes, it looks strange. So when I wrote my book about Judas Maccabees, I called him Judah instead—it's basically the same name, but those s's would have driven me crazy.

**Question marks:** belong only at the end of a direct question. *Did he still love her?* Not in this sentence: *She wondered if he still loved her.*

**Exclamation Marks:** Nothing marks a beginning writer more than an overabundance of exclamation marks. Use them rarely, and never use more than one at the end of a sentence. Reserve them for people screaming, burning houses, atomic bombs, etc.

I know that we often take punctuation for granted. We get into the writing groove and let the words flow, not caring too much about whether or not we're punctuating correctly. And that's fine—for the first couple of drafts. But at some point you have to put on your editor's hat and look at your manuscript with a narrowed eye, looking at the details—including your punctuation.

So give it a careful look, and don't rely on someone else to clean up your text. You don't want to accidentally write something slanderous about the Pope and Mother Teresa.

# ON HABITS, PERMISSION, AND POETRY.

**Write Well: #84**

**Word of the Week: inveterate (in-VET-er-et):**
Habitual, deeply-rooted, established by long experience. From the Latin *inveteratus* 'made old', based on *vetus, veter-* 'old'. *My mother was an inveterate romance reader. Inveterate* is related to *veteran* (an old soldier) or anyone who's been doing something for a long time. *She's a veteran hairdresser, an inveterate peruser of hair style magazines.*

## Q&A

**Question:** Can I use a poem at the beginning of my story or chapter without breaking copyright rules if I cite the author, or is there more to consider?

**Answer:** There is more to consider. In the case of poetry or song lyrics, "fair use" (what you could use without paying for a license or written permission) is based on percentage, not word count. So if you use 100 percent of a short poem, you definitely need to obtain a license and permission.

Some would say that even ten percent of a short poem is too much to use without a license.

The only way to be sure is to contact the poem's author or publisher (preferably the latter), explain how much of the poem you wish to use, how many copies of your book you plan to print, and ask for permission or information about a license.

Honestly, I've found it easier to write my own poetry for epigraphs and such. Don't know how to write poetry? Keep reading.

**Book Club Scam**

Recently I told you about the flood of highly complimentary AI-authored emails that are going out to writers of all sorts. There's another variant involving book clubs, and it's tricky because the sales pitch is not obvious in the first email. This is one I recently received:

Dear Angela Hunt,

I hope this note finds you well. My name is Jessica, and I organize the **Oakland/Berkeley New Fiction & Emerging Authors Book Club,** a community of passionate readers who love discovering fresh voices and supporting new and emerging authors.

On **September 28,** our group will be featuring *Rescued Heart (Book #1): Historical Biblical Fiction Set in Abraham and Sarah's Old Testament Era for Fans of The Chosen* as our monthly selection. We meet in the Bay Area to read, discuss, and celebrate contemporary fiction, with a focus on uplifting new and emerging voices.

Our club has become a vibrant hub for conversation, connection, and the discovery of exciting new works, and we are delighted to include your book in this journey.

Sounds wonderful, right? There was even a photo of

eager young women sitting around a table. So, to test my scam theory, I replied with a simple "thank you."

Then I received a response—this time Jessica wanted me to schedule my book for September 28, when the club would read and discuss it. I wrote back: "Wonderful! But since the book doesn't release until October 7th, how are you going to read it? And you should know that I don't pay for book club exposure—never have, never will."

And that was the last I heard from Jessica.

Be careful out there—don't believe every email in your inbox, especially if it's beautifully written and filled with flattery. If it could have been written with details in your Amazon blurb or a review, trash it. And never, ever pay for book club exposure.

### Quotes of the Week

"Poetry is emotion put into measure. The emotion must come by nature, but the measure can be acquired by art." — *Thomas Hardy, as quoted in The Later Years of Thomas Hardy by Florence Hardy.*

"Poetry is the best words in the best order"." — Samuel Taylor Coleridge

### Quote of the Week

Nobel Prize winner (in literature) **Shmuel Yosef Agnon** was born in what is now Ukraine (1888). He spoke Yiddish at home, and read Hebrew and German.

At a party for his 70th birthday attended by several hundred people, he spoke of his books and said: "I did not recount great things and wonders about myself. Who more than I knows of my impoverishment? I say this not from false modesty, but from my own opinion — that an author who believes he has great things to tell about himself misappropriates his mission. **The individual to whom God gave an author's pen must write of the acts of God and his wonders with human beings."** (From Garrison Keillor's THE WRITER'S ALMANAC.)

*Though I have dabbled in poetry in some of my books, I'm no expert, so I asked my friend **Betty O'Hearn** if she'd write about poetry for us. Betty is a published poet and I love her work. She was kind enough to contribute, so enjoy!*

## How to Write Poetry

Poetry is an art form that expresses emotions, ideas, and stories through rhythmic and often symbolic language. It allows the writer to convey deep feelings and thoughts in a tight and impactful way. Writing poetry can be a rewarding experience, offering a unique outlet for creativity and introspection. Whether you're a seasoned poet or a beginner, this guide will help you understand the essentials of crafting your verses.

Poetry is a literary genre that uses verse, meter, and often rhyme. Unlike prose, which follows a straightforward narrative structure, poetry relies on the aesthetic qualities of language. It can take many forms, from sonnets and haikus to free verse and spoken word. The beauty of poetry lies in its versatility and the freedom it gives the poet to experiment with words and structures.

**Meter:** The rhythmical pattern of stressed and unstressed syllables in a poem.

**Rhyme:** The repetition of similar sounds at the end of lines or within lines.

**Imagery:** Descriptive language that appeals to the senses and paints a vivid picture in the reader's mind.

**Imagery and symbolism** are potent tools in poetry. Use descriptive language to create vivid images that evoke emotions and thoughts in the reader. Symbols can add depth and layers to your poem, making it more meaningful.

**Theme:** The underlying message or central idea of the poem.

**Structure:** The organization of the poem's lines, stanzas, and overall form.

**Voice:** The tone and style of the poet's expression.

The first step in writing poetry is finding inspiration. Your lines can come from various sources, such as nature, personal experiences, emotions, or even other works of art. Keeping a journal or notebook to jot down thoughts, observations, and feelings can be helpful.

### Choose a Theme

Once you have found your inspiration, decide on the theme of your poem. What is the central idea or message you want to convey? Having a clear theme will guide your writing process and help you maintain focus.

### Experiment with Form

Poetry offers a wide range of forms to explore. Some common forms include:

**Sonnet:** A 14-line poem with a specific rhyme scheme and meter.

**Haiku:** A traditional Japanese form consisting of three lines with a 5-7-5 syllable pattern.

**Free Verse:** Poetry that does not follow a specific rhyme or meter.

**Limerick:** A humorous five-line poem with a specific rhyme scheme

Experimenting with different forms can help you discover the most effective way to express your ideas.

**Focus on Sound**

The sound of your poem is crucial. Pay attention to the rhythm, meter, and rhyme. Reading your poem aloud can help you identify areas where the sound may need adjustment. Consider using techniques such as alliteration, assonance, and consonance to enhance the musical quality of your poem.

**Tips for Writing Poetry**

Read Widely: Read diverse poetry to understand different styles, forms, and techniques.

Write Regularly: Practice writing poetry regularly to develop your voice and improve your skills.

Be Authentic: Write from the heart and be true to your emotions and experiences.

Embrace Creativity: Don't be afraid to experiment with language, form, and content.

Edit Ruthlessly: Be willing to revise and edit your work to achieve clarity and impact.

Stay Persistent: Writing poetry can be challenging, but persistence is key to growth and improvement.

Writing poetry is a deeply personal and creative endeavor. It allows you to explore your thoughts, emotions, and experiences uniquely and profoundly. By understanding the elements of poetry and following the steps outlined in this guide, you can craft verses that resonate with readers and express your innermost feelings. Remember, poetry is an art form that thrives on authenticity and creativity, so embrace the process and enjoy the journey of writing your poems. —Betty O'Hearn

**It's Fall**

The orchards glow with red and gold,
and nights are heavy with dew.
The mornings have a sharp chill.
The garden is at its brightest,
with salvia vivid and old-fashioned asters
looking cheerful from their beds.
The cornstalks have reached their highest point.
Apples everywhere show their red cheeks.
Darkness settles quickly after supper,
and the moon rises, large and yellow,
at the edge of town.
It's comforting to feel the warm,
patchwork covers and go to sleep.
There are a calm and sweetness in the air,
as if all living things sense the approach of winter.
You can almost see winter moving slowly in the
distance,
carrying his burden of ice and snow.
Every small blossom seems to put on its finest
appearance
before the frost arrives and the petals rest.
And the good old-fashioned asters
laughing at us from their bed.
The mountain highways are aglow
in what appears to be colors painted
from pots of primary colors.
The decor is possessed by the embrace of colors,
textures and shapes.
And next fall, it will be glowing
and the motif will be brand new.
Betty O'Hearn, St. Petersburg, FL
More of Betty's poetry can be found here. https://dead
mule.com/betty-ohearn-three-poems/

Few of us would attempt to write a novel without ever having read one, so if you are interested in writing poetry, make time to read it! I was fortunate enough to have an English teacher who emphasized poetry, and to this day I can quote passages of William Cullen Bryant and Wordsworth. Poetry sticks, and writing it is excellent discipline because it forces you to—as Coleridge said—*put the best words in the best order*. So give it a try! You may even be able to use your poetry in your novels and nonfiction works.

## ON LEGIT OFFERS, PUBLISHING PREP, AND GIFTING YOUR FUTURE SELF.

**Write Well: #85**

**Word of the week: fungible (FUN-jih-bul):**
interchangeable, easily replaced by something else. *Currency is fungible—a check works as easily as cash—but bank personnel are not.*

**Quote of the Week**

From the time she was a teenager, Marie Curie wanted to be a scientist, but her family could not afford her education. Her older sister, Bronya, wanted to be a doctor, so the two sisters struck a deal: Marie would work various jobs to support her sister's medical education, then, after Bronya was a doctor, she would support Marie.

So for five years Marie worked as a family governess, studying when and where she could. Bronya kept her word and supported Marie when she was finally able to enter the Sorbonne. She eventually graduated at the top of her class in physics and mathematics, and would become the first woman to win two Nobel Prizes—first in physics, and later in chemistry. She became known for her work with radioactivity.

"A great discovery," Marie Curie wrote, "does not issue from a scientist's brain ready-made, like Minerva springing fully armed from Jupiter's head; it is the fruit of an accumulation of preliminary work."

The things you did last year, yesterday, and today—reading, writing, editing, studying, attending a conference, talking with friends, dreaming, praying, pondering, and revising—are a gift to your future self. The efforts you make today will either be successful, or they will teach you what *not* to do next time. So keep working and doing all those things. —Revised from Billy Oppenheimer's 7-27-25 newsletter.

## Q&A

**Question:** How can I tell if a publisher's offer is legitimate or if they are just trying to get me to spend money on marketing?

**Answer:** Because you have received an offer (and because you submitted your work to this company), I assume you are not self-publishing. But traditional publishers don't ask writers to spend money on ANYTHING. The publisher pays for the editing, design, distribution, and marketing. That's why you give them a large share of the profits from the sale of your book and get a relatively small royalty percentage.

If your publisher's offer requires you to *spend* money, you are being courted by a hybrid or vanity publisher. You could self-publish, spend your own money on marketing, and save money by cutting out the middleman. Yes, there's a learning curve, but you had to learn how to write, didn't you? You might as well learn how to publish your book.

**Is your book ready to publish—or just finished?**

With NaNoWrMo (which has officially shut down, but you can still do it) around the calendar corner, perhaps it's time we considered the project you're currently working on.

How do you know if your work in progress is ready to publish or just *done*?

Before you hit that upload button or email that manuscript, let's run through a preparation checklist.

- **What kind of book are you finishing?** Is it a novel, a children's book, a devotional, or a nonfiction book? Do any of these genres tend to come out at certain times of the year? (A lot of devotional and children's books come out in the fall, to be available for sale during the pre-Christmas season. Does your book have any sort of holiday tie-in? Is this the best time of year for this book to be published? If your book is a summer beach read (and that's how you want to market it), then publish and start selling in the spring. If your book is an advent devotional, publish and start selling in the fall. If you're sending to a traditional publisher, don't worry too much about this. Your publisher will schedule your book according to their own publishing calendar.
- **What is your publishing plan?** (Self-publishing, traditional, hybrid?) Do you have a valid reason for attempting self-publishing first? Most people

try self-publishing first because they're in a hurry —and that can result in a missed opportunity and a sloppy launch. Don't be in a rush. If it took you a year to write your book, give yourself a year to sell it.

- **Have you revised the manuscript, and if so, how many drafts or rounds of feedback have you gone through?** Writing a book and then rereading it quickly isn't going to be enough to make sure your book is the best it can be. Trust me. I've outlined several steps of revision in my book The Art of Revision, and I suggest you check it out. *Writing isn't writing, it's rewriting.* One thing you must do: LISTEN to your book. Have the computer read it to you. Your ear will catch more mistakes than your eyes. My Book

- **Has the manuscript been read by anyone else?** (Beta readers, critique partners, editors?) Have you identified your ideal reader? Is it men? Christian women? Children ages 3-8? People who like dogs? People who like cozy mysteries? Try to find people who fit the description of your ideal reader, ask them to read and give their honest opinion of your book, then thank them appropriately.

Note: I wouldn't hire an editor if you are aiming for a traditional publisher. First, because they have an editor who will want you to do revisions--count on it. Second, because the acquisitions editor expects to see *your actual writing*, not a hired editor's revision. But if you are self-publishing, hiring an editor is a good idea.

- **What's your biggest hesitation or worry about publishing your work now?** Write down the answer to that question, then fix whatever is worrying you. Afraid there are too many typos? Fix them. Afraid it will offend an entire people group? Figure out a way not to offend them. Afraid you got a fact wrong? Do more research and get the facts right. There's nothing worse than reading a dozen Amazon reviews that claim that the author didn't do his homework . . .

About offending people: I'm pretty sure that every book I've ever written has offended someone, especially since people seem to be looking for offenses these days. I once wrote a novel about a woman president who had an affair, and later a church librarian proudly showed me a copy of that book with BANNED written across the cover. My lovely aunt was once offended because I had a little boy character say the word *fart* . Like I said, there's always something to offend someone.

**But you don't want to write something that will likely offend everyone in your ideal reader group.** Read that sentence again, and take it to heart. Know your readers, understand their sensibilities, and respect them.

Okay—if you're finished, or are about to finish a project, run through that list.

Now, for the nitty gritty (for a novel):

- Check your craft: Is your voice consistent, the pacing smooth, the character arcs complete, and the prose tight?
- Do you have solid story structure: Does your story open with an engaging obvious problem? Is

the inciting incident and your character's resulting goal clear? Is that goal film-able, and does it last throughout the story? Is the emotional ending satisfying?

For a novel *and* nonfiction:

- Can your book be placed in a clear genre? Does it fit easily, and is it unique? Who is the ideal reader?
- Have you done a spell and grammar check (both can be done in Word). How's your formatting? Is it double spaced? Please tell me you aren't using five spaces at the beginning of a paragraph when a tab would do. (Better yet, set up a "manuscript" style that automatically indents your first lines of paragraphs .25 inches.)
- If this is a proposal, is your query letter engaging? Did you spell the agent's or editor's name correctly? Did you confirm the address? Do you have a polished synopsis and three sample chapters?

Now--What scares you most about hitting publish?

# ON BOOK LAUNCHES, EARNING THE MONEY, AND THE IMPORTANT THING.

**Write Well:** #86

### Word of the Week: parochial (pah-RO-key-al).

Limited in range or scope, petty, provincial. The word was first applied only to ecclesiastical matters, but gradually came to mean any group who is short-sighted. From the Latin word for "parish." *The Women's Club was so parochial they refused to allow women who moved from north of the Mason-Dixon Line.* Related word: *parochialism*, having a limited point of view. A *parochial* school, however, is a church school.

### Quote of the Week

I recently read about a conversation between Chris Rock and a struggling young comedian. The young guy said he was having trouble landing gigs and building a following. So Rock said, "What do you do during the day?"

The young guy was confused. "Whaddya mean?"

Rock said, "What do you *do*? Do you write? Work on material? Listen to your set from the night before? Stand in front of a mirror and work on your delivery? Do you read books? Seek out and develop relationships with bookers, producers, club owners?"

The young guy admitted he didn't do anything of those things, and that was the problem. Rock said, "In comedy, we make the money during the day."

Writing is surprisingly similar. So many times I read about a writer with a breakout first novel, and when I read the bio, I see that he or she was a newspaper writer for twenty years . . . or a reporter . . . or a columnist. The novelist had been writing for years before deciding to write that story.

Novelists—and comedians—aren't born in a night, or even a year. They are people who have been writing and studying and working with words for a long time. They read. They write articles and sell them. They seek out and develop relationships with other writers and editors.

I say it all the time, but I'll say it again: **start writing smaller things**. Get a copy of **Writer's Market** and write and sell some articles and blog posts. Get your name out there. Join some writer's organizations. Develop a reputation for being fast, dedicated, and dependable. Go to conferences and learn. But most of all, write and publish and write again.

### Q&A

**Question**: What are some tips on how to write a query letter that will grab the attention of an agent or editor? How long should the letter be, and what should it contain?

**Answer**: A query letter to an agent or publisher should be about a specific project—a fiction or nonfiction book, or a series. Query letters don't need to be more than one page long, as editors are busy people.

In the letter, introduce your project in one paragraph, explain what it is, what genre it is, and give the hook that will make the editor want to ask for your proposal.

In a second paragraph, detail your writing experience—previous publications, books, or articles. If any of these were self-published, say so. If you have developed a following on social media, this would also be a good place to mention it. If you have a TV or radio program that would enable you to sell your book, mention that as well.

But do keep your query letter brief and to the point. And offer to send a proposal, not the entire manuscript.

### How to Launch Your Book

A solid book launch is important for traditional *and* indie authors, so here are some tips to help you through the process.

**Prepare for the launch—six weeks before the big day.**

- **Pick your launch date** (Tuesday is industry standard, but you can choose any date).
- **Indies: Finalize your product** (proofread, edit, format, upload if needed).

- **Create a dedicated landing page** for your book (with a preorder button if possible). You should have an author website—this landing page is *not* a separate *site* for your book, it's a page *within* your website. If you or your publisher have uploaded your book to Amazon, for instance, and included a preorder option, you can include a link to that Amazon page.
- **Email teaser campaign**
  - Send an email to your mailing list with behind-the-scenes information, title/cover reveals, a piece on why you wrote the book.
  - Ask for feedback/opinions to boost engagement
- **Build a launch team (aka street team or influencers):**
  - Invite fans to read the ARC (advance reading copy) or an early copy
  - Provide review instructions and share promo graphics
  - NOTE: Confession: I don't often do launch teams. I usually go to my Facebook page—which has regular visitors—and announce that I have 50 copies of my new book available to folks who want it *and* will promise to leave a review on an online site. (Overseas readers get a digital copy). I do this with every book, so my list always has different people, depending on who sees the invite and responds first. I think that's fair, and it prevents me from having a list of folks who automatically expect a free copy.

- **Create promo assets with Canva, Photoshop, or another graphics program**
  - Social media graphics
  - Author quote graphics
  - Countdown images
  - Pull quotes from the book to feature in the images
- **Line up early reviewers** (BookSirens, NetGalley alternatives, newsletter swaps). Note: the Independent Book Publishers Association has a program through which members can offer their manuscripts to reviewers and librarians through NetGalley. I recommend this heartily!
- **Plan your email launch sequence** (4–6 emails spread out)

Launch Week:

1. **Launch day email newsletter blast:**
   - Include buy link and a heartfelt thank-you to your list.
   - Ask for reviews after they've read the book..
2. **Social media blitz**
   - Daily social media posts (quotes, videos, testimonials, photos)
   - Use trending hashtags in your genre
3. **Engage your launch team/influencers:**
   - Remind them to post, review, and tag you
   - Share and celebrate their content in your social media
4. **If Indie publishing, run a launch promo:**
   - Offer a discounted price for launch week

- Offer a bonus digital gift for those who buy and email their receipt—or enter them in a giveaway for a prize
- Off a Limited-time bundle or an autographed edition

5. **Cross-promotion:**
   - If possible, appear on podcasts, blogs, newsletters of other authors
   - Consider group giveaways or newsletter swaps. Recently I've seen a spate of reader scavenger hunts, where several author offer presents for readers who visit a series of websites and look for clues.

After the Launch

1. **Send a "what's next?" email to your newsletter list**
   - Offer a book club discussion guide, behind-the-scenes tidbits, or deleted scenes
   - Ask for reviews again
2. **Post reader reviews/testimonials** (use screenshots or pull quotes)
3. **Pitch your book to bookstagrammers/booktokers/bloggers**
4. **Apply for promotional features**
   - BookBub deals, Freebooksy, Bargain Booksy
5. **Use ads strategically**
   - Consider Amazon ads, Bookbub ads, or Facebook/Instagram advertising (if you can afford them)
   - Start small; test copy/images; optimize over time

6. **Bundle with another product or lesson** (great for nonfiction or teaching authors)

It is a little dizzying, isn't it? Just remember that you don't have to do EVERYTHING on this list. These are ideas and suggestions—do what you're comfortable doing.

And never forget this—all the marketing in the world won't help if you haven't written an amazing book. **THE BOOK IS THE IMPORTANT THING.** You earn your money writing the book; you spend it doing the marketing. At some point, you will have to let your book market itself.

Because you have to get busy working on another one. :-)

# ON BOOK TITLES, FOCUS, AND RESPONDING TO CRITIQUE.

**Word of the Week: allay (ah-LAY)**

To lessen, alleviate, relieve. *Parents chase away monsters under the bed to allay their children's fears. To allay her doubts, he told her he loved her.* From the Old English *allecgan*, to "lay away." Synonyms: *modify, moderate, mollify, reduce, assuage.*

**Novel Sprint is born (instead of NaNoMaMo)**

I've never participated in National Novel Writing Month, but apparently it died over a kerfuffle about AI. So welcome **Novel Sprint!** The endeavor, designed to help writers complete a rough first draft in only a month, is new and here's the catch: participants must write their novel *on the site*, thus no copying-and-pasting from AI. Details, if you're interested, can be found here.

**Q&A**

**Question:** What would happen if two different books

were published with the same title? Which author would have to change his title?

**Answer:** Neither. Since titles are not copyrighted, absolutely nothing would happen and no one would have to change his or her title. The books would be by different authors and would be completely different.

I had a book come out this month: *Rescued Heart: The Story of Sarah.* A quick search on Amazon reveals that there are also books called

1. **Rescued Heart, a Last Chance Country Novel**
2. **Rescued Hearts: A Small Town Slow Burn Romance**
3. **Rescued Hearts**
4. **A Rescued Heart** (a couple of those, actually)
5. **Rescued Heart: A Puppy Love Romance**
6. **Rescued Heart: Indecent Proposal Book Six**
7. **Rescued Hearts: Emma's Story**
8. **The Rescued Heart** (a couple of those, too)
9. **Rescued Heart: A Titan World Novel**
10. And many other variations.

Incidentally, while having a subtitle helps make a book unique, I've noticed a tend on Amazon where publishers are listing tropes and other descriptors instead of the actual title. For instance, my publisher listed my book as **Rescued Heart: Historical Biblical Fiction Set in Abraham and Sarah's Old Testament Era for Fans of The Chosen (The Matriarchs).** The purist in me wishes they had stuck to the title, but I understand that the extra words have been added to attract a book browsing customer. The actual book simply says **Rescued Heart: The Story of Sarah.**

**Quote of the Week**

From Billy Oppenheimer's newsletter:

Jerrod Carmichael has excelled across a range of creative fields—from stand-up comedy and acting to creating sitcoms and directing feature films. Asked if he's noticed any common mistakes people make when they struggle in those fields, Carmichael said, "They focus on the wrong things. There are a lot of aspiring comedians, for example, who aren't funny or don't have stage presence, but they have excellent websites. They have excellent websites and the shiniest business cards and their head shots are impeccable. And who [cares] about those things. You know what I mean? They focus on the wrong things." As for the people who excel . . . they focus on the work. On the content. On creating something of substance."

Remember to focus on the *writing*. On the story. On creating something that will change hearts and lives. Having a nice headshot and good social media is great, but writing a great book is better.

**Handling Feedback and Reviews**

A few weeks ago, I told you to start submitting work where you could score—remember the basketball analogy? If b'ball players didn't have a basket, they'd never know if they were shooting well. Writers need an editor, someone to buy their material. Publishing professionals read thousands of pages per week, and their expert eyes will know if your work has the potential to reach the masses.

The comments you may get on Facebook or Substack don't have the same power or credibility. It's nice to get approving comments, but social media users aren't pledging to invest in your work.

If you're not ready to submit to an editor, don't worry—

there are other ways to get constructive feedback. Critique groups. Hired editors. So when you get that feedback, how should you respond?

First—consider the source. If you're hearing from a magazine or newspaper editor, or an acquisitions editor at a publishing house, you're hearing from a pro. You can trust his or her opinion. You may feel defensive at first, but get over it. Snap out of the funk and learn to see your work with new eyes.

I once wrote a short story for a magazine. A boy had thrown a suit jacket down a well and assumed it was lost forever, and later his grandpa had presented him with the suit jacket, all pressed and cleaned, and he sniffed as he did it. My editor queried me— "How'd grandpa get the jacket?" Surprised, I replied, "I thought it was obvious—he went down into the well and caught a cold—that's why he was sniffing."

My editor said, "I didn't get that at all," and I realized she was right. Sometimes you can be *too* subtle, and I certainly was.

The problem, you see, is that we are too close to our stories and essays. We know and remember every hidden motivation and association, but our readers don't have access to our brains. All they have is the words on the page, and those words have to communicate as completely as possible while resisting the dreaded "urge to explain." Respect your reader's intelligence. Show the facts—I could have shown Grandpa on a ladder climbing out of the well— but don't *tell* the reader what you want him to know.

(Now that I think about it, a smart Grandpa would have just snagged the jacket with a fishing pole and stayed dry.)

So my advice is to accept 95 percent of everything the editor says. And only object to the remaining 5 percent if you have a doggone good reason for doing so.

Typically, if your topic interests an editor, they will write and say yes, please send the article or manuscript proposal. You write it up. What happens if they buy it? If it's a book, you'll get a revision letter and you'll resubmit, but if it's an article, you may not. But eventually, you will see a copy of the finished, edited piece. You will read through it to make sure all is as it should be.

Don't go through and compare it with your last version. Just read it, and if it contains your intent and your ideas, and if it reads well, accept it and smile. Don't quibble over every little change unless the changes distort your meaning or your intention.

Later, after you've accepted the publisher's revisions, you can go back and view the work as a lesson, to notice what was changed so you can figure out why. Was your punctuation wrong? Did the editor substitute a better word?

But don't waste your emotional energy resisting the editor's changes if the piece reads smoothly and accurately. Life's too short to quibble—and you don't want to get a reputation as a quibbler.

I'll never forget the time a magazine editor sat me down

and pointed out—in person—all the things I was doing that needed improvement. I was so grateful for her instruction, and I resolved never to make those mistakes again. This is another reason why I urge you to start by writing and selling smaller pieces—you will have a variety of editors, and they're more likely to give you a helping hand and help you learn. Plus, making those sales and learning those lessons builds your confidence.

Remember—editors and publishers are actively looking for material to publish. They *want* to buy writing from people like you. So your job is to make sure your material is strong and meets their needs.

Another source of feedback is reader reviews—readers are not editors, but they can be vocal about what they like and don't like. Negative reviews tend to fall into two categories: reviews that point out weaknesses you can improve and reviews from people who aren't your ideal reader and never will be.

If your reviewer says, "I can't stand books written in first person" (or present tense, or books about dogs, etc.), take those words with a grain of salt. If they truly hated first person writing, they wouldn't have finished your book. But if they say, "This book doesn't work well for children because the story problem is never truly solved," go back and solve that story problem properly.

One of the wonderful things about self-publishing is that you can correct typos and even rewrite endings. If several readers point out a problem about a certain aspect of your book, you can always fix it and upload a revised file.

Occasionally, however, a reader will rip you up and declare that you are a waste of skin. If you are writing about God or animals or abortion or euthanasia or politics, there are readers who will write horrible reviews because they don't agree with your opinions and they don't want to be confronted with the opposing position. That's okay. We used to be allowed to disagree with each other, and we disagreed with civility and even defended the other person's right to disagree. Those days are almost gone, and if you're going to publish, you're going to have to develop a thick skin. Sometimes it's hard to shake off that sinking feeling, but a good night's sleep and a puppy will make you feel better.

If you have a website with a contact page (don't list your email address, or you'll get spam), you will also get emails. When you hear from someone who loved your book, thank them and thank the Lord for using your work. But what do you do when someone takes you to task?

A lot of my writer friends simply delete those emails, and that's okay. But most times I answer back. Once a woman was offended by one of my books and told me she was going to tell her Christian bookstore to pull ALL my books from the shelves. People like that don't seem to realize that with a traditionally published book, the story has made it through an entire TEAM of reviewers before hitting the shelves. (Apparently her offense meter was overly sensitive . . .)

I wrote back and asked only one question: "Did you pray before sending me this email?" She hadn't. She wrote back and apologized. Another woman saw the cover of my book, *Delilah*, and wrote to upbraid me for having a brown-skinned woman on the cover of a book "about an evil woman." She said that revealed my racial prejudice. I wrote back and asked, "Have you *read* the book?" After reading it, she wrote a lovely letter and apologized, because my Delilah wasn't evil, she was an abused woman trying to survive in a man's world.

If you choose to respond to a negative, angry letter, don't

resort to name-calling or anger yourself, just ask a question or two and let conscience do the rest. Or ignore the email.

I'm convinced that most readers don't think of writers as real people who actually read their emails—I often get messages that begin, "You probably won't read this, but . . ." They don't realize that the words they dash off in a fit of pique not only reach our inbox, but can actually wound us. A week or two later, they've probably forgotten about the email they sent. If only we could forget as easily! It's sad, but it's human nature: you can get 100 nice letters and one nasty one, but it's the nasty one you'll remember.

So—when those come in, either pray and answer them or forget about them. The sender of that message might have been having a really bad day. OR they have a valid point, and the Lord may be using them to tell you about something you've overlooked. But the helpful letters aren't angry, and the issues are presented in a constructive manner.

I hope this is helpful—if not now, then later. But if you find the courage to send your words into the world, you must find the courage to face the world when it responds. The Lord who gave you the courage to send can also give you the courage to receive.

**Write Well: On editing, ISBNs, and what readers want from a novel**
#88

**Word of the Week: puerile (PYU-rel or PYU-rile)**
Childish, silly, trivial. *The assemblyman offered puerile excuses for his inability to get the job done.* From the Latin *puer,* "child." Related words: *puberty, puerperal* fever (a fever that can occur up to six weeks after a woman has given birth).

Q&A

**Question:** Why is editing considered more of a creative process compared to proofreading, and what specific changes might an editor suggest to improve a manuscript?

**Answer:** There are different types of editing—*substantive editing*, which is focused on the content of a book or a novel, *copy editing* (sometimes called *line editing*), which focuses on line-by-line edits, checking every word and sentence for clarity, and then there's proofreading.

A **substantive editor** must understand the blueprint for story formation, if a novel, or the intent of a nonfiction book and judge whether or not the book will please a reader and sell in the marketplace. If the writer has no idea what the blueprint for his chosen genre is, he will need to make major revisions. If the story is unclear, or the characters not fully developed, he needs to rewrite.

In nonfiction, a substantive editor will make sure the material is well-organized and flows well. He should do some degree of fact-checking, and make sure all claims are substantiated. He will make sure the book provides what the reader expects, based on the title and the book's initial proposal. He may order a legal review, so the publishing company and writer are not subjected to a lawsuit. There are many things to consider in the editing process.

Editing and proofreading are two different processes. And no matter what the genre, *every* book needs other sets of eyes to evaluate if it is the best book it can be.

### Quote of the Week

Did you know that comedian Steve Martin is also a musician? After retiring from stand-up comedy, he set out to write his own songs, but his lyrics didn't match the quality of the work he'd produced in comedy. Then he read a book

—*The Stuffed Owl,* a collection of bad poetry. The book inspired him to write some bad poetry of his own. He had fun with it, and one day he looked at that bad poetry and thought, *This is bad poetry, but it might make some pretty good country songs ...*

Those songs became an album, *The Crow: New Songs for the Five-String Banjo,* which won a Grammy for Best Bluegrass album in 2010. Source.

Am I telling you to write bad poetry? Not necessarily—but if something's not working, maybe it's time to recast it as something else. Maybe that novel about the space-time continuum should be a nonfiction book. Maybe that short story should be a novel. Maybe that song should be a poem. Maybe that devotional should be a short story. Don't try to force something that isn't cooperating, but try to see it in a new light. You might be surprised at the result!

**Why does my book need an ISBN number?**

If you are traditionally publishing, you don't need to worry about getting an ISBN number for your book—the publisher will do that. But if you are self-publishing, you will need an ISBN number for each edition of your title (hardcover, paperback, and e-book).

The **International Standard Book Number**, or ISBN, is a 13-digit numeric code that serves as an internationally applicable unique identifier for books. The code captures information regarding the book's publisher, title, language, edition, and version. When a publisher buys a lot of ISBNs (and they are sold in bulk—large publishers buy hundreds of them), they enter information into a database that will give all pertinent information to any librarian or bookseller who scans the barcode associated with that ISBN number.

To buy an ISBN, go to www.bowker.com. If you are using

Amazon's KDP program or Ingram Spark to self-publish, you don't also have to buy a bar code—that will be generated when KDP or IngramSpark finalizes your book cover. Amazon KDP does not require that you purchase a separate ISBN for e-books, but if you don't use your purchased ISBN, the book will show as "Independently Published" on Amazon's Kindle page.

For more information about ISBN numbers, visit this website. https://www.editage.com/book-editing-services-arti cles/10-faqs-on-isbn-every-self-publishing-author-must-know

### What Do Readers Want from a Novel?

If you're writing a novel and aim to please your reader, it would be helpful to know what readers find pleasing, right?

Readers have personal and individual tastes, but certain elements consistently contribute to a fulfilling reading experience. Here are a few elements that make a novel satisfying . . . and keep readers coming back for more.

1. **Emotional Resonance:** Novels that evoke strong emotions—whether joy, sadness, or tension— tend to leave a lasting impact. Stories with

relatable characters or themes that connect to universal human experiences (love, loss, growth) often feel deeply rewarding. For example, classics like *To Kill a Mockingbird* or contemporary works like *The Nightingale* by Kristin Hannah are praised for their emotional depth.

2. **Engaging Storytelling**: A compelling plot with a clear arc—whether it's a hero's journey, a mystery, or a character-driven drama—keeps readers hooked. Pacing matters too; a balance of tension and release, as seen in thrillers like *The Girl on the Train* ensures satisfaction without overwhelming or boring the reader.

3. **Complex Characters**: Readers often find novels most satisfying when characters feel authentic, flawed, and dynamic. Books like *The Secret History* by Donna Tartt excel because their characters' struggles and growth invite empathy and investment.

4. **Intellectual Stimulation**: Novels that challenge readers with thought-provoking themes, moral dilemmas, or philosophical questions can be deeply satisfying, especially for those who enjoy literary fiction or speculative genres. Works like *Dune* or *1984* combine gripping narratives with conceptual ideas that linger long after the last page.

5. **Satisfying Endings**: A novel's conclusion doesn't need to be happy, but it should feel earned and cohesive. Whether it's the bittersweet resolution of *The Remains of the Day* or the triumphant closure of *The Lord of the Rings*, endings that tie up loose ends or leave purposeful ambiguity tend

to resonate. If you have a sad ending, however, be sure to leave your reader with a glimmer of **hope**.

6. **Immersive World-Building**: For genres like fantasy, sci-fi, or historical fiction, a richly detailed setting enhances satisfaction. Readers of *Game of Thrones* often cite the vivid worlds as a key reason for their enjoyment.

**Genre Preferences**: Satisfaction varies by reader. Romance readers might prioritize emotional payoff (*Pride and Prejudice*), mystery fans value clever twists (*Gone Girl*), and literary fiction enthusiasts often seek lyrical prose and depth (*The Goldfinch*). Genres like fantasy and mystery will always be popular for their escapism and the way they invite the reader to "play along."

Not every novel is for everyone. The most satisfying novel aligns with a reader's preferences while delivering a blend of

- emotional connection,
- compelling narrative,
- and intellectual or imaginative stimulation.

Does your work in progress hit those marks? I'm asking the same question of myself, so let's work to make it so!

# ON SMALL BITES, YOUR ESSENCE, AND WRITING IN CHUNKS.

**Words of the Week: mollify (MOL-ih-fie) and appease (a-PEAS).**

Both *mollify* and *appease* mean to placate, or soothe someone who has been angry, but there's a crucial difference. To mollify is to sooth someone who has been offended or put off by something said or done (or in the case of a crying baby, something *not* done), but *appease* means to satisfy or soothe someone who has made demands. You *mollify* your spouse; you *appease* the tax collector when he calls for your tardy taxes.

## Q&A

**Question:** As a new writer, should I work on perfecting my long novel, or on several smaller pieces to build my portfolio?

**Answer:** I have always advocated for serious writers to learn the business and craft of writing by working on short pieces first: anything that will get you an income (yea!) and editorial feedback. Get a copy of *Writer's Market* and submit articles to various periodicals. Once you learn what professional writing really is, you'll be much better prepared to tackle the world of traditional publishing in novels, etc.

I wrote articles and such for five *years* before I even considered writing a book. But once I submitted books, they sold without too much trouble—children's books, nonfiction, and yes, novels for children and adults. Why? Because writing all those small pieces had taught me the craft of professional writing.

Writing a novel without learning the craft through experience is like a surgeon attempting brain surgery before he's learned how to carve a turkey. A little hyperbolic, perhaps, but the principle is sound.

Want to be a professional writer? Start writing for professionals.

### Anecdote of the Week

For years, George Saunders tried to write stories that fit the "formula" for good writing. But publishers, editors, and even friends all reacted with some version, "You've worked really hard, and the story is interesting, but . . ."

One day, while on a conference call at his day job, out of sheer boredom he began to write short, funny stories and illustrated them as cartoons. By the end of the call he had completed ten of those stories. He almost threw them out, but instead he took them home and set them on the kitchen table.

Later, from another room, Saunders heard "the sound of genuine laughter"—from his wife, who was reading those little cartoons. "This was, I realized," Saunders writes, "the first time that anyone had reacted to my writing with pleasure."

The next day, he wrote a story in that new mode—"allowing myself to be entertaining, setting aside my idea of what a 'classic' story sounded like. When I finished the story, I could see that it was the best thing I'd ever written." Others also saw that it was the best thing he'd ever written and it became the first story in his first published book, *Civil War Land in Bad Decline.*

What made the difference in that story? It was pure George. He wasn't writing what he thought he was supposed to write, he was writing from his essence. They were *him*—with his humor and world view.

So don't be a slave to what everyone tells you is right. Learn the principles of good writing, certainly, but don't forget to add your essential essence. That is what will set your work apart.

**Getting the Piece—whatever it is—Written**

I married a man with ADHD. He's never been officially diagnosed, but he can't sit still. This is probably why he hasn't gained a single pound in all the years we've been married—he constantly burns calories.

The old writing adage—"How do you write a book? You put your rear in a chair and keep it there"—might be difficult if you have a busy life, many demands on your time, or a limited attention span. So how can you complete a project that will require hours and hours?

There's another old adage: "How do you eat a cow? One bite at a time." The key to writing a book is to break the task into small pieces. For someone with ADHD—or if you simply have trouble focusing, especially in the early drafts —the trick is to make those more manageable.

**Break the "chair" problem**

- **Don't aim for "hours"** in the chair. Aim for *sprints*—20–40 minutes of writing, then a break. This is the **Pomodoro technique** in action. The brain cooperates when it knows relief is coming soon.
- **The Pomodoro Technique** is a time management method developed by Francesco Cirillo in the late 1980s. It uses a kitchen timer to break work into intervals, typically 25 minutes in length, separated by short breaks. Each interval is known as a *pomodoro*, from the Italian word for *tomato*, after the tomato-shaped kitchen timer that Cirillo used while he was a university student.  Wikipedia
- **Use multiple stations.** Writing doesn't always have to happen at the same desk. Rotate: desk → comfy chair → standing desk → couch. Changing scenery resets attention.

**Externalize time**

- ADHD brains don't feel time passing normally. Use a **visual timer** or app so you *see* the minutes draining away. This makes writing feel like a game/beat-the-clock challenge. Something like this might help.

### Hack dopamine

- Pair writing with a "treat." Example: only drink your favorite coffee or play a certain playlist while writing. Your brain begins to crave the session.
- Break the big task into **tiny wins.** Instead of "Write chapter 5," aim for "Write 200 words" or "Draft the first conversation." Each micro-goal gives you a dopamine bump.

### Structure the project

- **Outline first.** ADHD brains burn energy making constant decisions. A map reduces decision fatigue. How to outline?
- **For nonfiction,** write out all the topics you want to cover on notecards, one topic per card. For instance, if you're writing a book on macarons, you might have cards for baking macarons, the history of the macaron, the proper technique for piping macarons, fillings for macarons, sweet macarons, savory macarons, etc. Then on each card, jot down subjects you want to discuss within that topic: for instance, under savory macarons, you might have spicy macarons, salty macarons, sweet and sour macarons, etc. When you have topics and subtopics and recipes for everything you want to cover, you can start writing!
- **For fiction:** start with an abbreviated **plot skeleton:** A protagonist (who?) is dealing with an interesting problem in his ordinary world (not the main story problem, just a problem); he overcomes that challenge, but is presented with a call to enter a **special world** (the world of —?), where he sets a **goal** (name it).
  But **complications** (list them) prevent him from easily reaching that goal, but he burns a bridge and makes a commitment to that goal because there's **a lot at stake** (what?) and things get really bad and he reaches a **bleakest moment** (a situation he cannot solve) where someone steps in to help, but not solve the problem (Who helps?). Then he **learns a lesson** (what?) and **makes a decision** (which is—?) to change

something about his life, and he returns to the ordinary world a different person—and you must show this change in action. Fill in those plot points, and you'll have a basic outline.

- For a more concrete explanation of plotting/out-lining/writing a synopsis, read The Plot Skeleton.
- **Chunk the work.** Instead of "write book," think "today: describe setting of the garden scene." Small, bite-sized tasks feel achievable.

## Use accountability

- ADHD thrives on **social pressure**. Try:
  - Writing sprints with friends on Zoom.
  - Daily check-ins with a buddy ("I wrote 500 words—your turn").
  - Public commitment (e.g., post daily progress on social media or in a writing forum).

## Tools that help

- **Dictation software** if sitting still is hard, walk and talk your draft. The legendary Gilbert Morris, author of more books than I can count, told me that he used to dictate his books while walking along the beach. His wife typed them up. Teamwork. :-)
- **Noise-cancelling headphones** + consistent playlist = cue for brain to enter writing mode.
- **Fidget tools** keep your hands busy when your mind drifts.

The key idea: you don't need to force yourself into a rigid

eight-hour writer's chair. Instead, design an environment where the *book gets written anyway*, in bursts, sprints, and chunks.

### ADHD-Friendly Daily Writing Ritual for Anyone
### 1. Prime Your Brain (5–10 min)

- Choose a **cue ritual** (same every day):
  - make coffee/tea
  - light a candle
  - put on a specific playlist

This tells your brain: *"Now we write."*

### 2. Set Your Micro-Goal

- Pick a goal small enough that success feels inevitable:
  - 200 words
  - one scene
  - 25 minutes of focus

Write it down. Crossing it off later = dopamine hit.

### 3. Writing Sprint #1 (25–40 min)

- Use a **visual timer** (like a Time Timer or Forest app).
- Write in "fast-draft" mode—no editing. Momentum matters more than polish. (This has been my mantra all along. First drafts should be fast and sloppy. Engage ONLY the creative side of your brain.)

### 4. Energizing Break (5–10 min)

- Move your body: stretch, walk, do a chore.
- Avoid scrolling—your brain will get hijacked.

### 5. Writing Sprint #2

- Another 25–40 min.
- If you're flowing, keep going. If not, micro-goal again ("write one paragraph of dialogue").

### 6. Reward Yourself (built-in dopamine)

- After 2 sprints, give yourself a treat: snack, coffee, short video, or hobby.
- Associate reward with writing success.

### 7. Optional Extra Sprints

- Stack up to 3–4 sprints a day. That's 1.5–2.5 hours of focused writing—plenty for steady book progress.

### 8. Closure Ritual (5 min)

- End the session with a mini wrap-up:
  - jot down where to start tomorrow
  - tidy your workspace
  - say "done" out loud (silly, but ADHD brains like closure)

### Weekly

- **Pick one "longer day"** (2–3 hours of sprints) if you can. Perhaps a Sunday afternoon?

- Track your progress visually—colored boxes, stickers, or a word-count chart. ADHD brains thrive on visible wins.

With this system, you'll never have to *force* yourself into a chair for endless hours. Instead, you'll build progress through short, focused bursts—stacking them until a book quietly appears on your computer.

Then, after you complete that first draft, you can break down the revisions in the same step-by-step method. Details can be found in my lesson, The Art of Revision.

# SPECIAL EDITION: GOD IS WRITING YOUR STORY, TOO.

**Write Well: Special Edition**

God is writing your story

You should, by now, be familiar with the handy dandy plot skeleton:

A story opens with a protagonist in his **ordinary world**, dealing with a **problem**. He shows us his **hidden need** and reveals his **admirable qualities** as he does this for the first act of the story.

Then he enters a "special story world," and soon after entering, he establishes a **goal**: "I want to . . . ." Then **complications** arise to test his mettle.

The complications lead to a **bleakest moment**, where he has no hope, but then a **helper** arrives, gives a push in the right direction, and the protagonist perseveres. In doing so, he learns a **lesson** and makes a **decision** that will affect the rest of his life. Finally, at the resolution, we see the character **living in his new resolve,** and his **hidden need** has been met.

The Plot Skeleton

## Now let's make it personal

The Bible tells us that God has written every page of our lives into His book. He is writing a story where *we* are the protagonist, He is the author, and *we* have our own individual plot skeletons.

If you have undertaken a writing project, you have set a goal—to finish it—and you have encountered complications. You know what they are.

And you may have already encountered your bleakest moment. Or maybe your bleakest moment is still ahead of you, when you sit down to read another rejection letter . . . or another not-quite-right manuscript . . . and feel all your motivation draining away.

But it's not really gone. It's still there, and you're simply having an attack of the *Fear of the Blank Page*. Or the *Needs-to-be-Revised* page. Or the *what-in-the-world should I write* fear.

The next stage of the plot skeleton is this: The **helper** steps in with words or advice—not to solve the protagonist's problem, but to give him a push in the right direction.

So I'll be your helper by saying this:

Fear not, my friend. If you have something to say, you are doing the right thing by learning how to say it well. If the Lord has met your needs thus far, then He will meet your needs and guide you to take the next steps.

What are your next steps? I don't know, but you do. If you don't know, ask the Lord and He will show you what they are.

Now is the time for you to verbalize the **lesson** you learned (what have you learned?) and **make a decision** to implement that knowledge in your life.

The final stage of the plot skeleton is the **resolution**, where you show that your protagonist is doing something he could not have done before this adventure.

We see Dorothy back from Oz and being happy to be on the farm.

We see Maria of the *Sound of Music* as the mother of a passel of children, giving her life in service to God by serving that family and her new husband.

We see the formerly helpless Sarah Connor warily eyeing the future and expecting the child who will be a leader against the coming Rise of the Machines.

What will you be doing next week or next month that is different from what you were doing before you entered the special story world of learning to write? What attitude of yours will be different? What actions will be different?

How will your prayers be different? I don't know, but you do. Because the Lord is writing your story, and you have the honor and privilege of living it as a writer—one who is responsible for communicating to the world God's precious, enormous love.

# ON CRITICISM, REVISION, AND RESISTANCE.

**Write Well:** #90

**Word of the Week: illusive (IH-loo-sive) and elusive (EE-loo-sive).**

*Illusive* comes from the Latin *illudere*, "to mock." Therefore an illusive dream is one that appears to be true, but isn't. Politicians promise many illusive results from their work. Related to the word *illusion*, which is similar to a mirage—you may see it, but it isn't real. *Illusory* is something that is false or deceptive. *Elusive* means "tending to slip away, or hard to grasp."

The mayor's promise of more tourists was *illusive*. Joe realized that Sally's affection was *elusive*.

## Q&A

**Question:** How do you deal with negative feedback or criticism on your work without losing motivation?

**Answer:** Develop a thick skin. You have to get used to negative criticism, because no one's work is loved by everyone. You will never be everyone's cup of tea.

Consider, however, that those who critique you may be offering sound advice. When you receive criticism, ask yourself whether it is merited. If there's a consistent theme in the feedback you receive, it probably indicates a flaw in your writing, and you'd do well to pay attention. Readers know what they like, and a good writer writes not for himself, but for his readers.

So receive feedback—all of it—with an open hand, seek the kernels of truth, make corrections or adjustments, and dismiss the rest. It's the best way to survive in the very public world of writing.

### After the Criticism: Quote of the Week

Do you remember seeing Lisa Kudrow in the pilot of *Frasier*? I don't, either. She was fired from the show, and being released really shook her self-confidence. She wasn't even sure she could continue acting.

Then she was offered a small part in *Mad About You*—a waitress with no lines. She nearly passed on the job, but she was broke, so she took the part. By the end of the week, the show producer was so impressed with her that he named the waitress—Ursula Buffay—and made the role a recurring part. That part eventually led to her role as Phoebe Buffay (Ursala's twin sister) on *Friends*.

Looking back at her period of discouragement, Kudrow said, "It's okay to be discouraged. But then you've got to pull yourself back up. You can't stay down. That can't be your mindset for too long, or otherwise, it won't work out. That down and discouraged mindset will win."

So if you encounter criticism and/or rejection, pull yourself back up, work harder, and persevere. You can't win if you stop playing the game.

## You Don't Have to Write in Only One Genre

You may be aware that most publishers prefer that their authors stick to the genre they do best—because that's where the steady sales are. But many writers grow tired of writing in the same genre, so they adopt a pen name and write in other genres, too.

Under the name A. M. Barnard, Louise May Alcott, author of the beloved book *Little Women*, wrote thrillers known as "sensation stories" focused on tough, feminist women. Researchers are still discovering new works from Alcott, including twenty poems and stories that were discovered in early 2024.

Agent Donald Maass recommends that new writers write **at least five novels in one genre** to develop a following and a core readership. After that, a writer can branch out into other types of writing, but his or her core readers may always prefer the original genre. John Grisham, for instance, made his name by writing legal thrillers—only natural for a writer who was also a lawyer. Eventually, after eleven legal thrillers, he convinced his publisher to let him write a more literary novel, *A Painted House*. Writing those thrillers gave him an audience for the more literary coming of age novel that was based on his own childhood. After *A Painted House*, Grisham went back to writing legal thrillers.

If you are moving into fiction or nonfiction, sketch out what books or topics might follow your work in progress. Are they similar in tone, concept, or genre? You might be wise to think long-term, so a publisher will want your second and third books as well as your first. Once you have established a solid readership, you'll have the freedom to branch out and try something new.

## Resist the Urge to Resist

I recently attended the ACFW national conference, where I chatted with a friend who had just finished her first manuscript. "I showed it to an agent," he said, "and she didn't have time to read it carefully, because she said my character wouldn't be thinking that her hair was brown. But I wrote it in third person and it's only the second sentence . . ."

I understand how frustrating it is when people point out problems in the manuscript you have labored over, but instead of looking for loopholes or exceptions, isn't it easier to fix the problem?

I was talking to some other multi-published writers who mentor new writers, and I mentioned the natural defensiveness that arises when we try to point out problems. "I know!" one woman said. "I see it all the time."

That's why today's mini-lesson is this: **resist the urge to resist.**

I know it's easy to get bad advice from other folks who haven't been published yet, but when you hear something from an editor, an agent, *and* other seasoned writers, just fix the problem. Don't create a molehill to die on in your second sentence. Or even your second chapter.

When you begin to write a novel, you don't know what you don't know. So when people are kind enough to point out something you didn't know, thank them and add that bit of information to your writer's toolbox. You will have to move through the stages of competence just like everyone else did.

**Stage one:** Unconscious incompetence—you don't know

what you don't know. You think your work is pretty good, but it's not ready for publication.

**Stage two:** Conscious incompetence—you realize how much you don't know, and you begin to learn it.

**Stage three:** Conscious competence—you have learned the skills, and you work hard to implement them.

**Stage four:** Unconscious competence—you have learned the skills, so you write well, but you *still* have to stay on your toes to learn new skills.

You might receive some bad advice occasionally because, after all, writing is an art and often subjective. But it is also a science, with accepted norms and best practices, so learn what those are and follow them. Once you know them, you'll be able to strain out the bad advice and follow the good.

And whatever you do, if your heart and mind are truly in this, don't quit. Just get back to your project, large or small, do excellent work, and offer it for publication. Write, submit, rewrite, submit, publish.

That's how you build a career.

# ON EYEBROWS, LITRPG, AND HIGH CONCEPTS.

**Write Well:** #91

**Word of the Week: supercilious (soo-per-SILL-ee-us).**

Scornfully superior and arrogant, exhibiting haughty contempt or indifference. From the Latin *supercilium*, eyebrow. Any word with the prefix super has to do with *above or beyond*, so think of a supercilious person as having beyond scornfully upraised eyebrows. Superciliary has to do with the area above the eye. Note: while a supercilious person may raise their brows, not all people who raise their brows are supercilious.

**Q&A**

**Question:** What's a simple trick to make an ordinary object feel unsettling in a story?

**Answer:** Easy—attach a troubling memory to the object in the reader's mind.

Suppose a ceramic bust of Pharaoh Thutmose is used to murder someone in scene ten. The murderer cleans up the statue and places it back on the shelf. Weeks or even months later, the victim's young daughter is curiously drawn to the bust of Thutmose, causing the murderer to wonder if she knows something . . . especially if she confesses that she's been dreaming of the statue, but she always wakes up before the dream "feels finished."

That would do it. The "troubling memory" could be someone drowning in a particular lake, falling from a cliff, dying in a certain kind of car or on a certain stretch of highway, or being killed by a certain kind of tree. And it doesn't have to be a murder—suppose Joe Smith breaks up with Maggie Jones beneath an oak tree. From that day forward, Maggie's stomach tightens whenever she walks beneath an oak.

The "troubling memory" can be in a character's mind, the reader's mind, or both. But if the reader knows the backstory of that object, he or she will feel tension whenever the object or location is mentioned.

**What is LitRPG? Where to Read and How to Write It**

Fantasy is a popular genre, especially among young readers, but the genre can be so far from reality that some readers find it hard to follow.

A new genre has entered the scene, and I first learned about it from Thomas Umdstadtt. I've never read or written it, but I aim to serve you, dear reader, so here it is: LitRPG.

LitRPG is the combination of gaming and reading. It brings the interactivity of an RPG to the certainty of a novel and gets you invested in the characters within the characters. Anyone can write LitRPG *if* they know where to start and what they're writing about.

**What is LitRPG?**

*Literary Role-Playing Games*, or LitRPG, is a bit of a misnomer. Rather than being the name of a series of games, it's the name given to a genre of books about a regular person participating in and playing a virtual role-playing game. These games are often fictionalized versions of real-world RPGs and MMORPGs (massively multiplayer online role-playing games).

Does that sound like Greek to you? Read more about it here or check out some of the books here. Leave a note in the comments if this is something you're aware of or interested in. I'm curious! https://en.wikipedia.org/wiki/LitRPG

**It's practice**

In his paper *The Mundanity of Excellence,* Daniel Chambliss tells the story of a group of coaches from around the world who visited a U.S. Olympic Team practice. "The visiting coaches were excited at first," Chambliss writes, "then soon they grew bored, walking back and forth, glancing down at their watches, wondering, after the long flight out to California, when something dramatic was going to happen."

"They all have to come to see what we do," the U.S. coach said. "They think we have some big secret."

You know what? There is no big secret. There rarely is. With things that appear magical, mysterious, or extraordinary, there's usually something simple and mundane actually going on.

I've been to so many writers' conferences where folks are looking for the "secret" to writing a best-seller. You know what? **There is no big secret.** The people who write best sellers work hard every day to write the best books they can. They study the craft, they read, and they practice. They put endless words on the page. And eventually the practice pays off.

### News Flash: Amazon KDP Translates!

Last week I got an email announcing that Amazon was now able to translate my KDP books. Spanish is currently the only language available, but I'm always quick to jump into beta programs, so I immediately went to my KDP book-shelf and started clicking the translate button. There are options: Translate into Spanish, translate into other languages as soon as they become available, and other buttons to select worldwide sales rights or specific country rights (which might affect you if you've sold rights to a foreign publisher). There's an option to change the price, and a button to set things in motion. Boom! Within a few minutes I had opted to translate my eligible KDP books (art/picture books are not eligible), and within a few hours most of them were published and available for sale in Spanish.

My mind boggles, frankly, at the knowledge that our books can now be available throughout the world, translated at no cost to us (other than the commission Amazon usually takes). This is amazing news.

Now—I know what you're thinking. How can we be sure the quality is good, especially if we don't speak the language? KDP has instituted a quality check, and at least fifteen of my books didn't translate because the translation failed said quality check. Amazon doesn't want returns or complaints any more than we do, so I'm trusting that their translation program is working as it should. I did run a few pages of my translated preview through Google translate, and the translation was spot on. Hoping for the best . . .

Note: they are releasing this program slowly in beta mode, but when it is ready, the "translate" button will be beneath your book title on your KDP bookshelf.

### High Concept Novels

According to agent Angie Hodapp, this is the composition of the average agent's slush pile:

- 85% of queries are quiet or derivative (e.g., generic vampire story) or blandly situational (e.g., watch someone deal with a divorce)
- 10% of queries are "whackadoodle" (so outside the norm that you can't even begin to imagine how to make it work)
- 5% of queries are "I must read more!" (offering something completely new or a completely new take on something—and this is where high concept lives)

You don't have to have a "high concept" novel to be part of that five percent—but high concept novels are attention grabbers.

What is a **high-concept novel**? A high concept novel is a story with a clear and easily communicated premise that typically appeals to a broad audience. It often revolves around a unique "what if" scenario that can be summed up in one to three sentences, making it easy to pitch and market.

Sometimes the concept can be summarized in a few words: "Jurassic Shark" becomes *Meg*. "Cowboys in Space" becomes the *Firefly* series. "Reality TV plus Game Show plus Politics" becomes *The Hunger Games.*

How do you come up with a high concept? Take a common situation and twist it. Angie Hodapp suggests the following:

- "It's a buddy cop story **but with** _____." (Or, to phrase it as a what-if question: "*What if* two diametrically opposed cops were suddenly [placed in a totally new and unexpected situation]?")
- "It's a teen girl's first romance story **but with** _____." ("*What if* a teen girl suddenly met [someone totally unlike anyone you would expect in a teen romance story] and they [did something totally unexpected]?")
- You can also phrase it as "X meets X," such as: "It's *Breaking Bad* meets *Outlander*." (However, Hodapp notes that you should probably avoid extremely popular or ambitious titles for the most part because they're difficult to live up to. There are exceptions, of course. George R.R.

Martin pitched the *Song of Ice and Fire* series as "*The Lord of the Rings* meets the War of the Roses.")

- "It's *Ferris Bueller's Day Off* meets *Firefly*." (This tells us that it's funny but has serious themes and probably takes place in space.) Source.

Your story does not have to have a high concept to be published. But if you can come up with a high concept that will appeal to a broad audience, and then you can write it well, you will have a winner!

### Speaking of eyebrows, let's talk about body beats

We all know that sometimes dialogue needs some physical action to indicate a pause, or just to give the reader a break.

"Come over here, cutie pie," creates a different feel than "Come over here—" he gave her a lecherous wink— "cutie pie."

Nothing wrong with body beats or other movements to break up lines of dialogue. But writers need to be careful of two things—first, don't get into a predictable pattern and 2) don't use the same body beats all the time.

I have a tendency to have my characters engage in eyebrow calisthenics—or at least I used to. But if you suspect that your characters are always lifting a brow, nodding, smiling, grinning or whatever, use the old search/replace trick to see how many times the same motion appears on two consecutive pages of text. If you're being too repetitive, either change the beats or cut them entirely.

Pattern? That's when you write something like this:

**"Nice to see you, George." Barry smiled. "It's been a hot minute, hasn't it?"**

"Sure thing." George nodded. "When was the last time we were together—that golf tournament just before Covid?"

"I think so." Barry fiddled with this tie, which suddenly felt too tight. "Right before my mother died."

Do you see the pattern?

Dialogue, beat, dialogue.

Dialogue, beat, dialogue.

Dialogue, beat, dialogue.

Nothing wrong with that, but don't get into the habit of using the same pattern for more than two or three lines. Using patterns like the one above will put your readers to sleep.

# ON REPETITION, POINT OF VIEW, AND THE VALUE OF LIVING.

**Write Well:** #92

### Words of the Week: respite and insouciance

I chose these two words because recently I heard them in the wild. *Respite*—a short period of rest or relief from something unpleasant—is frequently mispronounced (as it was when I heard it). It's **RES-pit**, not res-PITE. And notice that the rest or relief is not just a nap, it's a rest from something you'd rather not be doing.

*Insouciance* (in-SOO-see-ahntz) is an attitude of arrogant boredom. A casual lack of concern or indifference. *The difficult diva stepped from her limo with an air of insouciance, pretending not to notice the paparazzi she'd summoned to record her arrival.*

Useful words to have in your vocabulary.

### Q&A

**Question:** Why do publishers tend to avoid books that change perspective mid-scene, and is there a way to convince them otherwise?

**Answer:** Why is there a "one POV per scene rule?" Because otherwise readers get confused.

It would be easier—and better for the reader—to convince *you* to write differently. If you want to change point of view perspective, insert a scene break and continue. Problem solved.

Confused about point of view? Order my lesson here.

**Thought for the Week**

Asked what he would focus on if he were to teach a writing class, the great essayist Henrik Karlsson said, "Becoming a person who writes well. Writing is not really about having a technical skill set. It's deeper than that . . . . Figuring out grammar and adverbs or whatever—that is kind of easy. The hard part is **working to become a person who can think interesting thoughts.**"

That is the work he is primarily focused on in his own life. "The project I'm doing," Henrik said in another interview, "is basically turning myself into a certain type of person who is able to have the thoughts that turn into essays. The work is growing intellectually and emotionally. It's reading. It's talking to people. It's going out into the world and experiencing things. Cultivating the kind of mind that can have interesting thoughts—that's the real work. And the essays are just the exhaust from that process." Billy Oppenheimer, Six on Six

I love that thought. We writers are sponges—we absorb information, and when it's time to write, we release what we have absorbed. This is why older people have the potential to write more interesting books than younger people—we've seen more, we've learned more. Most first novels tend to be autobiographical because writers mine their own life experiences. Most young men write first novels featuring troubled adolescent males. Most of manuscripts I see from teens and young adults are fantasies with dragons—with little life experience, they are writing what they *read*.

If you are living an interesting life, if you are going into the world and talking to people, reading materials that both agree *and* disagree with your world view, if you are thinking deep thoughts, you can write books that attract the world.

If you are staying at home, if you don't know people who disagree with your perspectives, if you only read the Bible and religious books, your books are likely to only engage people who think like you do.

BUT—

In John 17, Jesus prayed for His followers: "**I am not asking that You take them out of the world,** but that You keep them from the evil one."

I would challenge you to write for the world that desperately needs the Truth you claim in your own life. Your nonfiction books, your novels—yes, there are times when you want to write for your tribe, **but are we not called to reach the world God loves?**

I may have said this before, but if your writing presents only one side of an argument, you are writing a form of propaganda. Even in something as simple as a romance, your protagonist faces a choice—life with the hero or life without the hero. You must make the choice of "life without the hero" seem absolutely as attractive as the opposite choice. And then you must make her decision to accept the hero seem rational and right because [insert compelling reason here].

[Aside: I was once in a seminar where the teacher said, "I hate rom-coms where the leads fall for each other just because they're cute and in a movie together." *Ah.* Lightbulb moment.]

In my book *The Pearl*, a woman was offered the chance to clone her five-year-old son, who had been killed in a freak accident. When I wrote the book, I knew that I was supposed to be against cloning, but I had no real idea why. But in my story, I had to make the argument for cloning as strong as the argument against it . . . so I had to do research, and then I had to make her decision rational and right.

If you want to become an interesting writer, if you want to have thoughts and stories people outside your sphere want to read, you have to expand your horizon to include the choices you *wouldn't* personally make as well as the ones you would. This is the chief problem I see in fiction that supports a particular world view, be it about climate change, slavery, women's rights, or whatever. Both sides of the argument must be fairly represented. Then you have to convince your reader that the protagonist is right to make the choice he does and *show* why he is right.

Each writer is different, and God leads each of us individually. But instead of assuming that you have to write a certain kind of book because that path is easier or because you know you'll have a built-in audience, prayerfully consider that perhaps you can write other books for the world at large—parables with deeper meanings, with challenging thoughts, with Truth wrapped in an entertaining story.

That's my challenge to you today—and to myself as well. When we sit at our desks, we could write ANYTHING—so choose your projects prayerfully and carefully.

## One plus one equals one-half

I doubt my male readers are familiar with this advice, but women should know it—when accessorizing an outfit, put on everything you want to wear—scarf, necklace, earrings, brooch, whatever—and then remove one thing. **Less is more.**

The same principle applies in writing. When ~~you're on a roll and~~ the words are flying from your fingertips, it's easy to ~~just~~ go with the flow. But when you ~~go back to~~ do your revisions, the editorial side of your brain needs to ~~kick in and~~ be ruthless. Look at your words, ~~your~~ adjectives, and ~~your~~ body beats, then cut out things that are repetitive. Keep the strongest phrase (and this will often be a subjective choice).

He was ~~exhausted—bone-tired, enervated,~~ as tired as a dog trying to pee on a corner in a round room.

She squatted ~~down~~ ~~to the floor~~, trying to get close to the ~~little~~ lizard.

Friends and neighbors, ~~ladies and gentlemen, students and scholars,~~ lend me your ears.

She sat ~~down~~ on the couch and whispered ~~softly~~ to herself.

He clutched the rope ~~tightly with both of his hands.~~

~~In my opinion, I think~~ The evidence ~~clearly~~ proves the point.

~~The reason why~~ she left ~~was~~ because she felt unwanted.

Now—your turn. Clean out the repetitious words or phrases in the following sentences:

The sun rose up over the horizon in the early morning dawn.

She was terrified—frightened, scared, filled with dread and panic.

The room was silent, utterly quiet, hushed and soundless.

This new policy is unfair, unjust, and not right.

He was angry—furious, enraged, boiling with wrath.

The storm was violent, ferocious, savage, brutal in its power.

**Remember: redundancy isn't intensity.** Writers often double or triple words because they're trying to add punch. But the smarter move is to choose the *one* word or image that says it best.

**Less is more. Especially when your Thanksgiving table is groaning beneath a load of food.**

# ON SCRIBES, CONFIDENCE, AND THE POWER OF ONE.

**Write Well:** #93

**Word of the Week: ascribe**

Ascribe (ah-SCRIBE) means to attribute to. The word suggests a characteristic, quality, value, opinion, etc., that is not outwardly apparent. *The police officer ascribed the accident to carelessness. The quotation should be ascribed to Patrick Henry.*

From the Latin *ascribere*, "to attribute." You probably recognize the root word, *scribe*, as a writer, or someone who records information. From the same root we get *scribble* and *scribbler*, as well as other useful words:

**inscribe:** to write or carve words onto something

**subscribe:** to sign one's name below or to support/agree to something

**prescribe:** to lay down a rule or direction, or recommend (as in medicine)

**describe:** to write down or depict in words

**transcribe:** to copy or write across

**conscript:** to enroll or draft into service
**conscribe:** to enroll or enlist (rare/archaic)
**circumscribe:** to draw a line around, limit
**rescribe:** to write back or in reply (archaic)
**proscribe:** to forbid or condemn
**postscript:** an addition written afterward (P.S.)
**script, scripture:** written text or holy writing

## Q&A

**Question:** Why do publishers return manuscripts without reading them or providing feedback?

**Answer:** Simple answer? Time.

Publishers don't have time to read all of the manuscripts, most of them *not* requested, that flood their offices. And if there's no time to read them, there is certainly no time to write a critique or provide feedback.

However, if a publisher requests your proposal (the proposal should consist of a synopsis or outline—if nonfiction—and three sample chapters, not the entire manuscript), they will at least read a page or two before rejecting it. If they like what they read, they'll read everything and request the entire manuscript.

You might be surprised at how easily you can discover a writer's skill in only a page or two. Once you know what good writing is, you recognize it right away.

## Quote of the Week

When Steven Pressfield first submitted his 800-page manuscript for his now classic epic novel *Gates of Fire,* his agent told him, "Steve, I can't sell this. You have to cut three hundred pages."

"I was shell-shocked," Pressfield writes in *Put Your Ass*

*Where Your Heart Wants to Be.* How could he possibly cut almost half the book? "I fell into depression and despair."

Then he got a hand-written note from Tom Guinzburg, then the president of Viking Press, one of New York's most prestigious publishing houses. Guinzburg had read the manuscript. "There is a first-rate novel in here," the note said. "I am confident you will pull this off."

"Sometimes it takes another person to believe in us," Pressfield writes. "That note changed my life. I taped it to the screen of my [computer] and took courage from it every day of the six months it took me to get three hundred pages out of that manuscript." From Six on Six, Sept. 7 2025

### Whose Story is It?

Once I read about "ensemble casts," and was determined to feature one in my novel **Uncharted**—because I like to try new things. So I came up with five college friends, moved ten or so years past their college graduation, and spun their story. Then I took it to a Don Maass intensive workshop, and Don read at least a few of the pages.

"You have too many main characters," he said (I'm paraphrasing).

"It's an ensemble cast," I said, feeling overly pleased with myself. "I'm telling five stories."

Don shook his head and said it wouldn't work. I needed ONE protagonist, and I needed to tell that person's story. The others could be *in* the story, of course, but I had to tell the story through one character's eyes.

Once I went back to the story, I realized the problem. I was trying to write five stories, with five inciting incidents, five goals, five sets of complications—in short, my story had become predictable and altogether too obvious. So I asked myself, "Which of these characters has the most to lose?

Which will be most emotionally affected by the events of this book?" Ah—Karen, the mother, because she had a teenage daughter who was at risk.

So I went back, cut all the extraneous material, and focused on Karen. The result? The book was a thousand times more powerful, emotional, and memorable.

I have noticed that "pantsers"—people who write "by the seat of their pants" --tend to have too many characters because they haven't taken the time to create a plot skeleton revolving around ONE person. Of course you can have multiple characters in your novel, but they are important only to the degree that they affect your protagonist. We don't care that John's mother has been scammed by a Nigerian hacker unless that scam somehow affects Marjorie, our protagonist. If John is upset by his mother's financial loss and therefore misses his date with Marjorie, okay, let us see him comforting his victimized mother. But if the situation never touches Marjorie, cut it.

Some stories seem to require a focus on two people—a thriller with a villain and a hero, a romance with a man and a woman, a buddy movie with two cops. But even in those situations, one must be the primary character. *Lethal*

*Weapon* is the story of grieving Martin Riggs, who found a family through his partner, Roger Murtaugh. *Jane Eyre* is Jane's story, though she falls in love with the powerful personality of Mr. Rochester. *Speed* is the story of Jack Traven, even though Sandra Bullock is charming and Dennis Hopper is a wildly wicked villain.

A novel is *one* person's story, and it is a wonderful way to tell big stories. Want to write about war? Write about one person's war. Want to write about infidelity? Write about one betrayed spouse. Want to write about aliens? Write about one man's encounter with an alien. The movie *Signs* is a great example of this—aliens threaten the entire planet, but we see the problem through the eyes of one man struggling to defend his family.

**One.** Let us, your readers, come to love and appreciate the protagonist in his or her ordinary world, then introduce us to the big problem in the inciting incident. We will feel it because we care about your main character, and we will live through the major calamity with him.

*The power of one.* Utilize it when writing a story, no matter what genre, no matter how long.

### Self-Publishing Resources

Though I don't usually recommend self-publishing as a starting point, if that's what you want to do, here are some good resources. Start by reading articles on Kindlepreneur: https://kindlepreneur.com/book-publishing/

There's also a free course on self-publishing from a site called Reedsy: https://reedsy.com/learning/courses/publishing/self-publishing-101

However—I would recommend that you not rush to self-publish before you have 1) polished your book so it is the best it can be and 2) submitted it to editors and/or agents and 3) revised it and resubmitted it again. Self-publishing is fast and easy, but it does not offer distribution to bookstores. And the operations that promise marketing will never do as good a job as you could do on your own.

Trust me on this, and give your project the best chance at reaching the most people. Isn't that why you wrote it?

# ON GREED, GRIFTING, AND HOOKING A PIRANHA.

**Word of the week: avaricious (ah-var-RIH-shus)**

*Avaricious* means greedy, prone to avarice. The man described as avaricious is not only greedy, but stingy. Charles Dickens painted Ebenezer Scrooge as an avaricious man. From the Latin *avarus* meaning *greedy*, which in turn comes from **avēre**, meaning "to crave" or "to desire."

Other words derived from or related to that same root:

- **Avarice** — extreme greed for wealth or material gain
- **Avariciously** — in a greedy or covetous manner
- **Avariciousness** — the quality of being greedy or grasping
- **Avid** — (from *avidus*, related to *avēre*) eager, enthusiastic, or desirous
- **Avidity** — keen eagerness or greediness
- **Avidly** — eagerly or enthusiastically

## Q&A

**Question:** What is one completely ordinary activity that sometimes brings a creative idea?

**Answer:** Taking a shower. There's something about the sound of water, and the fact that I don't have to *think* about the mechanics of washing, but I often get my best ideas in the shower. I've heard that I'm not the only one who finds the act of showering a creative wellspring.

## Quote of the Week

Asked while in the early stages of a project if he knew how it was going to end, the novelist E.L. Doctorow said that not even in the late stages of a project does he know how it's going to end. "It's like driving a car at night: you never see further than your headlights, but you can make the whole trip that way."

A big project, task, workout, assignment, goal, day—whatever it is: don't worry about the second step or the third. Start with the first. Start with the ground beneath your feet. Start with one bird or brick. Start close in. You can make the whole trip that way. Source.

## Christmas Gifts for Writers (a list to hide in plain sight)

If you're looking for a writerly gift, or if your spouse or kids want suggestions about what you'd like for Christmas or Hanukkah, here's a list for you! All gifts are under $50.

1. Jane Austen Writing Set: A beautiful, elegant writing set that evokes the craft and tradition of writing. Good for someone who values the tactile and aesthetic side of being a novelist . . . or someone who loves Jane Austen!

2. Threshold Desk Lamp with USB Ports: Practical but stylish—helps with workspace comfort and ambience, and the USB ports add utility for a writer who uses devices.

3. I'm Still Writing: Women Writers on Creativity: A book of inspiration and wisdom from women writers. Great for motivation, reflection, and creative encouragement.

4. The Writer's Toolbox: Creative Games & Exercises Kit: A fun, interactive kit of prompt-cards and exercises to help when a writer hits a block or needs fresh ideas.

5. Agatha Christie Writer's Journal: A themed, nicely designed journal with quotes from a famous novelist. Useful for planning, jotting down ideas, character sketches, or just daily writing.

6. Insignia Laptop Stand (Adjustable): Ergonomics matter. For novelists typing long hours, a laptop stand helps reduce strain and improve posture.

7. Genius Ideas Spiral Notepad: Affordable and stylish—perfect for brainstorming, capturing fleeting ideas, outlines, or random thoughts that can become novel threads. You may want to keep one of these in every room.

8. Words Are Hard Writing Prompt Deck: A deck of 150 prompts across genres—excellent for expanding creativity and playing with new directions in novel writing.

9. "Writing a Bestseller" Candle: Ambient gifts can make the writing space feel special. A candle that says "this is your writing zone" adds a nice touch.

10. "Scripturient" Dictionary Definition Necklace: A wearable, meaningful gift: the word *scripturient* means a strong urge to write. Symbolic and motivational.

11. Monogram Script Personalized Notepad: Custom stationery adds a personal touch and can feel like a professional writer's tool. Good for letter-writing, notes, or drafting by hand.

12. Lined "Note to Self" Journal: Simple but effective —a lined journal for reflections, self-prompts, daily writing rituals, or just capturing what's on your mind.

## Keep Them Turning Pages

Are you a fisherman? My dad took me fishing a couple of times when I was a kid, then years passed before I went fishing again. As it happens, the last time I went fishing I was in a dugout canoe on the Amazon River, fishing for piranha with a length of fishing line tied to a hook. Our guide could catch fish easily, as could Gaynel, my intrepid traveling companion. But no matter how hard I tried, I couldn't seem to manage the trick of hooking one of the little devils.

The technique seemed simple: you dropped the baited hook and line over the side of the canoe, you let it dangle in the water, and when you felt something tug at the bait, you set the hook with a jerk and hauled up your catch. I felt lots of tugs during our afternoon of fishing, but I was never able to bring up a fish.

(Excuse the AI hallucination. Piranha don't float in mid-air, though they might be easier to catch if they did.)

Maybe my subconscious didn't really *want* to catch a piranha. But I *do* want to hook my readers, and I know it's the tension on the line that hooks—and keeps—a reader.

What makes some books page-turners while others put you to sleep? The answer lies in a fascinating psychological principle called the *Zeigarnik effect*. It's our brain's obsession with things that are left unfinished, and the principle is simple: instead of explaining everything to your reader, throw out a "hook" by raising a question in your reader's mind. He will keep reading until he discovers the answer.

My book *Magdalene* opens with these paragraphs. I have inserted, in brackets, the questions that usually rise in the reader's mind as he or she reads:

Silence, as heavy as doom, wraps itself around me as two guards lead me into the lower-level judgment hall. *[Where is she?]* When I fold my hands, the *chink* of my chains disturbs the quiet. *[Why is she in chains?]*

My judge, Flavius Gemellus, senior centurion of the *Cohors Secunda Italica Civum Romanorum*, looks up from the rolls of parchment on his desk, his eyes narrow. I don't blame him for being annoyed. I am not a Roman citizen, so I have no right to a trial. *[Why is she on trial?]*

Besides, I have confessed and am ready to die. *[Why would anyone confess, and why is she ready to die?]*

Do you see how it's done? As a storyteller, your task is to raise questions in the reader's mind, not to reveal everything up front. Respect your reader's intelligence enough to let them figure things out, and don't reveal anything the reader doesn't absolutely need to know . . . yet. You need that tension to keep them "on the line."

Be careful, though--hooking the reader is not the same thing as *confusing* your reader. The reader isn't confused after reading the above passage; he's only asking questions. If the reader is confused because he can't figure out where or when or who the scene involves, he's likely to put your work down and not pick it up again.

Those three paragraphs of *Magdalene* paint a clear picture of a woman (we presume it's Mary Magdalene, because the reader always expects the first scene to be from the protagonist's point of view) in chains, standing before a busy Roman judge in a dank judgment hall. From just three paragraphs, we can safely assume the *where*, the *who*, and the *when*. We don't need a lengthy introduction to set the stage of a prison in ancient Rome.

The same principle works for **nonfiction**—introduce your topic with a story, and don't explain everything all at once. Raise questions in your reader's mind, and he will keep reading to discover the answer!

# ON CONCLUDING, DIME NOVELS, AND SUBTEXT.

**Write Well:** #95

**Word of the Week: denouement**

(DAY-new-maw(n) . . . but say the last syllable through the nose a la the French.) The *denouement* of a novel or a story is commonly known as the climax, or that point when all the loose ends are brought together: the crime is solved, the lovers unite, etc. It can be used in a non-literary sense if you talk about the culmination of a situation—the *denouement* of the senators' political posturing. The last syllable is not pronounced MENT, but in the same ways as macaron—the *n* in the final syllable is swallowed.

## Q&A

**Question:** Is it common for beginning writers to be traditionally published only after they've written one or two books? Why is that the case?

**Answer:** It is not *always* true, especially if the writer has been working in the field of writing for a long time, but it is often true. Why? Because that first book is a learning experience—you don't know what you don't know until you write a book and try—usually unsuccessfully—to sell it. Then you realize what you need to learn, you apply yourself to learning it, and you are better equipped to write your next book.

Some writer friends and I have compiled our stories of our first novels and put them into a book detailing our experiences—**My First Novel,** available on Amazon. In it we told the stories of writing our first books . . . and if we were ever able to sell them. You may find it helpful and inspiring.

### Story of the Week

On June 9, 1860, the first dime novel was published. It was called *Malaeska, the Indian Wife of the White Hunter*, by **Ann S. Stephens**, and it was the first of 321 dime novels published by Beadle & Adams. These early novels actually cost 10 cents, but soon the phrase "dime novel" came to mean any cheap, melodramatic pulp fiction, some of which sold for 15 cents.

Many authors of dime novels wrote nothing else, but some established writers tried their hands at writing pulp fiction. Louisa May Alcott published more than thirty dime novels under the pseudonym A.M. Barnard. To her friend Alred Whitman she wrote: "I intend to illuminate the Ledger with a blood and thunder tale as they are easy to 'compoze' and are better paid than moral and elaborate works of Shakespeare, so don't be shocked if I send you a paper containing a picture of Indians, pirates, wolves, bears and distressed damsels in a grand tableau over a title like this: 'The Maniac Bride' or 'The Bath of blood, A Thrilling Tale of Passion.'" (Adapted from Garrison Keillor's THE WRITER'S ALMANAC, June 9th.)

**The Quiet Power of Subtext: How to Make Your Dialogue Say More Than Words**

If you've ever overheard two people have a conversation and thought, *"Okay, they're talking about lost car keys, but something deeper is going on,"* you've already experienced the magic of subtext.

Subtext is what your characters *mean* but don't say. It's the emotion beneath the words, the tension between the lines, the history coloring every exchange. When it's missing, dialogue can feel flat, robotic, or overly on-the-nose. When it's present, dialogue becomes rich, layered, and alive.

Beginning and intermediate writers often focus so hard on getting characters to communicate information that they forget: people rarely say exactly what they mean. And the more dramatic the moment, the more likely they are to hide, blur, dodge, or soften the truth.

Subtext matters because it mirrors real life. It reveals your characters in the silent spaces between their sentences.

Let's look at how it works, why it matters, and how you can start using it today.

**Readers love subtext because it invites them to participate.**

What is it? Subtext is where your dialogue stops acting

like a list of exchanged facts and begins carrying emotional electricity. When characters dodge, hint, react physically, or circle around what they truly mean, the reader becomes an active participant in the scene—leaning in, decoding, and feeling connected. Instead of being spoon-fed the meaning, they enjoy the pleasure of connecting dots. It's like being part of an inside joke or discovering a secret hidden in plain sight. And readers who feel smart, engaged, and emotionally involved are readers who stay with you page after page.

Subtext also deepens characterization. When a character avoids the truth, circles around it, or expresses something sideways, we learn who they are. Do they deflect with humor? Retreat into silence? Lash out? Change the subject? People often reveal themselves most clearly when they're not being straightforward.

Finally, subtext creates tension—something we need to have on every page.

Anytime the reader senses *They're not really talking about the thing they're talking about,* the air between characters hums with unspoken energy.

**On-the-nose dialogue:**

"Are you mad at me?"

"Yes. You said something hurtful yesterday, and I'm upset."

"You're right. I shouldn't have said it."

"Thank you for apologizing."

Clear? Yes.

Compelling? No.

Now let's try subtext:

**Subtext version:**

"You're quiet today," she said.

"Just tired."

"Oh." She folded the dish towel. "Long night?"

He shrugged. "Been thinking."

"About yesterday?"

Another shrug. "Something like that."

What's going on? Tension. Emotional fog. Protective silence. Hurt feelings. Neither character says exactly what they mean, but both dance around something—and the reader feels the strain of the moment.

The point isn't to make dialogue cryptic or confusing. The point is to allow the **emotional truth** to shine through though the spoken truth does not. Subtext is not reserved for fiction—you can write characters using subtext into your nonfiction, too, especially if you fill your nonfiction with story-samples of situations.

1. **Subtext can reveal emotions characters can't say aloud.** Some truths feel too risky to voice. Subtext lets the reader feel the vulnerability without forcing the character to be explicit.

2. **Subtext can illustrate power dynamics.** Who has more control in a scene—the person talking or the person withholding? Often, silence is the louder weapon.

3. **Subtext can show the evolution of relationships.** Two people who used to joke easily may suddenly speak stiffly and formally. That shift is the story.

4. **Subtext can hint at backstory.** Subtext can gently uncover wounds, fears, old habits, or unresolved conflicts without dumping exposition.

5. **Finally, subtext can build tension and intrigue.** When readers sense a deeper conversation beneath the surface, they lean in. They want to know what's really going on.

**Three Simple Ways to Create Subtext in Your Dialogue**

**Body language:** Sometimes what the character *does* reveals what they feel more honestly than their words do.

**Example:**

"I'm not jealous," she said. But she kept rearranging the salt and pepper shakers, eyes fixed on the door. If the words and the behavior don't match, the reader will trust the behavior.

**Avoidance—when characters sidestep the real issue:** Think about how people act in real life when something uncomfortable comes up: they change the subject, joke, get sarcastic, retreat into silence, or suddenly announce that they need to check the laundry.

**Example:**

"Did you get the test results?"

"Oh! Speaking of tests, did you see Emma's science fair volcano? Thing nearly exploded." Dodge detected. Subtext created.

**Let characters speak *indirectly***

When something matters deeply, characters often approach it sideways.

**Example:**

Instead of saying, "I'm scared to lose you," a character might say:

"You're driving pretty fast."

Or

"Maybe you don't need to work so late tonight."

Or

"You okay? You seem . . . far away."

The surface meaning is simple, but the emotional meaning is much deeper.

Here's a snippet you can dissect. Imagine two siblings cleaning out their late mother's house.

**Version with no subtext:**

"I'm sad she's gone."

"Me, too."

"We should throw these clothes away."

"Okay."

**Version with subtext:**

"Her closet still smells like cinnamon."

"Yeah." He kept his eyes on the shoeboxes. "She never threw anything away."

"She thought she might need it someday."

He nodded. "Well. We . . . should start with the coats."

She pressed her lips together. "If you want."

"I didn't say I want to."

"You're the one holding the trash bags."

So much is happening here—grief, reluctance, old sibling roles surfacing—and none of it is stated outright. That's the goal of subtext: to open emotional depth without over-explaining.

You don't need to force subtext into every line of dialogue, but anytime the stakes are high—when emotions surge, when secrets press at the edges, when characters want something they can't quite admit—that's the moment for subtext. And remember—sometimes, the reader will know what the character cannot say, thus building tension even higher.

Let the silence speak.

Let the half-truths ripple.

Let the reader feel the heartbeat between the lines.

**Your Homework**

Pick a scene from your current project (or write a fresh scene) where two characters want different things.

Write **two versions:**

1. **On-the-nose** – the characters say exactly what they mean.
2. **Subtext-rich** – the characters speak indirectly, dodge, gesture, or hide their feelings.

Then compare them.

Where does the tension rise?

Which version feels more layered?

Which one pulls you in emotionally?

This simple exercise builds your subtext muscles fast—and once you start noticing subtext, you'll see it everywhere.

# ON BOOK COVER DESIGN, SOCIAL MEDIA, AND THE GIFTS GOD GIVES

**Write Well:** #96

**Word of the week: bon mot (bahn MOE).**

A *bon mot* is literally a "good word." It is a witty remark, delivered at just the right time. It's a witty riposte, a snappy comeback, though not snarky. *My friend James Scott Bell has a gift for presenting bon mot. Me, I have to practice being spontaneous.*

**Q&A**

**Question:** How is a new writer supposed to develop a following on Facebook, Instagram, Tik-Tok, YouTube, and X and write an excellent book at the same time?

**Answer:** Despite what others might want you to believe, you can't do everything—not well, at least. You should ask yourself, "Where are my ideal readers?" I know that mine— mostly readers of a certain age, mostly women—are on Facebook, so that's where I invest the majority of my social media time. If I were younger, I might focus on Instagram or even Tik-Tok. But there are only so many hours in a day, and it takes time to produce good social media. You can't have an excellent podcast, newsletter, social media posts, *and* focus on writing a great book unless you clone yourself.

So choose a main platform, develop content for it, and share it across different platforms if you can. But social media isn't so much about *finding* readers as it is *maintaining relationships* with the readers you pick up along the way. They seek you out AFTER they've read your book, not usually before.

I think I mentioned that a few years back I went into photography and was even a professional photographer for a time. But then I realized that in order to really develop the photography *and* write, I needed more time than I had to spare. So last week I started selling off the photography equipment. I'm glad I learned the craft (I might create a photographer protagonist someday), and I loved the creative aspect, but if you try to serve two masters full time, it's difficult to maintain a happy personal and family life.

**Three Dead Giveaways that a Book has been Self-Published**

1. **The book uses the wrong color paper.** If a nonfiction book has been published on cream paper, or if a novel is published on white, someone got it backward.
2. **There are blank lines between every paragraph and paragraphs are not indented.** This is not only bad formatting, but the design has created far too many pages for the book, thus increasing the price.
3. **The cover image does not properly reflect the book's genre.** This applies to fiction and

nonfiction. Study other books in the genre, and make sure the reflects the sort of book it is.

4. **The book is not a standard size.** Most novels are 5.5 x 8.5 inches. Some may choose 6x9 inches if the book is especially long and requires many pages (it's more economical to print a longer book in the larger size), but an oversized book stands out. Unless you *need* to use 6x9, use the standard 5.5 x 8.5. Novellas and gift books, on the other hand, are often published as 5 x 8 hardcovers.

I know choices can be confusing when you're getting ready to publish your book on KDP or Ingram Spark. So pick up a traditional book in your genre and use it as a guideline.

### Qualities of a Great Book Cover

I'm sure you realize how important it is to have an eye-catching book cover. It's the first thing people see when they are looking for a book, and a bad cover can turn a reader away unless they are sold on the author.

So what makes a great book cover? Here are a few tips:

**Circular design:** by this, I don't mean that the cover has to contain a circle, but that the text and images are laid out so that the reader's eye moves *around* the cover instead of left to right and down. Don't just stack title, subtitle, and author name at the top, middle, and bottom. Instead, put the text in the center and see if you can push images to the corners. This approach may not work for every book, but it's a great way to be creatively different.

Here's a cover that features an actual circle. Beth wanted to use the skyline of the protagonist's cities, so we used AI to create a depiction of the real cities. She has three books in the series, so each of them uses this skyline/circle motif. But as you look at this cover, notice how your eye moves *around* the image, not just up and down.

**Typography:** Use **no more than two fonts,** and make sure they contrast. If one is swirly and ornate, make the second font super simple. And don't use the far-too-common fonts that came with your computer. Find something better.

**Layers:** Make sure your cover has depth—at *least* three visible layers. First, building from the bottom up, a background. Even if it's not visible, its color will add depth to your image. Second, an image, and be sure it suits your genre. Third, texture. Top layer: your text. It can overlap the image to enhance this feeling of depth, but make sure it's still legible.

I created the cover below in Photoshop. A background layer adds depth. There's an image layer, and there's text that has been enhanced to look three-dimensional. Finally, if you look closely, you can see a texture layer—to give the appearance of age, I applied a cracked fresco texture that suggests the image is ancient. In Photoshop, the texture was applied *beneath* the font to affect only the image, not the text.

Whenever I use a photo image on a cover, I always apply some kind of texture, otherwise it looks like someone just

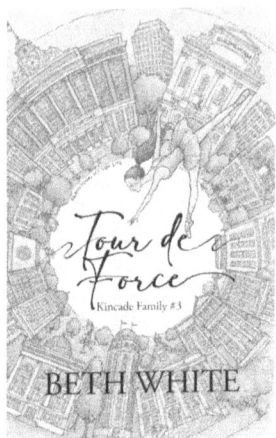

stuck a stock photo on a book. I want it to look like the work of an artist.

When I published a series of colonial novels back in the 1990s, the publisher actually hired a renowned artist to create oil paintings for the book covers. Yep, it was expensive, but they wanted the look of fine art. In this era, when we're using clip art, stock photos, and AI to generate images, why not make our covers look like someone took the time and trouble to create *art*?

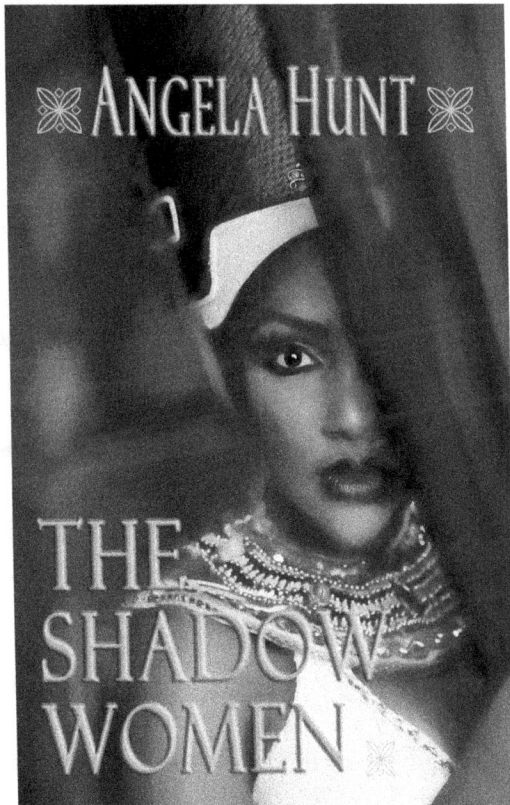

If your book is being traditionally published, the professional designer should do a great job. These folks usually know what's right for the market.

If rights ever revert to you, or if you are self-publishing your book, you'll be responsible for either designing a cover or hiring someone to do it for you. In either case, I hope you find these tips helpful.

## The Gifts God Gives Us

At Christmas, our minds naturally turn to gifts—the ones we wrap, the ones we hope for, the ones we give with love. But for those of us who write, there is another kind of gift we might overlook amid the ribbons and sparkle: the quiet, holy gifts God places within us long before December arrives. Gifts that don't sit beneath a tree, but shape the way we see the world and speak into it. Gifts meant not for display, but for ministry.

Writers of faith have been entrusted with the sacred ability to **see**. While others pass by moments without noticing, we catch the flicker of emotion on a stranger's face, the way winter light slants across a kitchen table, the weary courage in someone's voice. We notice small things—beautiful things, heartbreaking things—that whisper, *Pay attention*. This is not an accident. It is a divine endowment, given so we can reflect God's heart with clarity that stirs others awake.

We have also been given the gift of **feeling**. Writers are sometimes told we're "too sensitive," but heaven sees differently. Sensitivity is not a flaw; it is a responsibility. God entrusts certain hearts with deep wells so that compassion, ache, joy, and hope can run deep enough to overflow onto the page. We feel intensely so we can speak into the hurting places of the world with authority and tenderness. We suffer so we understand how to describe suffering. It is one of God's greatest gifts to us—and one of His greatest gifts *through* us.

And then there is the gift of **pondering**—of holding things in our hearts and minds the way Mary did after the angels visited and the shepherds came running. A writer ponders the meaning beneath moments. We turn ideas over, look at them from new angles, sit quietly with questions others rush past. This slow, thoughtful attention is not laziness or overthinking. It is participation in the creative nature of God, who delights in mystery, reflection, and revelation.

But when writing feels heavy—or when doors remain closed, manuscripts languish, or progress seems invisible—we sometimes forget these gifts. We compare ourselves to others. We wonder whether anything we write is good enough. We fear we may never find our place in a world overflowing with voices.

If that is where you find yourself this season, take heart. The gifts God put within you are not seasonal. They don't depend on trends, platforms, or applause. They are steady because *He* is steady. They are purposeful because *He* is purposeful. And they are needed because this world is hungry—desperate—for words shaped by truth, compassion, and holy imagination.

So as you wrap gifts this Christmas, remember the ones God has wrapped up in you. The ability to see what others overlook. The capacity to feel what others suppress. The instinct to ponder what others forget.

These are not small things. They are the foundations of every story that has ever changed a life.

May you rest in that truth this season. And may the One who called you continue to guide your hands, strengthen your heart, and breathe new courage into your words.

# ON REJECTION,
# ACCEPTING A CHALLENGE,
# AND RESOLUTIONS.

**Write Well:** #97

**Word of the Week: Auld Lang Syne.**

We hear it every year, but how do you pronounce it and what does it mean? It's pronounced almost exactly as it's spelled: *auld-lang-zyne*. And when people sing the song and lift a glass, they are drinking to the good old days, as the phrase literally means "old long since" (say it with a dashing Scottish accent).

If you're a reader like me, you probably learn words through osmosis, but you aren't sure of how they're pronounced. That's one reason I do these words of the week . . . so you will know the exact meaning of words and phrases, and how to say them without fear that you're mispronouncing them.

## Q&A

**Question:** Have you ever written a manuscript and had it rejected?

**Answer:** Oh, yes. Twice I have handed in manuscripts to

fulfill a contract, then heard from the editors that the story just wasn't working. One was for my book *The Novelist*, because it was my effort to illustrate a theological doctrine, and my first effort was too intellectual—not suitable for a novel. So I rewrote the entire thing, opening my heart about a family situation and pouring it out on the page—not something I had intended (or wanted) to do, but something that needed to be done in order for that book to work.

Another time I was contracted to write a book about a troubling social issue, and I wrote a book about so many troubling social issues that it was too dark and unfocused. When I was told it wouldn't work, I put that book in a drawer and went with another topic. I am completely rewriting that first book now, and though it's still not perfect, it is coming together.

### Take the Dare

After Lin-Manuel Miranda's "In The Heights" ran on Broadway and won four Tony Awards, he was with one of his mentors, the composer Stephen Sondheim. Sondheim asked Miranda what he was going to do next and Miranda said, "I'm working on this hip-hop album, like a 'Jesus Christ Superstar' concept album about Alexander Hamilton."

Sondheim threw back his head and laughed, then he said, 'No one will expect that from you. That's amazing. Keep writing that.'"

When nearly everyone else was telling Miranda that anything to do with Alexander Hamilton was a terrible idea, he said, "That laugh was enough to power three years of writing."

In a similar vein, my husband and I were once watching a TV special on Koko, the gorilla who spoke sign language. I was hit by a bolt of inspiration and turned to my husband. "Wouldn't it be neat if we could teach an animal to talk and it testified about God?"

He looked at me and said, "That's the dumbest idea I've ever heard."

I smiled and accepted the challenge. The idea became *Unspoken*, and Sema the gorilla is my favorite character ever.

**Ten Ways Writers Sabotage Themselves—And How Not to Do It in 2026**

Every January brings the same hopeful hush. Fresh planners. Blank pages. A sense that perhaps this will be the year when everything finally clicks and you get published. You hit the bestseller list. You break out of your sales pattern. You manage to finish the book you've worked on for years.

Yet many writers don't realize that the biggest obstacles they face aren't craft problems, industry complications, or even time constraints. More often than not, the things that hold us back are the subtle, invisible ways we sabotage our own progress.

The good news? We can fix that.

As we begin a new year, here are ten common patterns that quietly derail writers—and how to leave each one behind as you step into a new year of possibility.

## 1. Waiting for Inspiration Instead of Building a Habit

The myth of the muse is persistent and seductive. We picture brilliance striking out of the blue, words flowing effortlessly, ideas dropping like ripe fruit from the heavens. Trust me, that's an invention. Yes, sometimes inspiration does strike, but most stories and books are created with thoughtful intention and planning. Rely on the muse, and you'll finish far fewer pages than if you just show up to work.

**How not to do this next year:**

Create a steady writing habit. Fifteen minutes a day or a few sessions a week can build remarkable momentum. Let consistency invite inspiration—not the other way around.

**Resolution:** *I will write consistently and trust creativity to meet me in motion.*

## 2. Revising the First Chapter Twenty Times Instead of Finishing the Draft

Writers endlessly polish early pages for many reasons: fear of the unknown, discomfort with messiness, uncertainty about where the story goes next. But perfectionism disguises itself as diligence, when it's just procrastination wearing a fancy coat. Endless revising halts progress—and sometimes kills projects.

**How not to do this next year:**

Let the first draft stink. You can always clean it up later. Push forward. Finish the story. You'll revise more wisely once you can see the entire shape.

**Resolution:** *I will choose momentum over perfection.*

## 3. Comparing Yourself to Other Writers

Comparison is a creativity killer. The moment we

measure our progress against someone else's achievements, joy drains away. You see their launches, awards, clean prose, or booming platforms—and suddenly your work feels small. But someone else's success is not your failure.

**How not to do this next year:**

Follow writers who inspire rather than intimidate. Celebrate their victories without treating them as judgments on your own worth. You are one link in a long chain of writers that includes the apostle Paul and Charles Dickens, so accept your place in the chain and write on.

**Resolution:** *I will stay in my lane and grow at my pace.*

**4. Ignoring Feedback—or Taking All Feedback to Heart**

Some writers shrink from critique; others rewrite their story every time a new opinion arrives. Both extremes steal your power. Healthy writers treat feedback as information to use or ignore, they don't build an identity from it.

**How not to do this next year:**

Choose a small group of trusted readers. Listen with humility. Keep the notes that strengthen your work. Release the ones that derail your vision.

**Resolution:** *I will welcome guidance and stay anchored in my voice.*

**5. Waiting to "Feel Qualified" Before Acting Like a Professional**

Many writers hesitate to submit work or introduce themselves as writers because they don't feel "official" yet. They're waiting for a book contract, an award, or a degree to confirm what they secretly fear they are not. But it's not as difficult as you think to become a "professional" writer. Write an article or a devotional. Submit it, revise it if necessary, and get paid for it. Done! You're a professional writer.

**How not to do this next year:**

Respect your writing life. Set goals. Track progress. Learn the business. And always, always look for places to sell your work. Don't focus on one project if you want to build a career.

**Resolution:** *I will write small pieces, get paid for them, and know I am a professional writer.*

### 6. Forgetting the Joy—Letting Pressure Replace Play

Writing begins in wonder. But life piles on pressures—deadlines, platform-building, revisions, expectations—and suddenly the delight drains away. When writing becomes nothing but duty, creativity shrivels.

Joy is not optional; it's fuel.

**How not to do this next year:**

Every week, treat yourself to a creative activity you enjoy. Every morning write three "artist's pages" in a notebook no one but you will ever read. Or try a new genre. Write a scene you may never publish. Let curiosity, not pressure, lead you again.

**Resolution:** *I will protect the joy that brought me to writing in the first place.*

### 7. Believing You Must Write Alone

The stereotype of the lone writer—the quiet room, the dim lamp, the isolation—hurts more than it helps. Creativity thrives in connection. Without community, it's easy to get discouraged and quit. Encouragement, accountability, and a fresh perspective don't weaken your work, they strengthen it.

**How not to do this next year:**

Seek connection: a critique group, an online community like ACFW or RWA, a conference, a local writing group. Writing with others doesn't dilute your voice; it deepens it.

**Resolution:** *I will grow in community, not isolation.*

### 8. Consuming More Than You Create

It's easier to read another Substack than write a chapter. Easier to watch a craft video than revise a scene. Easier to scroll writing tips than draft a messy paragraph. But you can't learn to play the piano without a keyboard. You will never learn to apply what you've learned until you put your hands on the keyboard and start writing.

**How not to do this next year:**

Set limits. For every hour of learning, spend two hours creating. Let writing be your main diet; reserve the writing advice for seasoning.

**Resolution:** *I will create more than I consume.*

### 9. Quitting Too Soon (Especially in the Muddled Middle)

Every project has a point where excitement fizzles and doubt swells. The middle feels impossible. The plot tangles. The characters go silent. This is the point where many writers abandon ship and chase a shinier idea. Trust me, the only way out is through the mess.

**How not to do this next year:**

Expect the middle to be messy. When it hits, pause, breathe, revisit your plan or plot skeleton, and re-engage. The magic often returns on the far side of perseverance.

**Resolution:** *I will stick with my work in progress—even when it stops being easy.*

### 10. Treating Setbacks as Stop Signs Instead of Stepping Stones

Rejections, stalled drafts, negative reviews, missed opportunities—these can feel like proof that you're not meant for writing. But setbacks aren't stop signs; they are mile markers. Every writer you admire has met plenty of them along the road. The presence of struggle is not evidence of failure—it's evidence of *effort*.

**How not to do this next year:**

Reframe setbacks as signs of growth. Let them make you resilient, not reluctant. Your writing life will unfold one decision at a time.

**Resolution:** *I will not be* defined *by setbacks, but* refined.

**A New Year, A New Way of Being a Writer**

You don't need a flawless January to begin again. You don't need perfection, certainty, or the "right conditions." You only need awareness, willingness, and the determination to keep going.

As the new year dawns, I hope you greet it like a clean white page—open, hopeful, and ready to receive the stories and information only you can relate.

May we release the habits that hold us back.

May we embrace the practices that move us forward.

And no matter where we are in this writing journey, may this be the year we write with fresh courage, consistency, joy, and grace.

## WRITING LESSONS
## FROM THE FRONT

*The Plot Skeleton*, Book 1
*Creating Extraordinary Characters*, Book 2
*Point of View,* Book 3
*Track Down the Weasel Words*, Book 4
*Evoking Emotion*, Book 5
*Plans and Processes*, Book 6
*Tension on the Line,* Book 7
*Writing Historical Fiction*, Book 8
*The Fiction Writer's Book of Checklists,* Book 9
*Writing the Picture Book*, Book 10
*The First Fifty Pages,* Book 11
*The Art of Revision*, Book 12
*Writing Dialogue*, Book 13
*The Business of Writing*, Book 14
*Beginning and Ending Your Novel*, Book 15
*Show and Tell,* Book 16

*A Christian Writer's Possibly Useful Ruminations on a Life in Pages,* supplemental volume

# ABOUT THE AUTHOR

Angela Hunt writes for readers who have learned to expect the unexpected from this versatile writer. With nearly six million copies of her books sold worldwide, she is the best-selling author of more than 165 works ranging from picture books (*The Tale of Three Trees*) to novels and nonfiction.

Now that her two children are grown, Angie and her husband live in Florida with Very Big Dogs (a direct result of watching *Turner and Hooch* too many times). This affinity for mastiffs has not been without its rewards—one of their dogs was featured on *Live with Regis and Kelly* as the second-largest canine in America. Their dog received this dubious honor after an all-expenses-paid trip to Manhattan for the dog and the Hunts, complete with VIP air travel and a stretch limo in which they toured New York City. Afterward, the dog gave out pawtographs at the airport.

Angela admits to being fascinated by animals, medicine, unexplained phenomena, and "just about everything." Books, she says, have always shaped her life— in the fifth grade she learned how to flirt from reading *Gone with the Wind*.

Her books have won the coveted Christy Award, several Angel Awards from Excellence in Media, and the Gold and Silver Medallions from *Foreword Magazine*'s Book of the Year

Award. In 2007, her novel *The Note* was featured as a Christmas movie on the Hallmark channel. She has completed her doctorate in biblical literature and another in Theology.

When she's not home writing, Angie often travels to teach writing workshops at schools and writers' conferences. And to talk about her dogs, of course. Readers may visit her web site at www.angelahuntbooks.com and her Substack at ange lahunt.substack.com.